1/03

Ambassadors
of Progress

American Women
Photographers in Paris

1900–1901

CONTRIBUTORS

VERNA POSEVER CURTIS
Curator of Photography, Prints and Photographs Division, Library of Congress,
Washington, D.C.

BRONWYN A. E. GRIFFITH
Assistant Curator, Musée d'Art Américain Giverny

LAURA ILISE MEISTER
Art Historian

MICHEL POIVERT
President, Société Française de Photographie, Paris
Senior Lecturer, Université de Paris I Panthéon-Sorbonne

ANDREW ROBB
Senior Photograph Conservator, Library of Congress,
Washington, D.C.

Ambassadors
of Progress

American Women
Photographers in Paris

1900–1901

Edited by
BRONWYN A. E. GRIFFITH

Essays by
VERNA POSEVER CURTIS,
BRONWYN A. E. GRIFFITH,
MICHEL POIVERT and ANDREW ROBB

Biographies by
LAURA ILISE MEISTER

Musée d'Art Américain Giverny, France
In association with the Library of Congress, Washington, D.C.

Distributed by University Press of New England
Hanover and London

Published in conjunction with the exhibition

Ambassadors of Progress: American Women Photographers in Paris, 1900–1901

organized by Bronwyn A. E. Griffith, Musée d'Art Américain Giverny
in collaboration with Verna Posever Curtis, Library of Congress, Washington, D.C.,
and with the participation of the National Museum of American History,
Smithsonian Institution, Washington, D.C.

Exhibition Venues
Musée d'Art Américain Giverny, France
September 13–November 30, 2001

Terra Museum of American Art, Chicago
January 26–April 14, 2002

Hood Museum of Art, Dartmouth College, Hanover, New Hampshire
January 11–March 9, 2003

Front cover: Amelia Van Buren. [Profile portrait of woman draped with a veil], ca. 1900.
Back cover: Paul Bergon. *À l'exposition*, in *La Revue de photographie* 2 (1903).

Produced by the Department of Publications of the Musée d'Art Américain Giverny

Edited by Francesca Rose
Designed by Laurent Romano
Production by Francesca Rose with the assistance of Claire Guilloteau
Translation of essay by Michel Poivert by Bernard Wooding
Copy-edited by Bernard Wooding

Published by the Musée d'Art Américain Giverny
99, rue Claude Monet, 27620 Giverny, France (www.maag.org)

Distributed by University Press of New England, Hanover, N.H., 03755
ISBN 0–932171–22–2

Printed in France

Library of Congress Cataloging-in-Publication Data

Ambassadors of progress: American women photographers in Paris,
1900-1901 / edited by Bronwyn A.E. Griffith ; essays by Verna Posever
Curtis ... [et al.] ; biographies by Laura Ilise Meister.
    p. cm.
  Includes bibliographical references and index.
  ISBN 0-932171-22-2
  1. Women photographers—United States—History—20th
century—Exhibitions. 2. Women
photographers—France—Paris—History—20th century—Exhibitions. 3.
Johnston, Frances Benjamin, 1864-1952—Photograph
collections—Exhibitions.   I. Griffith, Bronwyn. II. Curtis, Verna
Posever. III. Meister, Laura Ilise. IV. Musee americain Giverny. V.
Terra Museum of American Art. VI. Hood Museum of Art.
  TR139 .A42 2001
  770'.82'0973—dc21
                                                    2001038514

CONTENTS

In just six weeks, Frances Benjamin Johnston organized a presentation of work by nearly thirty American women photographers for the 1900 Universal Exposition in Paris. Perhaps it is fitting then that we should have just one year to coordinate the many phases of a collaborative effort to conserve, publish and exhibit the original works housed in her personal collection, for an exhibition opening in France.

The Terra Foundation for the Arts, dedicated to the preservation and interpretation of American art, immediately recognized the value of funding the conservation of works in the Frances Benjamin Johnston Collection when approached by Linda Ayres, former Chief of Prints & Photographs at the Library of Congress. Plans for an exhibition were then initiated by Derrick Cartwright, former Director of the Musée d'Art Américain Giverny, and Verna Curtis, Curator of Photography at the Library.

It is the transatlantic collaborative efforts between our institutions which have brought about the extraordinary opportunity to view these works generously loaned by the Library of Congress and the National Museum of American History. While Verna Curtis and Andrew Robb, Senior Photograph Conservator, carefully oversaw the conservation of the objects and prepared them for loan at the Library of Congress, Bronwyn Griffith and Francesca Rose of the Musée d'Art Américain Giverny worked tirelessly to organize the exhibition and produce the publication.

Musée d'Art Américain Giverny, dedicated to furthering the understanding of American art in France, seems the ideal venue for the partial reconstruction of Frances Benjamin Johnston's exhibition, allowing the original works, gathered in Washington by Johnston for her Paris presentation, to chart the same course a century later. It is with great pleasure that we present *Ambassadors of Progress: American Women Photographers in Paris, 1900–1901*, which honors the collaboration between our institutions and celebrates the women photographers so worthy of exhibition.

Elizabeth Glassman
Interim Director, Musée d'Art Américain Giverny

The Frances Benjamin Johnston Collection at the Library of Congress is a rich research resource. Her papers, comprising some 19,000 items, are housed in the Manuscripts Division, while her wide-ranging photographic materials are in the custody of the Prints & Photographs Division. During her lifetime, Johnston's photographs entered the Library through various means: copyright deposit, legal deposit, and gift. A resident of Washington, D.C., her interest in the Library as a repository for her work began as early as 1905, when she donated a portrait of industrialist Andrew Carnegie. But the bulk of her photographic collections—including the works by other women that she assembled and exhibited in Paris in 1900—were acquired in 1953 from her estate by gift and purchase.

The Johnston collection in the Prints & Photographs Division numbers some 25,000 items. Organized into over 110 groups arranged by subject, it contains photo prints (including silver gelatin and cyanotype proofs), glass and film negatives, and lantern slides, as well as artistic photos by other photographers, family photos, albums, graphic ephemera, and architectural and watercolor drawings. Additional special collections within the division that incorporates photographs by Johnston include the Carnegie Survey of the Architecture of the South and the Pictorial Archives of Early American Architecture. It is a pleasure to share with a wider audience a distinctive aspect of the Library of Congress' remarkable Frances Benjamin Johnston Collection. She was indeed an "ambassador of progress."

Jeremy Adamson
Chief, Prints & Photographs Division, Library of Congress, Washington, D.C.

This exhibition and publication are the result of the generous contributions of dozens of people who recognized the value of conserving, exhibiting and documenting Frances Benjamin Johnston's rich collection of work by women photographers housed in the Library of Congress and the National Museum of American History, Smithsonian Institution.

The grant from the Terra Foundation of the Arts for the conservation of the photographs in the Frances Benjamin Johnston Collection at the Library of Congress would not have been possible without the interest and efforts of the Board of Trustees of the Terra Foundation for the Arts, Linda Ayres, formerly Chief of Prints & Photographs Division, Derrick Cartwright, Director of the Hood Museum and Catherine Stevens.

Both the conservation and the exhibition stages of the project were greatly aided by the kind assistance of the staff of the Library of Congress in the Prints & Photographs Division: Jeremy Adamson, Chief of Prints & Photographs Division, Doris Lee, Secretary, Harry Katz, Head of Curatorial Section, Carol Johnson and Beverly Brannan, Curators of Photography, Elisa Bourdonnay, Curatorial Intern, Yvonne Burton, and Sarah Rouse, Greg Marcangelo, Woody Woodis, Donna Collins, Richard Herbert and Cheryl McCullers in Technical Services; Department of Conservation: Andrew Robb, Senior Photography Conservator, Mary Wootton, Senior Book Conservator, Rikki Condon, Julie Biggs, Anne Fuhrman, Lisa Barro, Conservation Intern, Martin Salazar, Conservation Fellow, and Marita Clance, Conservation Photographer; Interpretive Programs Office: Tambra Johnston and Margaret Brown; Department of Publications: W. Ralph Eubanks, Director of Publishing, and Athena Angelos; Photoduplication Services: Jim Higgins and Denise King; Information Technology Services: Domenic Sergi, Jade Curtis and Glen Krankowski; European Division: John Van Oudenaren, Chief, and Harry Leich, Russian Specialist; Manuscripts Division: Frederick Bauman and Jeffrey Flannery, Reference Librarians, Mary Wolfskill; Rare Book and Special Collections Division: Gerald Wager, Head Reference Section; Music Division: Gail Freunsch.

The staff of the National Museum of American History, Smithsonian Institution also made great efforts to assist this project, in particular, Michelle Delaney, Shannon Perich and Helena E. Wright, Photographic History Collection; David Burgevin, Photographic Services; Margaret Grandine, Outgoing Loans Manager, Lynne Gilliand and Katie Speckart, Loans Office.

This project is heavily indebted to the professional assistance of the following people: Dennis Barrow, Fairfield Historical Society; Jennifer A. Watts and Dan Lewis, Huntington Library, San Marino, California; Fern Eddy Schultz and Jim Rogers, La Porte County Historical Society, La Porte, Indiana; Christian Peterson, Minneapolis Institute of Art; Andrew Eskind, Editor of the George Eastman House Database; Becky Simmons, Richard and Ronay Menschel Library, George Eastman House; Anne Havinga, Erica Hirshler and Ellen Roberts, Department of American Art, Museum of Fine Arts, Boston; Nicole Bouché, The Beinecke Rare Book and Manuscript Library, Yale University; Jessica L. Roscio, National Museum of Women in the Arts; Cheryl Leibold, Pennsylvania Academy of the Fine Arts; Jean McDaniel, The Robbins Hunter Museum; Dan Bourdon and Una Gibson Whyte Museum of the Canadian Rockies; Jean Nielsen Berry, Margaret Clapp Library, Wellesley College; Karen Holmes, Grace Hudson Museum, Ukiah, California; Mary Ann Curtis, Photograph Archives, J. Willard Marriott Library, University of Utah; Lorna Condon, Society for the Preservation of New England Antiquities; Marie-Helen Gold, Schlesinger Library, Radcliffe College; Patricia Fanning, Norwood Historical Society; Barbara Grubb, Special Collections and Carol W. Campbell, College's Collections, Bryn Mawr College; Pam Roberts, The Royal Photographic Society of Great Britain; Sarah J. Weatherwax, Curator of Prints and Photographs, Library Company of Philadelphia; Anne Caiger, Manuscripts Division, UCLA Library Department of Special Collections; Leslie Calmes and Shaw Kinsley, Center for Creative Photography, The University of Arizona; Madeleine Viljoen, Philadelphia Museum of Art; Karen Papineau, Currier Gallery of Art, Manchester, New Hampshire; Jack Von Euw, Bancroft Library, University of California, Berkeley, California; Donna Humphrey, Cory Amsler and Betsy Smith, Mercer Museum/Bucks County Historical Society; Doylestown, Pennsylvania; Kathy Erwin, Warren and Margot Coville Collection, Bloomfield Hills, Michigan; Nina Kohser, Licking County Historical Society, Newark, Ohio; Mary Delmonte, Buffalo State University of New York, Buffalo; Linda Kennedy, Buffalo and Erie County Historical Society, Buffalo, New York; Varney Greene, Buffalo Public Library; Sally Pierce, Boston Atheneum; Amy Hezel, Albright-Knox Art Gallery, Buffalo; Lisa Leibfacher, Ohio Historical Society; Dan Sponseller, Columbus Metropolitan Library, Ohio; Margaret Baughman, Cleveland Public Library; Abby Bridge, California Historical Society, San Francisco; the staff of the Department of Fine Arts and the Department of Microtext at the Boston Public Library. Thanks to Nancy Newhouse for providing accesses to private archives and collections.

The research and writings of several scholars laid the groundwork for this catalogue and when consulted on numerous occasions they freely shared their knowledge. Thank you to Peter E. Palmquist, Women in Photography International Archive; Suzanne L. Flynt, Memorial Hall Museum, Deerfield; Peter Bunnell, Curator of Photographs, Princeton University Art Museum; Gillian Greenhill Hannum, Manhattanville College; Barbara L. Michaels, Toby Quitslund, Jain Kelly, Naomi Rosenblum, Janice Sanford Beck, Diane VanSkiver Gagel.

The Russian articles were found due to the efforts of Miriam Dandamayeva, Galina Vasilenko and the staff of the Russian State Library. They were translated by Thomas Hoisington and Harry Leich, Library of Congress.

A few people deserve special mention for their commitment to the exhibition and the catalogue: Derrick Cartwright, Director of the Hood Museum, for initiating the exhibition which led to this transatlantic cooperation; Verna P. Curtis for collaborating throughout and seeing to innumerable details at the Library of Congress; Laura I. Meister for seeking out information about the lives of these fascinating women; Andrew Robb for overseeing the conservation of the photographs; Michel Poivert, Président de la Société Française de Photographie, for his contribution to the catalogue; Elizabeth Whiting and Stephanie Mayer, colleagues at the Terra Museum of American Art in Chicago for conducting research; Jeanne Bouniort, for translation and associated research; Hugues Fontenas, architect, and Cyrille Fourmy, graphic designer, for the design of the exhibition in Giverny; Elizabeth Glassman, Interim Director, and Sophie Lévy, Chief Curator, Musée d'Art Américain Giverny, for guidance and support; Claire Guilloteau, for help on the catalogue; Francesca Rose, Head of Publications, who orchestrated the production of this publication, for her constancy and dedication.

These acknowledgements are written on behalf of the contributors to the catalogue, who are also sincerely grateful to the dozens of research librarians and archivists, too numerous to mention, who assisted with every stage of this project and whose interest was an on-going source of encouragement.

Optimism prevailed at the close of the nineteenth century. The concept of "progress" infused nearly every component of the Universal Exposition of 1900. Technological advances were thought to contain the potential for the future happiness of mankind and accordingly had a strong impact on the concepts of modernity as the world prepared to enter a new century. Eager to view what the future might hold, Americans flooded into the French capital to attend the Exposition. The presence of Americans in Paris by 1900 had become so conspicuous that, for some, the word *American* became the generic term for foreigner.[1] Yet, the presentations of the prospering United States held great interest as the young republic seemed to be charting the course of the future, striving forward and surpassing Europe in nearly every field.

The exhibition of American women photographers organized by Frances Benjamin Johnston in 1900 combined the fascination with the "new woman," almost by definition American, with the interest in technology—the burgeoning field of photography. It is not surprising, therefore, that its presentation at the International Congress of Photography in Paris at the Universal Exposition of 1900 garnered wide attention. Indeed, the crate containing the women photographers' works so piqued the curiosity of the delegates to the International Congress of Photography that it was opened before the arrival of its representative, Frances B. Johnston.[2] The photographs, which numbered between 150 and 200,[3] were then returned to their case until the presentation by

Johnston two days later. In the official report of the Congress, Sosthène Pector invoked the catchword of the era when praising the photographs, referring to the authors of the photographs as "friends of progress." The women were examples of both social and photographic advancement: the accomplished techniques were proof of their photographic expertise and the fact that so many of them were professionals proof of the independent "new woman."

The present exhibition was organized with two objectives: to document the recently conserved Frances Benjamin Johnston collection of photography by American women photographers housed at the Library of Congress and to explore the initial presentation of many of these works at the Universal Exposition in 1900 and the Photo-Club de Paris in 1901 by adding photographs from Johnston's archive now housed at the National Museum of American History, Smithsonian Institution. The catalogue, which includes biographical texts and exhibition histories, assembles the photographs by each of the female photographers represented in Frances B. Johnston's personal archive, which is now divided between two institutions. The catalogue essays address the historical contexts and political influences behind the Paris exhibitions, Johnston's contributions to the Universal Exposition, the French critical reception of the women photographers and the conservation treatments performed on the photographs and mounts. Whenever possible the original works assembled by Johnston are exhibited. However, in some instances it was necessary to display other examples of work by these photographers from that period. Despite thorough research in the United States and France in preparation for this exhibition, many questions remain unanswered. This is largely due to an absence of detailed records and to unknown variations of the original exhibition as it traveled to three additional venues. The following is a brief explanation of what is known about the works assembled by Johnston in Paris and exhibited in three other venues in 1900 and 1901. Further details are found in the essays.

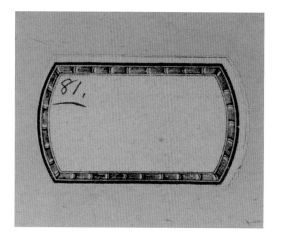

Fig. 1. Example of the labels used to number the works before the Russian exhibitions. Washington, D.C., Library of Congress.

Following the scheduled presentation at the congress, the photographs, in addition to work by Frances B. Johnston, was exhibited briefly in the Palace of Letters, Science and Art.[4] After viewing the presentation of the works, W. I. Sreznewsky, a Russian attendee, requested a loan of the works for exhibition in St. Petersburg and Moscow, where Pictorial photography was little known. Johnston honored the request. In preparation for the Russian exhibitions, Johnston's mother labeled (fig. 1) and numbered 142 works by 31 photographers[5] and made a corresponding alphabetical list of photographers in her *Wanamaker Diary of 1900*, indicating the number of works included by each photographer (figs. 2 and 3).[6] This list of exhibitors for the Russian venues briefly fixed the number of works included. By comparing the labels on the original works with the numbered lists it is possible to determine many of the works shown in Russia. As 75 of the 142 photographs were carefully preserved by Johnston and now reside in the collections of the Library of Congress and National Museum of American History, it is assumed that the other prints were returned to the photographers at their request or disappeared over time.

In addition to the labels and list of exhibitors created by Mrs. Johnston, other sources were consulted and cross-referenced to ascertain what other works may have been exhibited. Seven reviews of the exhibition (four in France and three in Russia) at the various venues were useful as they illustrate, mention and describe particular works. The reception of the photographs in Russia was laudatory, revealing an appreciation of the artistic prints and mounts. Of particular note are the two detailed reviews of the Russian exhibitions. One article was previously cited in an earlier exploration into Johnston's exhibition.[7] The second, heretofore unknown, was discovered by a researcher in Russia

FIGS. 2 & 3. *The Wanamaker Diary of 1900.*
Washington, D.C., Library of Congress, Manuscripts Division.

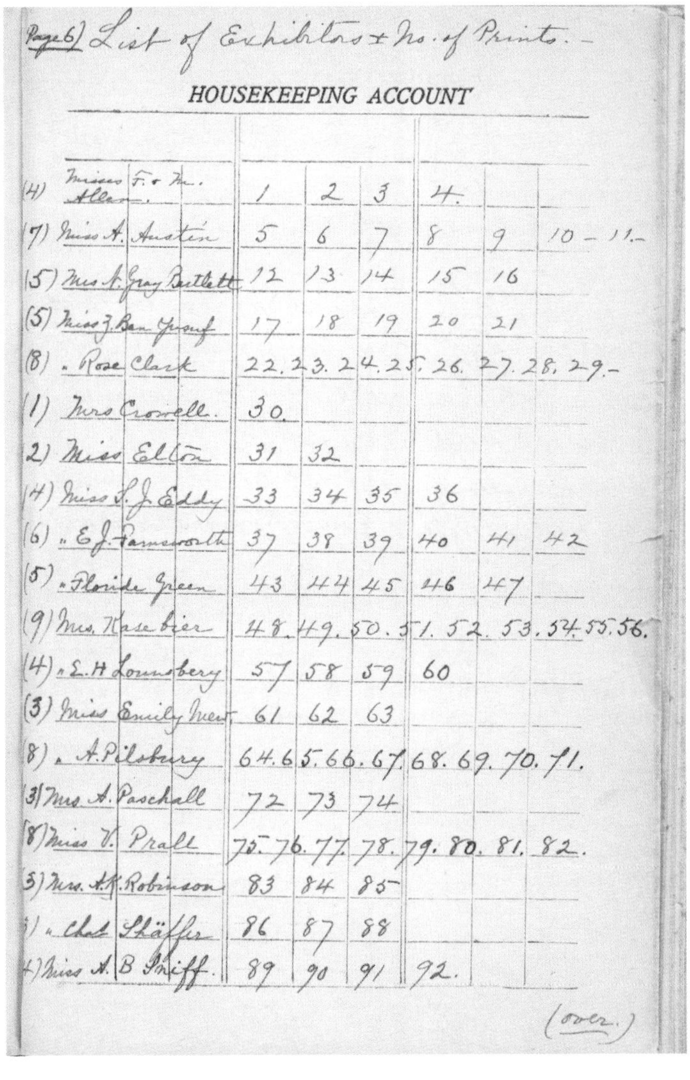

Page 6) List of Exhibitors & No. of Prints.–
HOUSEKEEPING ACCOUNT
(4) Misses F. & M. Allen. 1 2 3 4.
(7) Miss A. Austin 5 6 7 8 9 10 – 11.–
(5) Mrs A. Gray Bartlett 12 13 14 15 16
(5) Miss Z. Ben Yusuf 17 18 19 20 21
(8) " Rose Clark 22.23.24.25.26.27.28.29.–
(1) Mrs Crowell. 30.
(2) Miss Elton 31 32
(4) Miss S. J. Eddy 33 34 35 36
(6) " E. J. Farnsworth 37 38 39 40 41 42
(5) " Floride Green 43 44 45 46 47
(9) Mrs. Kasebier 48.49.50.51.52.53.54 55.56.
(4) " E. H Lounsbery 57 58 59 60
(3) Miss Emily Mew 61 62 63
(8) " A. Pilsbury 64.65.66.67.68.69.70.71.
(3) Mrs. A. Paschall 72 73 74
(8) Miss V. Prall 75.76.77.78.79.80.81.82.
(3) Mrs. A. K. Robinson 83 84 85
(3) " Chas Schäffer 86 87 88
(4) Miss A. B. Sniff 89 90 91 92.
(over.)

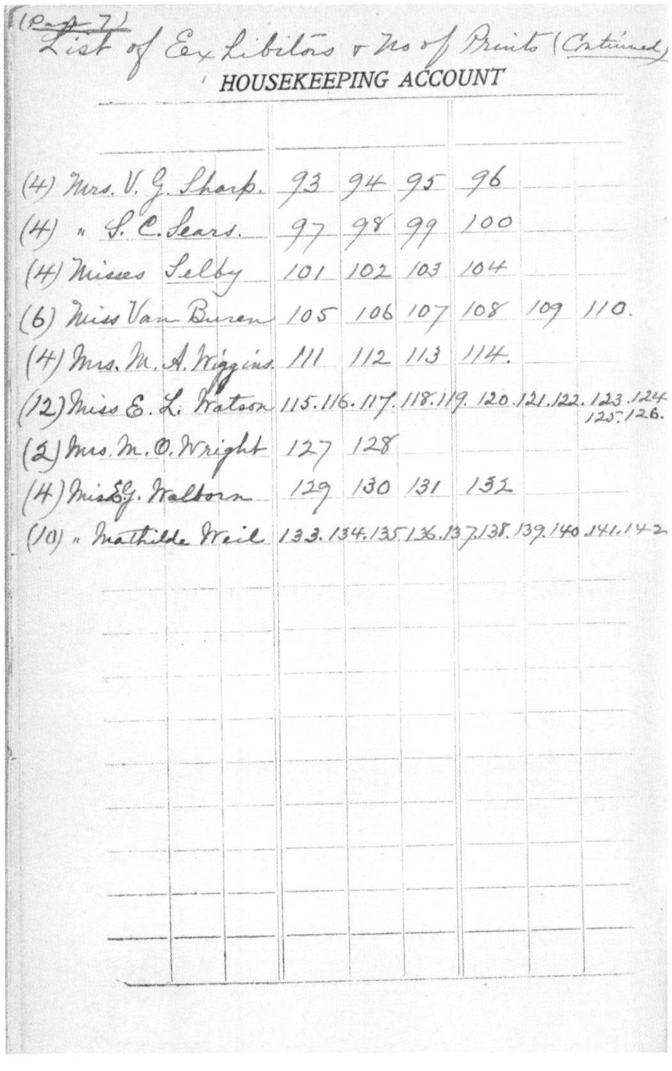

(Page 7) List of Exhibitors & No of Prints (Continued)
HOUSEKEEPING ACCOUNT
(4) Mrs. V. G. Sharp. 93 94 95 96
(4) " S. C. Sears. 97 98 99 100
(4) Misses Selby 101 102 103 104
(6) Miss Van Buren 105 106 107 108 109 110.
(4) Mrs. M. A. Wiggins 111 112 113 114.
(12) Miss E. L. Watson 115.116.117.118.119.120.121.122.123.124 125.126.
(2) Mrs. M. O. Wright 127 128
(4) Miss E. G. Walborn 129 130 131 132
(10) " Mathilde Weil 133.134.135.136.137.138.139.140.141.142.

assisting in the preparation for this exhibition. Though not at the heart of this exhibition, which focuses on the Parisian presentations, the Russian essays shed new light on the photographs, citing particular works, techniques and descriptions of mounts[8] and are therefore published in their entirety in the appendix.

In January 1901, the unframed works[9] returned to Paris for a public exhibition at the Photo-Club de Paris. Once again the exact number of works exhibited becomes unclear. French Pictorialist Robert Demachy added work by at least one photographer, Mary Devens, to the work selected by Frances B. Johnston.[10] In the various reviews of the exhibition, the following photographers were mentioned: Frances and Mary Allen, Alice Austin, Mary Bartlett, Zaida Ben-Yusuf, Elise Pumpelly Cabot,[11] Rose Clark, Mary Devens,[12] Sarah Jane Eddy, Fannie Elton, Emma Farnsworth, Floride Green, Gertrude Käsebier, Edith Lounsbery, Emily Mew, Mary Paschall, Anne Pilsbury, Virginia Prall, Addie Robinson, Mary Schäffer, Sarah Sears, Emily and Lillian Selby, Virginia Sharp, Amelia Van Buren, Eva Walborn, Eva Watson,[13] Mathilde Weil, Myra Wiggins and Mabel Wright. Therefore, the exhibition seems to be little changed from the works sent to Russia.

Curiously, despite the praise they garnered in the four showings abroad, which confirmed the established reputations of these women photographers in 1900, the exhibition has been virtually ignored in the annals of photographic history. Through the exhibition of these exquisite works and this accompanying publication, we hope to document Johnston's remarkable presentation of photographs by American women photographers, to reveal new information and details about these women and their work and, ultimately, to encourage scholars to explore the history of women photographers still further.

B. G.

NOTES

1. Harvey Levenstein, *Seductive Journey. American Tourists in France from Jefferson to the Jazz Age* (Chicago: Chicago University Press, 1998), p. 150.

2. Sosthène Pector, *Congrès international de photographie, tenu à Paris du 23 au 28 juillet 1900. Procès-verbaux sommaires.* Ministère du Commerce, de l'Industrie des Postes et des Télégraphes. Exposition Universelle Internationale de 1900 (Paris: Imprimerie Nationale, 1900), p. 9; discussed further in Bronwyn Griffith, *"L'Œuvre à accomplir et les obstacles à vaincre." An Exhibition of American Women Photographers at the Third International Photographic Congress in Paris at the Universal Exposition of 1900,* unpublished Masters thesis, Columbia University, 2000, p. 39, and in M. Poivert's text in this publication.

3. Both editions of the official report mention the presentation and crate, but the number of works is alternately listed as 150 and 200, without mention of particular photographs or photographers.

4. Joseph T. Keiley, "La Classe 12 à l'Exposition universelle," *Bulletin du Photo-Club de Paris,* 1900, p. 209.

5. Often errantly listed as twenty-eight because Rose Clark and Elizabeth Flint Wade, the Allen sisters and the Misses Selby are listed as a single entry.

6. *The Wanamaker Diary of 1900,* entry for August 5, 1900, continued under May 22; for detailed discussion and quotes see text by V. Curtis in this publication.

7. Toby Quitslund, "Her Feminine Colleagues. Photographs and Letters Collected by Frances Benjamin Johnston," in *Women Artists in Washington Collections* (College Park, MD: University of Maryland Art Gallery, 1979).

8. Fortunately many of the original artistic mounts were preserved in Johnston's personal archives. Those included in the exhibition are reproduced in the color plates of this catalogue.

9. Griffith, *op cit.*, p. 40, note 66; based on review by Wallon, "L'Exposition des artistes américaines au Photo-Club," *Photo-Gazette,* (February 25, 1901), p. 62.

10. Frances Benjamin Johnston Papers, Manuscripts Division, Library of Congress, Washington, D.C.: One unpublished letter from Mary Devens to Frances Benjamin Johnston, August 22, 1901. In which she mentions that Demachy added some of her photographs to the exhibition.

11. No correspondence or other documentation confirm her participation which was mentioned by C. Puyo in a review which primarily covered the *New School of American Photography* in which she exhibited.

12. Added by Demachy for the Photo-Club de Paris exhibition (January 1901). See Frances Benjamin Johnston Papers, Manuscripts Division, Library of Congress, Washington, D.C.: One unpublished letter from Mary Devens to Frances Benjamin Johnston, August 22, 1901.

13. Married in 1901, and thereafter known as Eva L. Watson-Schütze.

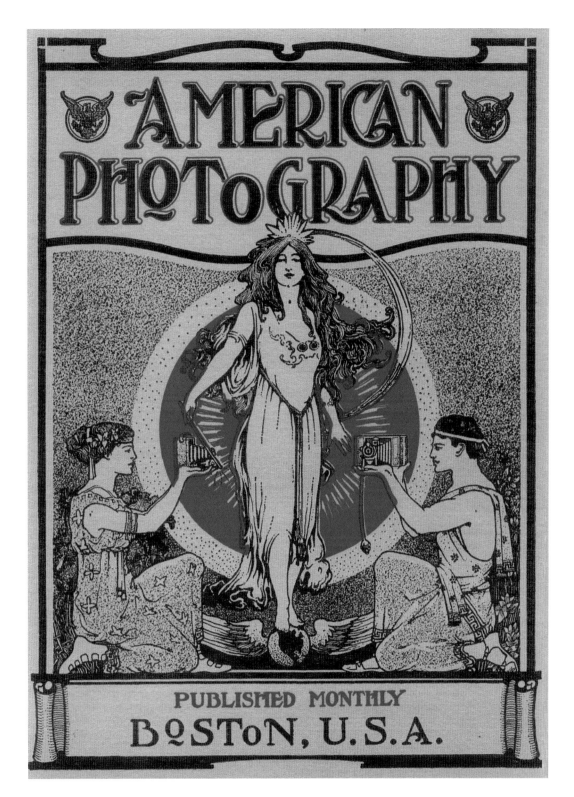

Cover of *American Photography* (August 1911).

"DAINTY AND ARTISTIC OR STRONG AND FORCEFUL—JUST AS YOU WISH"[1]
AMERICAN WOMEN PHOTOGRAPHERS AT THE UNIVERSAL EXPOSITION OF 1900

BRONWYN A. E. GRIFFITH

In 1900, the world turned to Paris for the unveiling of the extravagant Universal Exposition which was to embody a century of progress. National delegations assembled from all over the world to make their contributions to the ostentatious display of advancements, brimming with anticipation of what further developments the future might hold. The fundamental theme at the turn of the century was that of "progress," and the desire for the world to continue evolving dominated the exposition. Among the countries emphasizing this doctrine, following its unprecedented economic growth and reflecting a determination to assert itself, was the United States of America.

The porch of the United States Pavilion was crowned with the allegorical figure of *Liberty Driving the Chariot of Progress* (fig. 1), while the portico just beneath was decorated with a mural depicting *America Unveiling Her Natural Strength*. Both were clear visual indications of the proud aspirations of the burgeoning republic.[2] One of the many demonstrations of "progress" presented by the United States delegation at the Universal Exposition was a presentation of work by American women photographers, organized by Frances Benjamin Johnston, a pioneering photographer herself, for the International Photographic Congress held from July 23-28. The presentation, cel-

ebrated at the time but nearly forgotten since, has been studied by various scholars, all of whom have remarked upon its originality but remain divided about its consequences or even the particularities of its organization. The numerous explanations range from the sheer novelty of the exhibition to the particular place of American women within the international Pictorialist movement in photography and finally to the near omission of women photographers from the annals of photographic history. To some contemporary critics and some present day scholars, it appears to mark a turning point for American women photographers by garnering attention previously denied. Further inquiry proves otherwise, however. The exhibition organized by photojournalist Frances B. Johnston did not unveil the talents of American women photographers for the first time, as many of the participants were already known in the international photographic community. Rather, it illustrated the distinctive role of the American woman photographer at the turn of the last century as a representative of both social progress for women and the evolving definition of photography as art. Furthermore, the exhibition of American women photographers and the accompanying speech by Frances B. Johnston corresponded with the complex and far-reaching nationalist agenda of the United States Delegation to the 1900 Universal Exposition in Paris. Thus, to properly place the maverick exhibition in context, it is necessary to consider the social and political influences behind its presentation.

"What a Woman Can Do with a Camera"[3]

The turn of the last century was a period of transition for women in Western societies, marked by major societal shifts from nineteenth-century conventions toward "modern" twentieth-century sensibilities. A clear example was the rising popularity of photography among American women at this time, which can be attributed to a strong economy, increased leisure time and social changes such as the

FIG. 1. Alexander Phimister Proctor. *Quadriga: Liberty Driving the Chariot of Progress.* Stereograph. Washington, D.C., Library of Congress.

formation of associations and access to education, both of which stimulated women's desire to explore the world outside the narrowly circumscribed domestic life delineated by Victorian mores. Economic prosperity and the American fascination with technological inventions (such as the sewing machine) relieved women of time-consuming domestic chores and allowed them to develop more personal interests, some of which would eventually draw them out of the home. The increased access to secondary and university education was unquestionably the single largest advancement for women, and this in turn instigated other changes.[4] The increased sense of independence and opportunity permitted women to resist the limitations imposed by the Victorian values of home, piety and beauty, freeing them to explore areas of personal interest and the possibility of a career (fig. 2).

A world-wide increase in the number of books and periodicals published for the feminine audience reflected the shifting societal roles and the growing demand for information on careers and hobbies for women. Publications responding to the female curiosity about professional possibilities, such as in *What a Woman Can Do* by Mrs. M. L. Rayne (1884), often included mention of photography as a viable option. As an activity that could be practiced and, indeed, was most often practiced within or near the home, photography did not upset strictly defined gender roles. In fact, it was curiously compatible with the central role occupied by women in the home, providing a means to document the activities of the family. Domestic responsibilities that could prove advantageous in photography, such as orderliness and thoroughness, were often highlighted in articles encouraging women to practice photography.[5] Between 1885 and 1900, articles devoted to women in photography were published regularly, not only in photographic journals, but also in a wide variety of publications, including *Ladies' Home Journal, Demorest's Family Magazine, Munsey's Magazine* and others. Capable of satisfying Victorian sensibilities as a "charming, practical, and fulfilling amusement,"[6] photography provided women with the possibility of visual expression and, most unusually, a remunerative career. As women progressively mastered the new art, they began both to recognize the creative and professional possibilities of photography enjoyed by their male colleagues and to enter the ranks of professionals and serious amateur photographers.[7]

In addition to social changes, technological advancements in photography also helped to open up the field to women. In particular, the invention of the dry plate eliminated the need both for bulky equipment and a portable darkroom. In the second half of the nineteenth century, photography represented a new activity as yet undefined by either gender. Lighter outfits replaced the cumbersome equipment once required, thereby making the practice of photography less physically challenging for women and thus more accessible. The increasing feminine interest in photography did not go unnoticed as advertisers of the new apparatus sought new markets. Traditionally, the operation of mechanical things remained firmly within the masculine sphere, but advertisers, eager to exploit new business opportunities, focused on minimizing social stereotypes that might deter women from attempting photography. Recognizing women's changing role in society, particularly their increased independence and purchasing power, advertisers aimed to turn it to their advantage. Kodak and other companies launched campaigns featuring women with cameras, demonstrating the ease of operation (fig. 3).

FIG. 2. Unknown female photographer at work, Southern California, ca. 1900. Stereograph. Peter E. Palmquist Collection.

In publishing promotional brochures like "Women Who Use Kodaks" (1891), George Eastman, the founder of Kodak, consulted the accomplished photographer Frances B. Johnston.[8]

Though geographically spread across much greater distances than their European counterparts, American women photographers developed ways to efficiently share information with their peers across the country. Using all possible means of communication and inspired by a shared passion, they established an extensive informal network that helped bridge geographic distances and lessen isolation caused by domestic obligations. Articles written for women gave purely technical advice, detailing how to convert closets or other spare rooms into darkrooms and what accessories they could provide for themselves and others.[9] Intent on sharing information and serving as examples, successful women photographers, such as Eva Watson, Sarah Jane Eddy and Elizabeth Flint Wade, actively contributed to photographic bulletins and other journals, providing straightforward, practical advice, and encouraging other women to enter the field. In "What a Woman Can Do with a Camera," Frances B. Johnston spoke from personal experience, encouraging women with training in the fine arts whose "talents do not lift their work above mediocrity" to consider photography as a profitable livelihood.[10] Catherine Weed Ward, née Barnes, an editor at both *American Amateur Photographer* (fig. 4) and *Photogram*, went one step further when she stated matter-of-factly that any "reasonable, well-edu-

cated, naturally refined, more or less artistic woman" should try photography.[11]

Caught between the traditions of the nineteenth century and the trends of the twentieth century, women entering photography encountered resistance and at times expressed ambivalence about embarking on this new practice. At times, it was women themselves who leveled some of the staunchest arguments for women to remain within the home, predicting that their natural limitations would subvert those who dared to venture out into the workforce. Also evident are self-contradictions characteristic of the era as found in the article "Women and Their Cameras" by Margaret Bisland. She touted that "women with their cameras surpass all traditions and stand as the equals of men in their newly-found and now most ardently practiced art."[12] However, the reasons cited to support this claim were firmly rooted in the Victorian values of women as associated and defined by the home. She concludes, "Photography makes a strong appeal to woman for the reason that she may study and practice it in her own home, in the very corner of her room; yet it does not interfere with daily duties or pleasures."[13] Such criticism failed to dissuade thousands of women from exploring photography within and beyond the confines of their homes and becoming actively involved in the photographic community.

The economic prosperity in the United States at the end of the nineteenth century contributed to the influx of women entering the field of photography. Most were from the ever larger middle class with more time for leisure, thereby fuelling the vogue for clubs and associations. Along with fraternal associations and clubs for other activities, like the popular bicycling club, photo clubs were founded throughout the United States and were

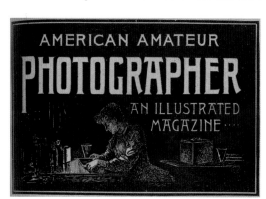

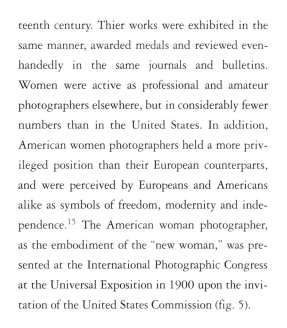

unquestionably instrumental in the broad development of photography. Clubs provided facilities, libraries, exhibition spaces and, perhaps most importantly, criticism and advice offered by experienced photographers. In the 1880s and 1890s, societal mores separated men and women in most clubs. Fewer in number, the female members were relegated to a secondary role, with more limited hours and fewer opportunities to assemble.[14] However, by the end of the 1890s the segregation of women within the photographic clubs began to dissipate in the United States, following the recognition of the high quality of their work and other concurrent social changes. When allowed to participate equally in the clubs and to exhibit at salons beside their male peers, the technical skills and artistic accomplishments of women photographers quickly received official recognition. Participation in photographic clubs, particularly those with facilities, combined with the interchange of ideas via publications and correspondence, allowed for a rapid collective advance by American women photographers. It expedited their technical advances and drove them to pursue more ambitious work.

American women photographers participated alongside their male colleagues with remarkable success in international photographic exhibitions and salons during the last two decades of the nine-

teenth century. Thier works were exhibited in the same manner, awarded medals and reviewed evenhandedly in the same journals and bulletins. Women were active as professional and amateur photographers elsewhere, but in considerably fewer numbers than in the United States. In addition, American women photographers held a more privileged position than their European counterparts, and were perceived by Europeans and Americans alike as symbols of freedom, modernity and independence.[15] The American woman photographer, as the embodiment of the "new woman," was presented at the International Photographic Congress at the Universal Exposition in 1900 upon the invitation of the United States Commission (fig. 5).

"The beautiful and graceful with the progressive and strong"[16]

As with all World Fairs, the Universal Exposition of 1900 was closely tied to political agendas, allotting spaces for each nation to construct an image of itself for the world at large. The emerging nation-states, such as France and the United States, used the international fairs as cultural battlefields,[17] with extensive committees and subcommittees carefully screening and approving each component to be included. Following the disruptive and divisive forces of the American Civil War, violent labor and class conflicts, the Spanish-American War and economic depressions, the United States government seized the occasion of the Universal Exposition to promote a nationalist agenda. The objective was to demonstrate to those abroad, as well as those at home, that the "newly constructed American nation-state had come of age as an imperial power."[18] The strongly worded essay in the official catalogue clearly reveals this agenda:

"Beyond all considerations such as we have discussed it was recognized by every intelligent man of affairs that the time had fully come when the United States of North America should assume its proper place in all the international assemblings of the nations of the world. ...all the elements of national greatness are present in such degree as to make it incumbent upon her to assert her position among the nations... and to have a voice in deliberations which concern the welfare of the world."[19]

The United States invested more money than any other government in its national exhibition and made its presence felt in the months leading up to the Exposition. Frequently appealing to the French committees for additional space to house the various pavilions and exhibitions, the persistence of the United States delegation succeeded in making the American presence a strong one. A certain amount of trepidation was expressed in the January 1900 issue of *The Nineteen Hundred*, the official journal established in 1895 to document the preparations for the exposition:

"The American Union will triumph, indisputably, at the Universal Exposition of 1900. The Latin nations, inactive and on their decline, England with her economic power shaken, Russia overflowing with young sap, but still doomed to limited exchanges, the gigantic efforts of Germany, victorious in Europe and Asia, will be confronted with the Republic of the New World with her prodigious industry and constantly increasing commerce, her prompt filling of export orders and her universal acquisitions of new markets.

They are about to come among us… Several old countries whose confidence hitherto nothing or almost nothing had shaken, will be able to learn from them many a serious and profitable lesson. A whole world unknown to our Parisians who do everything by routine will spring up on the Quai d'Orsay with mysterious and terrible threats. It is a world of 70 millions of men accustomed to persistent labor and to whom defeat is unknown."[20]

This sense of foreboding was also accompanied by a measure of admiration for the American spirit and determination that had brought such rapid growth and expansion. Realizing the possibility that the prosperity of the United States was eclipsing the European nations, from which the majority of her citizens had immigrated, articles in the French press expressed curiosity about this emergence. Some suggested that the European nations could learn from American ambition and work ethic: "the American people stand before us, not as a formidable 'unknown,' but as a living proof of what human determination can accomplish… Old Europe must learn from this example, shake off the dust of time and without renouncing the past

which made it famous, look towards the future which shall bring its happiness."[21]

It was not merely the economic presence of the United States that pervaded the exposition; American strength and confidence were also felt in the cultural exhibitions. An entire pavilion was built for celebrated American dancer Loïe Fuller, who was already known in Paris and was sure to draw crowds. John Philip Sousa and his band played concerts regularly on the esplanade of Les Invalides to the "most enthusiastic crowds ever brought together in Paris"[22] and at ceremonies dedicating the statues of George Washington and Marquis de Lafayette, for whom Sousa wrote "Hail to the Spirit of Liberty." The formal dedication ceremonies, symbolic of the changing political climate, were gestures of diplomacy between two countries that had been fiercely debating trade agreements at the close of the century. Throughout the Exposition, articles in the French press reflected a growing interest in the United States and American art while attempting to explain and contextualize this phenomenon.[23]

The United States Commission for the Fine Arts selected works "to demonstrate not only America's new cultural status, but also its economic, technological, imperial and agrarian riches."[24] John B. Cauldwell, Director of the Department of Fine Arts, formally acknowledged in his official report that many American artists had been influenced by the European art schools where they had studied, but controversially asserted that since the Universal Exposition of 1889, where Americans took home more medals than any other country, American art had "emancipated" itself from European influence.[25] Léonce Bénédite, curator of the Musée National de Luxembourg, agreed. In a letter to Cauldwell he stated, "I have no difficulty observing in your brilliant exposition a strong movement, unknown to us, less in contact with European centers, more local, and which no doubt marks the beginning of a real national school."[26] Once again awarded more medals than any other nation in 1900, the American artists succeeded in differentiating themselves from their European peers despite the fact that most had studied in Europe.[27]

In industry, music and the arts, the United States had come into its own and was redefining each field, setting new standards and presenting itself as a rival to the European countries that had long nurtured it. Every image of American society represented was consistently "progressive," and this, coupled with the economic success of the United States, embodied for most visitors to the Universal Exposition of 1900 a vision of the future. One author noted: "The Republic is rapidly developing a highly perfected as well as a soundly organized civilization, and particularly that it promises to solve, to the satisfaction of all, that problem which has so long annoyed Europe and the world and all ages, viz, the practical and satisfying combination of the artistic with the utilitarian, the aesthetic with the enduring, the beautiful and graceful with the progressive and strong."[28]

"Persona non grata" [29]

Less apparent within this concept of progress was the place of American women. Following the 1893 World's Columbian Exposition in Chicago, where the Women's Building gave women, especially those of the white middle and upper classes, a visible presence and a forum for expressing their concerns for social issues, American women expected to have some control over how they were represented at the Universal Exposition of 1900 in Paris. However, not a single woman was appointed to the United States Commission, something that caused the Head of the Board of Lady Managers for the World's Columbian Exposition, Bertha Honoré Palmer, to declare publicly her discontent over the absence of women from the commission. Mrs. Palmer eventually obliged Ferdinand W. Peck, the Commissioner General and a fellow Chicagoan, to provide an explanation for this decision. He reasoned that the United States Congress had not mandated that women be appointed to the commission as it had for the Chicago Exposition and, moreover, "it would be embarrassing to the ladies [because] the appointees would likely be 'persona non grata' to the French officials."[30] Other officials of the United States opposed the participation of women, declaring the possible presence of women a "fifth wheel" and asserting that "we have no such funds to spend in such a useless direction."[31] Even Edward Bok, editor of the *Ladies' Home Jour-*

nal, opposed a separate building for American women at the Paris exposition, stating that it would most likely be a "hen house." Some opposition was directed toward the concept of separatism, but the fact remains that the American concept of women displayed at the 1893 Exposition in Chicago, more progressive than anywhere else in the world, was not officially present at the Universal Exposition of 1900 in Paris. Women participated in each of the fields to a certain extent, but without an independent voice. For the Exposition in France, the United States reverted to the Old World conception of a woman's role in society—one to be strictly defined by men.

Ultimately, Mrs. Palmer's continuing complaints compelled President McKinley to appoint her as one of the eighteen honorary commissioners for the United States Delegation to the Universal Exposition of 1900, hoping to quell her voice with the honorific post just a few months before the inauguration. Mr. Peck also tried to pacify Mrs. Palmer with the news that the French had agreed to allow a Woman's Pavilion, though his own chief lieutenant Frederick Skiff admitted it was "a miserable fake… more of a comfort station than a serious exhibition hall."[32] Inspired by the Woman's Building in Chicago, the Parisian pavilion took on a very different form and encouraged women to continue in the traditional roles of wife and homemaker.[33]

In her new position, Mrs. Palmer was determined that the social advances of the American women be represented and charged her secretary, Ellen Henrotin, with finding twenty-five American women who were specialists in their fields to serve as United States delegates in Paris. As discussed above, photography was a rapidly expanding field and provided good examples of accomplished "modern" women. It was with this aim that Henrotin wrote to Frances B. Johnston, a pioneering photojournalist, asking her to assemble a representative exhibition of American women photographers to demonstrate that they had "accomplished such unique work."[34] The invitation was accepted with enthusiasm and an exhibition was prepared. Surprisingly, due to conflicting ideas on the classification of photography at the Paris exposition, this proved to be the only representation of American artistic photography.

FIG. 6. Alice Austin.
[Portrait of a woman], ca. 1900
(cat. 29).

FIG. 7. Amelia Van Buren.
[Woman with urn], ca. 1900
(cat. 170).

In 1900, a fierce debate was raging within the American photographic community, dividing it into two distinct groups: those that considered photography as a new art, capable of personal expression, and those that believed that photography was nothing more than a scientific tool, incapable of artistic creativity. The periodical literature of the period, rife with conflicting viewpoints, reveals both arguments. One recurring enigma was the very definition of photography as it evolved in different directions, with some photographers pulling away from "straight photography" and instead following their desire to be more creative. An example is found in a review of the Chicago Photographic Salon of 1900: "Here is the point round which the battle rages: if the fog is accidental the picture is not artistic; but if the fog was got deliberately then it is."[35] The need to differentiate between the two schools of thought led some writers to begin referring to artistic photographers as "painter-photographers" and clammering for recognition of the artistic merit of the medium by comparing it to painting. The following quote, praising the work of Gertrude Käsebier as more "artistic" than many contemporary painters, reflects this point of view:

"There are painters that live under the laws, the eternal, immutable law of creative art; but they are few in number. There are photographers, myriads of them, who are but button-pressers or tricksters; but, while one may scrutinize endless exhibitions of pictures in oils and water-colors, and find no such conscientious art work, here is one (and there are many others) who, working in an almost undeveloped medium, contending against technical difficulties inherent in the mode, yet goes back to the fundamental laws of the great old art and uses them for the production of results that are justly and exactly artistic."[36]

The conflict had escalated, making the high-profile Universal Exposition of 1900 the perfect stage for a dramatic boycott by American "painter-photographers," or Pictorialist photographers as they would come to be known. When asked to choose American photographs for inclusion in the Universal Exposition, Alfred Stieglitz seized the opportunity to promote his agenda: the elevation of photography to the level of fine arts.

As a challenge to the organizers, he requested that the standard of selection for photography be the same as for other arts, so that any photographs judged worthy by the American Art Jury, in charge of selecting the paintings and sculptures to be included, would then be exhibited beside the selected paintings and sculptures. Not surprisingly, the request was denied, infuriating Stieglitz and prompting he and other 'progressive' photographers from the United States to boycott the event.[37] This highlighted the rift within the photographic community and was a harbinger of the formal split that would come two years later with the formation of the Photo-Secession.[38] As a result, the women photographers presented by Frances B. Johnston formed the only collective representation of American Pictorialist photography in Paris until F. Holland Day's exhibition of the "New American School of Photography" in February 1901.[39]

"The Foremost Women Photographers of America"[40]

It is a testament to Frances B. Johnston's central position in female photographic circles that, within a collapsed time frame, she organized a large exhibition of work by leading women photographers, both professionals and amateurs. A professional herself, Johnston did not believe that professional photography was without artistic value, so she contacted women solely on a basis of merit. As a result, she exhibited professionals and amateurs jointly, transcending the heated debates dividing the American photographic community and presenting a cross-section, which revealed the varied styles causing such scandal in American photographic circles.

The women invited to participate in the exhibition received a simple letter from Johnston outlining the exhibition, requesting a biographical sketch, a portrait photograph and asking them to specify rights of reproduction. The women Johnston contacted were active members of the national photographic community as amateurs and professionals and had found success in international photographic salons as established as London and as exotic as India. Many had successful professional photography careers and had already committed to other major exhibitions that year. The demands upon these women to provide work for various salons and exhibitions was evident through their correspondence with Frances B. Johnston in preparation for the Paris exhibition. Many women expressed regret at having so little time to prepare and apologized for having already sent some of the finest examples of their work to other exhibitions. Considering that sixteen of the women Johnston invited participated in more than three major exhibitions that year, ten in five or more, and Eva Watson submitted work to nine, it is not surprising to find the same images listed in other concurrent salon and exhibition records.[41]

At the close of the nineteenth century, photographers were more or less divided into three categories: amateurs, professional artistic photographers and professionals. The women included in Johnston's exhibition reflected these divisions. The amateurs approached photography from an aesthetic perspective and did not use it as a means to support themselves. Inevitably, serious amateurs were economically privileged, often receiving a traditional art education, which encouraged composition and artistic interpretation and influenced their photography. The most notable amateurs in Johnston's exhibition were an art collector Sarah Choate Sears, a member of Boston's high society, friend of John Singer Sargent, and Virginia Sharp,

who studied at the Museum of Fine Arts in Boston with Eastman Johnson and in Paris at the Académie Julian.

The professionals who defined themselves as "artist-photographers" wished to differentiate themselves from the "cheap-johns"—the professionals who entered photography with purely commercial goals and took photographs without careful consideration of composition or artful printing. The title was also a means of attracting a select clientele.

FIG. 8. Alta Belle Sniff. [Portrait of a man with mustache in a tuxedo], ca. 1900 (cat. 154).

FIG. 9. Fannie Elton. [Oval portrait of a woman with a flower in her hair and a corsage], ca. 1900 (cat. 72).

Fig. 10. Emma J. Farnsworth. *In the West Wind Blowing*, ca. 1894 (cat. 87).

Fig. 11. Frances and Mary Allen. [Illustration] *For Alice Morse Earle's "Home Life in Colonial Days,"* ca. 1898 (cat. 14).

As found in the commercial brochure of Estelle Huggins,[42] educational institutions and professors were often listed to substantiate artistic training. Several women from Johnston's exhibition fell into this artistically skilled professional category. The most prominent were Gertrude Käsebier, Zaida Ben-Yusuf, Alice Austin (fig. 6) and Amelia Van Buren (fig. 7) all of whom were highly artistic photographers, and received recognition for their skillful compositions, innovative printing techniques and artistic matting. The skills of professional photographers like Käsebier caused rifts in the photographic community, in particular with members of the Stieglitz circle, of which she had been a member. Even though these were undeniably beautiful images, they believed that any photograph taken for commercial purposes could not be considered artistic, since the impetus behind its creation was commercial.

Also included in Johnston's exhibition were professional photographers who held to more straightforward representations, like Addie Robinson (fig. 8) and Fannie Elton (fig. 9). Elton described her traditional methods in a letter to Johnston, "I do not strive to make odd 'freaky' things, but stick close to nature."[43] The portraits, though carefully posed, do not embrace the aesthetics of the Pictorialist movement. Rather, they strive to capture a likeness. In comparing the styles of portraiture, one can see the variety available to

the American public, with some photographic portraits achieving the originality previously mastered only through the traditional arts of painting and sculpture. The Pictorialist, or "progressive," interpretations of professional portraits caught the attention of French critics because they crossed the boundary between professional and amateur circles, something uncommon in France. In his review of the Photo-Club exhibition, the critic Étienne Wallon remarked that, unlike in France, it was difficult to distinguish upon first glance the work of the professionals from the work of the amateurs and he attributed the development of a more interpretative style of portraiture to a more demanding clientele.[44]

Illustration was a common practice among the professional women photographers included in the exhibition. Whether for advertisement, storybooks and poems, or the re-creation of allegories, the scenes were carefully composed and constructed. Inspired by Old Master paintings, Myra Albert Wiggins re-created Dutch interiors through meticulous attention to detail, covering the walls of her home with burlap, sewing costumes and laying down wide wooden planks on the floor, as seen in *Hunger ist der Beste Koch* (plate 75). Emma Justine Farnsworth dressed her models in Classical costumes to create images depicting allegories and poems (fig. 10). A deliberate orchestration of composition is revealed in two photographs by Sarah Jane Eddy, *Contentment* (plate 21) and *A Welcome Interruption* (plate 20).

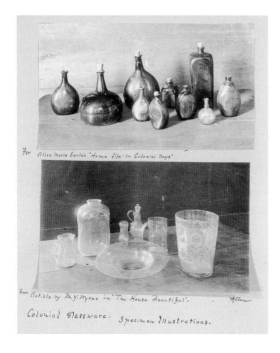

Taken in the same diffused light from the same viewpoint, the photographs have subtle differences that were carefully adjusted. Mary and Frances Allen, former schoolteachers, also practiced the "straight" style of photography, using it to document their community and illustrate historic articles and books (fig. 11).

Several professional photographers included by Johnston were not modest about their success when they wrote their biographies for her, boasting about the prices that they could command and the number of assistants in their studio. A good example can be found in a letter to Frances B. Johnston from Alta Belle Sniff. She bragged: "I receive the highest prices paid for photographic work in our city [Columbus, Ohio] and keep two ladies besides myself busy all the time."[45] Professional demands seemed to weigh heavily on some of the photographers, such as Sarah Jane Eddy, who did not wish to have a biography included in the presentation, reasoning that "To be known means more care and more demands upon me and I have too many already."[46] Respecting the professional integrity of the photographers, Johnston asked specifically about rights of reproduction. Eighteen of the photographs submitted were already copyrighted and three photographers forbade any reproduction whatsoever, demonstrating business savvy and the need to protect their livelihood.

In order to share the cost of equipment and a studio, it was common for professional photographers to enter into partnerships. Among the professional women photographers included in Johnston's archive were six former or current partnerships: Van Buren and Watson, Clark and Wade, Johnston and Käsebier, The Misses Selby, Mary and Frances Allen, and Mary and Katharine Stanbery. Other photographers included in the Johnston archive, such as Elton, Desmond and Walborn, also had business partnerships at one time with other photographers. It is also worth noting that photography was a second career for several of the women, including the Allen sisters, Mathilde Weil, Elizabeth Flint Wade and Ema Spencer; the first had been teachers, the second had read manuscripts and the latter two had been writers.

Though all photographers included were active in various associations, nine of the women exhibitors, both amateurs and professionals, only participated in a few, if any, additional exhibitions. One of the unique aspects of Johnston's exhibition was the fact that it assembled works by women photographers beyond those who were already participating in salons and exhibitions. The inclusion of these photographers gives a broader view of what women photographers were creating at the time. One must not overlook the continuing demands that familial responsibilities still placed upon women and the constraints that this put on their photographic work. In their letters to Johnston, many of the women attributed the delay in responding or the lack of more recent prints to frail health, the transit to summer residences or to other familial obligations. For most married women, even successful professionals, photography was second to domestic duties. Mary Bartlett, for example, wrote to Johnston about the demands of motherhood and how it pulled her away from her interest in photography: "I would enjoy doing some new printing of pictures. But this is a busy month—my boys & girls busy in various ways about their schools & all of us in a hurry to get to our lake home so I cannot do as I would like."[47]

As the constraints of family life remained strong, it is not surprising that twenty of the thirty-one women were unmarried at the time of the exhibition and that eighteen never married. These figures are consistent with the trends of professional women of the era. A few of the married

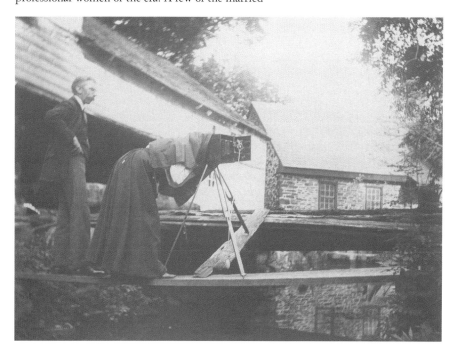

FIG. 12. *The Editor and His Wife* (Alfred Paschall watching his wife Mary Paschall photograph). Doylestown, Penn., Mercer Museum, Bucks County Historical Society.

FIG. 13. Cover of *American Amateur Photography* (June 1899).

women photographers were aided by their husbands or were pleased to recount the supportive role that their husbands played in their pursuit of photography (fig. 12). The advanced printing techniques of Mary Bartlett, for example, were due in part to the assistance of her husband, a well-known chemist. Virginia Sharp and her husband were both photographers and participated in the same photographic salons on a number of occasions. Some women also mentioned their husbands in their letters to Johnston, telling of the "kind co-operation" which allowed them to pursue photography.[48] Mabel Osgood Wright, after requesting a simple Kodak, received a fancy tripod camera from her husband, who advised her "Don't be a snap-shot nuisance, if you wish to take up photography, begin at the right end."[49]

"Progress in Photography" [50]

By 1900, American women photographers had become symbols of the "new woman," though in many ways the majority of them were far from avant-garde beyond their passion for photography. It is important, therefore, not to make the errant assumption that "interactions between women in photography were related to political, feminist or reform causes"[51] or that they wanted to be differentiated from men within the photographic community. Many saw the benefits of exhibiting alongside male photographers and, when approached by Frances B. Johnston to participate in an exhibit of exclusively women, were wary of being segregated. Eva Watson made clear that she did not want her photographs to be presented as "women's work," but instead "judged by only one standard irrespective of <u>sex</u>."[52] One must not remove these women from their historical context. Indeed, it is more interesting to consider them within it. In certain respects they were exceptional, but in most ways they were representative of American women of the era: on the cusp of social change, caught between Victorian traditions and the trends of the future. The added particularity is that these women were also involved in the simultaneously shifting definition of photography, which was developing technically and undergoing transition from a strictly documentary practice to an art form.

The exhibition organized by Johnston was significant not because it gave recognition and displayed the work by American women photographers for the first time. In fact, most had long been publicly exhibiting their work and already receiving widespread recognition. Rather, the primary objective was to highlight the particularly marked success of American women photographers at the turn of the century. It encapsulated what American women photographers were producing at the time and was held up as an example of "progress in photography."[53] Frances B. Johnston, upon the invitation of Bertha Honoré Palmer, made certain that an example of the modern woman or the "new woman," as part of the American national identity, was represented as a symbol of social progress. The exhibition at the Universal Exposition of 1900 is often misinterpreted as a comparison of works by female and male photographers, but it was not an attempt to prove that women could master photography. Instead, it was to boast the mastery of *American* women in photography (fig. 13), something that had happened to a much lesser degree elsewhere. It was thus a presentation to demonstrate of the supremacy of American women photographers "in triumph over the remainder of the world."[54]

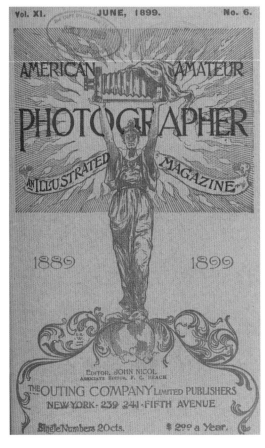

The basis of this essay comes from my Masters thesis, *"L'Œuvre à accomplir et les obstacles à vaincre."*
An Exhibition of American Women Photographers at the Third International Photographic Congress in Paris at the Universal Exposition of 1900
(Columbia University, 2000), which also explores the French reception of the works discussed more extensively in this catalogue by Michel Poivert.
Thank you to both David Griffith and Ezekiel Edwards for thoughtfully editing this text.

1. Advertising pamphlet for Estelle Huntington Huggins, n.d. Frances Benjamin Johnston Papers, Manuscripts Division, Library of Congress, Washington, D.C.

2. Fischer, Diane P., "L'Invention de l' 'École Américaine' en 1900" in *Paris 1900, Les Artistes Américains à l'Exposition Universelle* (Paris: Paris-Musées, 2001), p. 31. The statue was by Alexander Phimister Proctor and the mural was painted by Robert L. Reid.

3. The title of an article by Frances Benjamin Johnston, *Ladies' Home Journal* (September 1897), pp. 6–7.

4. Fifty percent of women who received a college education between 1890 and 1920 remained unmarried. See Jane C. Gover, *The Positive Image: Women Photographers in Turn of the Century America* (Albany: State University of New York, 1988), p. 3.

5. Catherine Weed Barnes, "Women as Photographers," *American Amateur Photographer*, 3 (September 1891), p. 338.

6. Gover, p. 20.

7. The census of 1900 contained a section dedicated to "Women at Work" that listed 3,500 women as professional photographers. As cited in Gover, p. 17.

8. Beaton, Cecil, and Gail Buckland. *The Magic Image. The Genius of Photography from 1839 to the Present Day* (Boston: Little & Brown, 1975), p. 84.

9. "Women's Work in Photography," *The Photographic Times and the American Photographer*, 17:287 (March 18, 1887), pp. 127–28.

10. Frances Benjamin Johnston, "What a Woman Can Do with a Camera," *Ladies Home Journal*, 14 (September 1897), p. 6. An education in the fine arts, often in Europe, was popular among upper class women and Johnston, who studied in Paris at the Académie Julian, typified this trend.

11. Catherine Weed Barnes, "Women as Photographers," *American Amateur Photographer*, 3 (September 1891), p. 338.

12. Margaret Bisland, "Women and Their Cameras," *Outing*, 17 (October 1890), pp. 36–38.

13. Bisland, p. 38.

14. Gover, pp. 69–70.

15. For further discussion of the French perception of American women, see "La Belle Américaine" in *Une Fascination Réticente. Les États-Unis dans l'opinion française* by J. Portes (Nancy: Presses Universitaires de Nancy, 1990) and C. de Varigny, "La Femme aux États-Unis" in *Revue des Deux Mondes* (January 15, 1893), pp. 391–428.

16. "Three Annexes to the United States," *The Nineteen Hundred*, 10:6 (June 1900), pp. 17–18.

17. Robert Rydell, "Gateway to the 'American Century': The American Representation at the Paris Universal Exposition of 1900," in *Paris 1900, The 'American School,'* catalogue for a traveling exhibition beginning at the Montclair Art Museum, edited by Diane P. Fischer (New Brunswick, New Jersey: Rutgers University Press, 1999), p. 124.

18. Rydell, pp. 120–24.

19. *Catalogue of Exhibitors in the United States Sections of the International Universal Exposition, Paris, 1900* (Paris: Société Anonyme des Imprimeries Lemercier, 1900), pp. 4–5.

20. M. Paul Louis, "The Economic Grandeur of the United States," *The Nineteen Hundred. Illustrated Journal of the Paris Exposition*, 10:1 (January 1900), pp. 14–15. [The journal was published in Paris, and nearly every article appears in both French and English in each issue and prices for subscription are given for France, Great Britain and the United States.]

21. Alfred Schweizer, *Les États-Unis à l'Exposition Universelle de 1900* (Paris, Imprimerie P. Dubreuil, 1900), p. 82.

22. Frédéric Maye, ed., *The Nineteen Hundred*, 11:1 (July 1900), p. 9.

23. For further discussion, see Gabriel P. Weisberg, "The French Reception of American Art at the Universal Exposition of 1900," in *Paris 1900: The 'American School' at the Universal Exposition*, catalogue for a traveling exhibition beginning at the Montclair Art Museum, edited by Diane P. Fischer (New Brunswick, New Jersey: Rutgers University Press, 1999), pp. 153–70.

24. Fischer, p. 177.

25. *Report of the Commissioner General for the United States to the International Exposition, Paris, 1900*, 6 vols. (Washington, D.C.: Government Printing Office, 1901) cited in Weisberg, pp. 164–66.

26. *Report of the Commissioner General for the United States to the International Exposition, Paris, 1900*, 6 vols. (Washington, D.C.: Government Printing Office, 1901) cited in Weisberg, p. 164, note 53.

27. For further discussion of the American art presented at the 1900 Universal Exposition, see *Paris 1900, The 'American School' at the Universal Exhibition*, catalogue for a traveling exhibition beginning at the Montclair Art Museum, edited by Diane P. Fischer (New Brunswick, New Jersey: Rutgers University Press, 1999).

28. *Report of the Commissioner General…, op. cit.,* vol. 1, p. 69.

29. Peck as quoted in Rydell, p. 138.

30. *Ibid.*

31. As quoted in Rydell, p. 138.

32. Skiff as quoted in Rydell, p. 139.

33. Indeed, according to reports in *The Nineteen Hundred* and the official catalogue, the Palais de la Femme housed restaurants, a hair dressing salon, sitting rooms and other amenities. The exhibitions housed were "women's work," hygiene, the feminine *toilette* and feminine elegance. Photography, which could be practiced within the home, fell within the acceptable activities and was thus presented as a hobby for the public in the pavilion.

34. Unpublished letter from Ellen Henrotin to Frances Benjamin Johnston, April 12, 1900, Frances Benjamin Johnston Papers, Manuscripts Division, Library of Congress, Washington, D.C.

35. F. Dundas Todd, "The Salon Pictures. The Chicago Salon," *The Photo-Beacon*, 12:6 (June 1900), p. 151.

36. R. A. Cram, "Mrs. Käsebier's Work," *Photo-Era*, 4:5 (May 1900), p. 134.

37. Pictorialist photographers from Germany, Belgium and Austria also boycotted.

38. A group of Pictorialist photographers founded in 1902 by Alfred Stieglitz with the intention of advancing photography to the status of fine art. Of the women in Johnston's exhibition the following were members: Alice Austin, Zaida Ben-Yusuf, Gertrude Käsebier, Sarah Sears, Ema Spencer, Mary and Katharine Stanbery, Eva Watson-Schütze, Myra Wiggins, and Frances Benjamin Johnston herself.

39. Only professional photographers participated in the official exhibition, which according to Sreznewsky was just as well, as "artistic works would most likely not have been noticed at the exhibition, since the building allocated to American photography was even worse than that for Russian photography—cramped and completely dark." W. I. Sreznewsky, "Kollektsiia fotograficheskikh kartin, ispolnennykh amerikanskimi liubitel'nitsami fotografii," trans. by Harry M. Leich, *Fotograficheskoe obozrienie*, 6:1 (November 1900), pp. 1–5. See appendix.

40. Frances Benjamin Johnston, "The Foremost Women Photographers of America. A Series of Picture-pages Showing What Women Have Done with the Camera," *Ladies' Home Journal*, a series of seven articles profiling women photographers published from May 1901 to January 1902.

41. For example, nine photographers in Johnston's exhibition submitted several of the same works to the Chicago Photographic Salon of 1900 (Johnston and four other women included in her collection also submitted work to this salon).

42. Advertising pamphlet for Estelle Huntington Huggins, n.d. Frances Benjamin Johnston Papers, Manuscripts Division, Library of Congress, Washington, D.C.. See biographical entry for listing of professors.

43. Unpublished letter from Fannie Elton to Frances Benjamin Johnston, June 23, 1900, Frances Benjamin Johnston Papers, Manuscripts Division, Library of Congress, Washington, D.C.

44. E. Wallon, "L'Exposition des artistes américaines au Photo-Club," *Photo-Gazette* (February 25, 1901), p. 62.

45. Unpublished letter from Alta Belle Sniff to Frances Benjamin Johnston, June 23, 1900, Frances Benjamin Johnston Papers, Manuscripts Division, Library of Congress, Washington, D.C.

46. Unpublished letter from Sarah Jane Eddy to Frances Benjamin Johnston, June 18, 1900, Frances Benjamin Johnston Papers, Manuscripts Division, Library of Congress, Washington, D.C.

47. Unpublished letter from Mary A. Bartlett to Frances Benjamin Johnston, June 6, 1900, Frances Benjamin Johnston Papers, Manuscripts Division, Library of Congress, Washington, D.C.

48. Unpublished, undated letter from Addie Kilburn Robinson to Frances Benjamin Johnston, ca. June 1900, Frances Benjamin Johnston Papers, Manuscripts Division, Library of Congress, Washington, D.C.

49. Unpublished letter from Mabel Osgood Wright to Frances Benjamin Johnston, June 19, 1900, Frances Benjamin Johnston Papers, Manuscripts Division, Library of Congress, Washington, D.C.

50. "Progress in Photography. Collections of Specimens for the Paris Exposition. All the Work of American Women—A Proposed Exhibit in This City," *The Evening Star* (Washington, D.C., July 6, 1900), p. 1.

51. Gover, p. 55.

52. Unpublished letter from Eva Watson to Frances Benjamin Johnston, June 10 [1900]. Frances Benjamin Johnston Papers, Manuscripts Division, Library of Congress, Washington, D.C.

53. "Progress in Photography. Collections of Specimens for the Paris Exposition. All the Work of American Women—A Proposed Exhibit in This City," *The Evening Star* (Washington, D.C., July 6, 1900), p. 1.

54. *Ibid.*

FRANCES BENJAMIN JOHNSTON IN 1900
STAKING THE SISTERHOOD'S CLAIM IN AMERICAN PHOTOGRAPHY

VERNA POSEVER CURTIS

*The women in this country are certainly
doing great photographic work & deserve much
commendation for their efforts.*

ALFRED STIEGLITZ TO FRANCES B. JOHNSTON, June 8, 1900[1]

FIG. 1. Frances B. Johnston. *Self-portrait in her studio*, ca. 1900. Modern gelatin silver print from Johnston negative. Washington, D.C., Library of Congress, Prints & Photographs Division, LC-USZ62-64301

Frances B. Johnston (1864–1952) was a trailblazing photographer. She took charge and she took chances. By the age of thirty-six, she was a celebrity with many firsts to her credit: first woman member of the Washington, D.C., Camera Club, first woman to conquer underground photography, first White House photographer (fig. 1). A prolific author as well as camera worker, she had achieved distinction on behalf of her sex and photography. Readers of popular illustrated magazines in the 1890s could hardly miss seeing her articles or pictures.

In 1900, the United States Commission invited Johnston to be one of four delegates to the International Congress of Photography to be held during the celebrated Universal Exposition in Paris.[2] Johnston was the only woman to attend this historic meeting. She spoke about the distinctive work of American female photographers and illustrated her talk with a unique display of approximately one hundred and fifty photographs. Her own photographs from commissions to depict instruction in the progressive schools of Washington and at Hampton Normal and Agricultural Institute, Hampton, Virginia, were on view elsewhere on the grounds of the Exposition.

Although confirmation of her lecture came only six weeks before she was to sail, Johnston was able to gather enough work and biographical material from thirty-one women photographers to incorporate into her lecture. Members of the Congress greeted the women's work enthusiastically. Wiacheslav Izmilovich Sreznewsky, a Russian attendee, even arranged to take the collection to his country, where not much work in the Pictorialist or artistic style had been seen. Later, the photographs that had gone to Russia—not Johnston's own work—were shown at the Photo-Club de

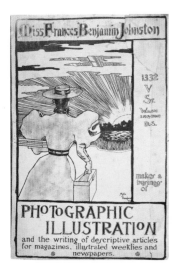

FIG. 2. Mills Thompson. *Miss Johnston makes a business of photographic illustration and the writing of descriptive articles for magazines, illustrated weeklies and newspapers*, 1895. Lithograph [poster]. Washington, D.C., L. C., P & P Div., LC-USZC4-1444

Paris in January 1901, where they made a powerful impact. Europe had no comparable group of women photographers.

Johnston's bold steps onto the global stage were in keeping with her character. Bolstering America's nationalist cause as the ambassador of the country's women photographers, she proclaimed their camera skills to the world. Her own work on display at the Universal Exposition proved her special effectiveness as a communicator; the photographs showed the success of public instruction in the United States for all its citizens. Although she is known today principally as an architectural photographer, her underappreciated role as a leader in American photography at the turn of the nineteenth century warrants review.

By the time of the Exposition, Johnston had already enjoyed a decade of success in a career that had initially been devoted to illustration and writing, but soon embraced the pioneering field of photojournalism (fig. 2). She knew the value of publicity and on the eve of her departure news of her trip to Paris broke in her hometown paper, *The Evening Star* of Washington, D.C. The article "Progress in Photography" reported that Johnston expected "to illustrate fully the wonderful ability of American women who have been… students of the camera and its possibilities and to startle the old world with a revelation of what the women of this country have accomplished in triumph over the remainder of the world."[3] Johnston had the clout to be triumphant. Female readers avidly followed her contributions to *Demorest's Family Magazine*, *Ladies' Home Journal*, *Cosmopolitan*, *Frank Leslie's Magazine* and *Harper's Weekly*. They saw the results of her descents deep into the Kohinoor coal mine in Pennsylvania and the Mammoth Cave in Kentucky in total darkness, using a camera and flammable flash powder with considerable technical skill to capture the subterranean scene.

Such achievements justified her reputation for spirited independence. Coincident with America's imperial aspirations, Johnston acted on her own ambitions. Mixing business with pleasure on a European trip in August 1899, she scored the first of many photojournalistic coups. In Naples, she gained entrée aboard Admiral George Dewey's flagship, USS *Olympia*, on its way home from Manila Bay in the Philippines and victory in the Spanish-American War. She sympathetically portrayed the commander at rest and scenes of male camaraderie on board. Viewers responded warmly to the images she captured showing the seamen's vigor and her photographs helped to foster patriotism at home.[4]

Dubbed the "American court photographer," Johnston had produced portraits of Presidents Grover Cleveland, William McKinley, Jr., and their families, as well as senators, diplomats and numerous other government officials, often in their office settings (fig. 3). Established in 1894, her photographic studio had become financially successful and highly regarded in political and social circles in Washington, and also by photography colleagues near and far. Carefully planned as an addition to the back of the home Johnston shared with her parents, her skylit studio with its Arts and Crafts-style earth-toned interior was furnished with revival furniture and contemporary

decorative arts. It was a showcase of fashionable bohemianism. On Wednesday afternoons, cordial "at homes" were a regular social feature (figs. 4, 5).

By the time the Universal Exposition opened in Paris, Johnston had gained considerable stature as an art photographer. She had exhibited her photographs nationally and internationally as far as Calcutta and had served on the first all-photographer jury for the Second Philadelphia Salon in 1899.[5] In her own career, she had bridged the gulfs between amateur, professional and Pictorialist or art photographer, gulfs that soon developed into political impasses between them. Greatly admired in her own country both for her initiatives as a working woman with remarkable professional achievements and for her patriotism, she was perfectly positioned to represent her female colleagues in Paris as the premier ambassador of their progress.

The Universal Exposition ran from April 15 to November 12, 1900, and welcomed the new century in grand style. Larger than the previous Paris Universal Exposition in 1889 that inaugurated the colossal Eiffel Tower, it occupied 270 acres. Encompassing nearly 83,000 official exhibitors and 25,000 to 30,000 exhibitions, it was a huge nationalistic as well as technological and commercial extravaganza. Like world's fairs, there were pavilions for nations, but a new arrangement allowed similar productions from different countries to be shown side by side. Exhibitions were

FIG. 3. Frances B. Johnston photographing a governement official at the State, War and Navy Building [now Old Executive Office Building], 1888. Cyanotype. Washington, D.C., L. C., P & P Div., LC-DIGID: ppmsc-04839

FIG. 4. Frances B. Johnston. Interior of Frances B. Johnston's studio (1332 V Street, Washington, D.C.), probably 1890s. Modern gelatin silver print from Johnston negative. Washington, D.C., L. C., P & P Div., LC-DIGID-ppmsc-04835

FIG. 5. Frances B. Johnston serving tea to Elbert Hubbard (center) and another visitor to her studio, probably 1890s. Modern gelatin silver print from Johnston negative. Washington, D.C., L. C., P & P Div., LC-DIGID-ppmsc-04832

classified into eighteen groups, and separate buildings or palaces, such as those for Education and Instruction, Social Economy, Electricity, Optics, and Costume, were erected to display them. Planning for the Universal Exposition in America had begun in 1898, after the United States Congress authorized the nation's participation, appointed officials and appropriated a staggering $1.3 million dollars to fund it.

Having participated in the 1893 World's Columbian Exposition in Chicago, Johnston was no stranger to these periodic spectaculars. She had recorded the construction of the grandiose buildings in the neo-Renaissance "White City" built around lagoons near the shore of Lake Michigan and reported on it in *Demorest's Family Magazine.* During the Exposition, photographs from her survey of the United States Naval Academy at Annapolis, Maryland, were displayed in a remarkable replica in brick of the USS *Illinois*, and she served on a government team photographing the myriad exhibits.

Johnston's familiarity with Paris, the burgeoning art capital of Europe, stretched back to 1883. After high school graduation (from Notre Dame Convent School in Govanston, Maryland), she had spent two years in Paris improving her French and studying art at the famed Académie Julian. During summers in the 1890s, she often returned for further study and recreation.

On July 7, 1900, three months after the Universal Exposition had opened, Johnston, her mother Frances Antoinette Benjamin Johnston, and her beloved, widowed aunt, Cornelia Benjamin Hagan ("Nin"), boarded a Holland-American Line ship, the *Potsdam*, docked in Hoboken, New Jersey, for the voyage to Rotterdam. They were among throngs of Americans headed for Europe and the Universal Exposition that summer season. In a lengthy letter to her father Anderson D. Johnston, a clerk in the United States Department of the Treasury, she detailed business affairs she wanted him to handle for her, as well as instructions for workmen refurbishing the family's living quarters.[6] During the absence of his usual female companions, she also wished "Faddie" well. The family nicknames—hers was "Fannie"—indicated their closeness and mutual support.

Mrs. Johnston was a strong, independent woman in whose footsteps her daughter clearly followed. A career woman herself, she had been a reporter and a drama critic in Baltimore. The diary of her 1900 trip with her daughter, "Fannie," was peppered with colorful opinions about different nationalities and places they visited (fig. 12). She duly recorded the steamer's ten-day progress across the Atlantic, noting such highlights as the "patriotic [singing] demonstration" after an evening band concert and the sighting of *The Deutschland*, "the largest vessel afloat." Prior to first docking at Boulogne, "Fannie"—not being one to miss the opportunity to publicize photography and to charm and enlighten potential clients—had "her photographs out on a table in the Saloon" for passengers to view.[7] This display presaged her promotional activities in Paris.

Less than three months earlier, Johnston had begun receiving letters from Mrs. Charles Henrotin in Chicago at the Office of the United States Commission to the Universal Exposition inviting her to be a delegate to the week-long International Congress of Photography to be held from July 23 to 28.[8] Working with a Professor Gore of Columbia University, chairman of the committee in charge of appointing the American leaders at the various congresses, Henrotin was writing on behalf of Mrs. Potter Palmer, the famous philanthropist and collector of French Impressionist paintings. Palmer, who had been Head of the Board of Lady Managers for the Women's Building at the World's Columbian Exposition, was honorary commissioner of Illinois for the Universal Exposition in Paris, one of eighteen such appointees from various states. The approach to Johnston was part of an effort to place twenty-five women specialists among those representing the United States at the various congresses. Palmer had already invited Chicagoan Beatrice Tonnesen, a professional photographer in partnership with her sister, who was to deliver a paper on "Artistic Photography for Use in Advertising."

Henrotin suggested Johnston "present a more or less technical paper,"[9] advice she rejected. Nonetheless, Johnston represented the work of American women at the Universal Exposition in significant ways. Besides the display of her photographs relating to schools in Washington, the ambitious organizers of the American Negro Exhibit had purchased studies she had taken that winter at the Hampton Institute for their exhibition within the United States section in the Palace of Congress and Social Economy.[10] Visiting the Exposition just after it opened in April, Johnston's press agent, George Grantham Bain, negotiated for her photographs to be admitted for competition,[11] and she herself inquired about acting as a member of the jury.[12] By June, Johnston was officially a delegate to the photographic congress and

her topic, "The Work of the Women of the United States in Photography," confirmed. She would give a short talk presumably in French and show "an exhibit" of photographs.[13] Owing to the sudden death of her mother, Tonnesen, the other female delegate, never made it to Paris, although she asked that her paper be read.[14]

Publicizing the "New"

Johnston's participation in the Universal Exposition of 1900 was the culmination of her activities during the previous decade. In both her career and through the subjects she photographed, she was riding the waves of what had gained currency as "new" in American society: the "New Woman," the "New Education," the "New Negro" and the "New School of American Photography."

Johnston's displays at the photographic congress and the Universal Exposition concerning progressive subjects placed her at the center of current social thinking. Besides the plans already underway for 150 platinum prints in the American Negro Exhibit, Johnston was to have 350 of her recently executed Washington school photographs (featuring the city's four high schools, Central, Eastern, Western, and Business) appear in the international displays of education and instruction. Although it is unclear whether she included her own work in her presentation to the photographic congress, she was to present the work of at least thirty-two other women, mostly professionals or amateurs of the "new school."

With little time to prepare, Johnston strove valiantly to select a fair representation of women then flourishing in photography. She scrambled to assemble a strong group of outstanding women, to obtain a survey of their work and to secure permission to reproduce their images. Anticipating that her official activities could create further demand for their photographs, she understood (as a professional businesswoman herself) that approval would be necessary before she could publish or otherwise promote their works.

In late May of 1900, Johnston began sending "circulars" to the women. Her three-page letter requested "hearty co-operation and support by the preparation of a brief biographical sketch and the loan of a few prints showing your most individual and distinctive work."[15] Return correspondence from twenty-nine photographers whose work she showed in Paris remains among her extensive papers at the Library of Congress. Judging from her notes and the replies to her letters that arrived too late, she may have contacted many more.

With an eye toward presenting a stimulating display, it would seem, her early list of potential women included those who photographed a variety of subjects.[16] She favored those engaged in art photography, including Catharine Weed Barnes Ward, Emma Farnsworth and Gertrude Käsebier from New York; Mathilde Weil and Amelia Van Buren from Pennsylvania; Eva Gamble Walborn from Ohio; Sarah Sears, Alice Austin and Virginia Sharp from Massachusetts; Sarah Jane Eddy from Rhode Island; and Myra Wiggins from Oregon. Furthermore, Johnston felt it essential to show the work of the Allen sisters (Massachusetts), Zaida Ben-Yusuf (New York) and Mabel Osgood Wright (Connecticut), whom she considered professionals like herself.

There was a good reason why pioneer Catharine Weed Barnes Ward appeared at the top of the list, for her activities in some ways paralleled those of Johnston. She began in 1886 in fine art and amateur photography in Albany, New York, launching a column for "Woman's Work" in 1890, and later editing for the *American Amateur Photographer* in New York City. In 1893, Ward (then Miss Barnes) had been a delegate to the photography congress at the World's Columbian Exposition. By 1900 she was married to Snowden Ward, editor of *The Photogram*, and living in London, where she continued to work with her husband. Ward sent photographs for Johnston to present at the photography congress in Paris, but they arrived the very evening the sessions concluded and were never shown.[17]

At about the same time as Johnston was writing to the women, she canvassed leading men in the field by sending them her list and asking for names of other outstanding women. Juan C. Abel, editor of *The Photographic Times*, and Osborne Yellott of *Photo-Beacon* responded, as did respected photographers Henry Troth and F. Holland Day (with whom she had served on the Second Philadelphia Salon jury in 1899; fig. 6), and the acknowledged leader of the American Pictorialists, Alfred Stieglitz. In general, they concurred with her choices. Troth acknowledged: "Those you have sent your circular to are undoubtedly the best and most artistic women workers," but he added the names of six others "who have done more or less good work."[18] Planning a major group exhibition of his own in London later that fall, Day judged that her presentation would be incomplete without Rose Clark and the Boston amateurs, especially Margaret Russell and Elise Pumpelly Cabot, but also Mary Devens.[19] Stieglitz, complaining of overwork, nonetheless supported her and the "great photographic work" of American women. He corroborated that her list was "complete," and pronounced, "I can think of no one that you may have overlooked. I'd certainly ask them all."[20]

Exactly which women photographers Johnston finally contacted is not known. However, it appears that she took at least some of the suggestions that she received. Zaida Ben-Yusuf probably proposed the Selby sisters, who, like Ben-Yusuf, worked out of a commercial portrait studio in New York City.[21] Yellott may have influenced Johnston's inclusion of professional portraitist Addie Kilburn Robinson. Troth put forward Mary Schäffer, a wildlife photographer, and Mary Paschall, a specialist in flowers, gardens and genre

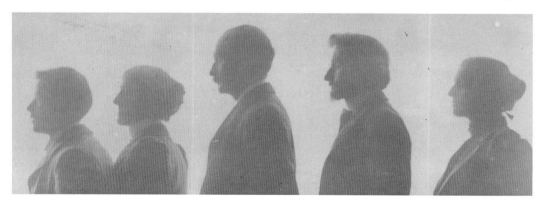

FIG. 6. Eva Watson. Jurors, Second Philadelphia Salon (left to right: Clarence H. White, Gertrude Käsebier, Henry Troth, F. Holland Day and Frances B. Johnston), 1899. Platinum. Washington, D.C., L. C., P & P Div., LC-DIGID-ppmsc-04838

scenes. Of the four women whom Day considered "musts," only Clark was among those ultimately included, although Johnston contacted both Russell and Devens. The former apologized that she had given all of her best work to Day for his fall exhibition of "The New School of American Photography" in London. The latter was traveling in Europe, and like Emma Fitz, another amateur from Boston, could not be reached in time.

Johnston had difficulty obtaining work from Gertrude Käsebier, perhaps the most highly respected of all the women photographers. Käsebier too had committed her strongest work to Day, and it took unusual persistence, including a personal visit to her New York studio, to secure original work. According to Joseph Keiley, a great admirer of Käsebier, Johnston went to extraordinary lengths to obtain examples. In a letter to Stieglitz, he described how "Miss J resorted to tears and finally tried to buy a print from a customer to whom Mrs. K had just delivered it in Miss J's presence."[22]

While Johnston could not show everything she may have wanted to in Paris,[23] she did manage to gather a lively group of about 150 photographs from female workers in the East, Midwest, California and Oregon. They represented a wide variety of photographic processes, styles and artistic or "pictorial" effects that characterized the work of her sex. The diverse photographs included many posed portraits, as well as more casual pictures of adults and children. There were some everyday scenes and allegories, and a smaller number of still lifes, nature studies and landscapes. In her notes for her lecture, Johnston described women of dissimilar habits and approaches—those who had worked but a few short years, others who made photographs for their own pleasure when family obligations permitted, and some who were running commercial operations. Her presentation featured prizewinners, professionals and successful businesswomen.

In addition to the photographs already on display at the Universal Exposition, Johnston—dedicated self-publicist that she was—must have brought other examples of her work to Paris. She certainly had displayed photographs aboard the *Potsdam*. However, in the absence of supporting evidence, we cannot determine whether she actually included any of hers in the presentation at the congress.[24]

Johnston and the "New Woman"

Most of the women in Johnston's presentation chose their own photographs, but amid warm congratulations for her appointment in their letters, the majority tended to describe themselves modestly. For example, Mary Paschall from Doylestown, Pennsylvania, whose tender views of children and adults in rural settings were unlike any in Johnston's group, called herself "very old-fashioned in my ideas."[25] On the other hand, nearly one-third of the women, particularly those for whom photography had become a vocation, described their activities with the kind of assurance, confidence and independence that revealed an emerging breed of woman. By "dint of hard work" and "devotion" to the popular "physical culture" movement that promoted bodily strength and fitness, portrait photographer Fannie Elton declared that she ran "one of the prettiest studios" in Cleveland, "with a very select trade."[26] As another portraitist, Alta Belle Sniff from Columbus, Ohio, put it, "I am thoroughly in love with my work and think it is a woman's vocation in every sense… I consider the field of photography very large and comparatively unworked, as 'a profession' for women."[27] When it came to recognition, however, a few, like Eva Watson (later Watson-Schütze), objected to being isolated as "women."[28]

It was true that the field of photography, in particular, offered women life-fulfilling possibilities. The will to experiment in a promising endeavor motivated those seeking their independence in the last quarter of the century. Photography allowed women to show their mettle in socially acceptable ways without being bound to predominantly male patronage or to the academic tradition of the fine arts. Qualities that were advantageous to the picture-taking, developing and mounting processes—such as deftness, attention to detail, good taste, patience and perseverance—were regarded as innately female, or at least were reinforced through training in such household arts and crafts as spinning or needlework. Indeed, mastery of photography required what was then expected of the female sex. In photographic portraiture, to cite one area, women who radiated graciousness and tact were at a great advantage with sitters.

By the end of the nineteenth century, new photographic processes and equipment had made the field physically less demanding than had previously been the case. Beginning in the 1870s, photography increasingly became easier: collodion wet-plate photography that had to be developed on the spot in a portable darkroom was replaced by the simpler gelatin dry-plate method. By the end of the next decade, celluloid film negatives began to replace heavy glass plates. In the 1890s, less cumbersome cameras and other technical improvements coming onto the market made things even easier for the amateur and newcomers to photography as a profession. Despite technical advances, though, many photographers preferred older methods and were slow to accept new equipment and processes.

Johnston stood out as being quite versatile. With the invention of the simple Kodak box camera in 1888, rolls of film could be sent off for convenient developing, and the resulting flood of novice button-pushers created a whole generation of amateurs. For many of them, the Kodak would be a first step toward a more serious interest in photography. After acquiring a Kodak from George Eastman himself in 1889, Johnston soon became an agent for the company. She was keen to take commercial advantage of the new product. By the 1890s, advertisers like Kodak were pairing two novel technologies in their promotions—the portable camera and the bicycle—and helping to create a market of modern women like those Johnston represented.[29]

Like numerous other female photographers, Johnston entered the field through the fine arts. When she set out for Paris in 1883 at the age of nineteen, the city was the cosmopolitan art center to which young art students from around the world flocked. For two years she was enrolled at the celebrated Académie Julian. Since women were considered dilettantes rather than serious students with a professional bent, classes were segregated by sex. But in the crowded atelier, Johnston learned the basics of art, while in the city itself she absorbed the cultured life of France. Immediately upon her return, she became active in the newly organized Art Students League of Washington, D.C. (now the Corcoran College of Art and Design), serving as treasurer and devoting herself to crayon portraiture.

Johnston's professional start in the late 1880s came in magazine illustration. Through a wide circle of friends and connections in Washington's art, social and political circles, she began receiving commissions from various publications. Her entry into the field coincided with the advent of illustrated magazines aimed at a mass market. These publications were beginning to incorporate the new half-tone printing technology for the reproduction of photographs. Johnston "found that the pencil had taken [its] place behind the camera, and the editorial cry was general 'only what cannot be photographed must be portrayed by drawing.'"[30]

Probably around 1888, Johnston took advantage of the private instruction in photography that Professor Thomas Smillie, first curator of photography at the Smithsonian Institution, intermittently offered. By 1889, she was the only female member of the Washington Camera Club. She began to exhibit with other members in 1891 and acted as their delegate to a photographic convention in New York. American camera clubs, where enthusiasts could learn about new equipment and gain access to a darkroom, were just beginning to allow women to join, albeit tentatively as "corresponding members." By 1891, Johnston had achieved national distinction in the field of photography and, in the words of one commentator, had "in a measure found professional recognition from her excellent work with the camera" in contrast to "the average feminine enthusiast in the pretty art."[31]

For someone who wanted to succeed as a self-supporting businesswoman, Washington was an ideal place. Johnston belonged to the Business Woman's Club, the first organization of its kind for women. In 1895, as head of its committee on decoration, she organized a well-publicized exhibition and sale of artworks by women, covering all areas of the fine and decorative arts. The following year, she lent posters from her own extensive collection for a show that she organized at the club. As an illustrator, Johnston had a strong interest in the poster movement.

It is a little-known fact that the earliest photography salon to feature artistic photography in the United States was held in Washington in 1896, two years before the landmark Philadelphia Salon was staged. Included in the groundbreaking "Washington Salon and Art Photographic Exhibition" were recent works by Frances B. Johnston. They were subsequently among the first photographic artworks acquired by the National Museum (now the Smithsonian Institution), the earliest such collection in America.

Johnston's successes in photography helped make her a role model for younger women. Her widely read article, "What A Woman Can Do with a Camera," written in 1897 for the *Ladies' Home Journal*, offered encouragement and practical tips in artistic photography, while promoting it as a profitable business. Art and enterprise were a combination at which Frances B. Johnston, a "new woman" herself, excelled.

The "New Education"

According to the announcement about the United States' educational display shipped to the French capital for the Exposition, Americans were convinced that Johnston's photographs of schools would "generate some new ideas among the Gallic public in regard to both the public school system in the United States and American photographic art."[32] The progress of the American public school "free and open to all from kindergarten through high school" was a proud achievement of the 124-year-old democracy. Indeed, school officials meeting in Washington at the suggestion of the government's Bureau of Education had planned to prepare special exhibits to illustrate progressive instructional methods.

William Bramwell Powell, the veteran superintendent of Washington's schools, outlined his "broad" and "enlightened" approach: "the mind of the child is an embryonic possibility to be nourished and developed, to be made to grow in desire for knowledge and in power, and to get and use knowledge, and not a receptacle to be filled."[33] Powell's "new education" emphasized the child's needs and made learning agreeable. Admiration for Johnston's portraits of Admiral Dewey and his sailors helped to win her the commission to document Washington's public education system, then considered to be among the best in the country. Photography, administrators believed, could offer the world a taste of the successful classroom methods in and around the capital city.

Working with the supervising principals of Washington's schools, Johnston spent six intensive weeks at the end of the 1899 school year making approximately 700 negatives. With characteristic energy, she produced a comprehensive survey. In elementary and high schools, she captured activities in the classroom, the gym and the dining hall, and photographed outdoor sporting events, nature tours and trips to nearby museums. Her photographic vision of school life was not only broad, it also captured the specifics of lessons and demonstrated well-ordered educational settings. Local school officials greeted her photographs with abundant praise.

During a trip to Europe that summer, Johnston showed samples to M. Berloy, the official photographer of Paris, who was surprised to discover that the students were not "selected types" and were "so healthy, happy and earnest in their work, so different from the Parisian 'ecolies' [*sic*]."[34] Her photographs showed students engrossed in cooperative tasks, interacting with teachers, and guided to learn by doing and experience. The viewer could easily imagine that their devoted labors and healthy competition would result in a sense of personal accomplishment.

Johnston had arranged for the photographs to be featured in a series of pamphlets aimed at teachers. *The New Education Illustrated*, published by B. F. Johnson in Richmond, Virginia, and issued semi-monthly during 1900 and 1901, allowed the photographer to profit from her school commission while spreading the word about her work and modern pedagogy (fig. 7). When presented at the Universal Exposition, the well-lighted interiors, showing the children and their activities in clear focus, won a gold medal.

The "New Negro"

In all likelihood, the success of the schools project in Washington in the spring of 1899 prompted the commission to undertake similar work at

FIG. 8. Frances B. Johnston. Students Conducting Electrical Experiments with Batteries, Western High School (Washington, D.C., School Survey), 1899. Cyanotype. Washington, D.C., L. C., P & P Div., LC-DIGID-ppmsc-04891

FIG. 9. Frances B. Johnston. *The Screw as Applied to the Cheese Press* (Hampton, Va., Hampton Normal and Agricultural Institute), 1899–1900. Platinum. Washington, D.C., L. C., P & P Div., LC-DIGID-ppmsc-04892

Hampton at the end of the year. Previous assignments had proven Johnston to be a master of the kind of photographic reportage that served her clients well. While the early instructions to her did not explicitly mention an intended display in Paris, Hampton expected the photographs to be "of real assistance in giving to the public an idea of what [they] were trying to do."[35]

Hampton Normal and Agricultural Institute (now Hampton University) was founded after the Civil War in 1868 by General Samuel Chapman Armstrong, the son of New England missionaries, to educate freed slaves in the South—and later Native Americans—for agriculture, elementary school teaching and other vocations. In 1893, the mantle of authority passed to the Reverend Hollis Burke Frissell, who strengthened Hampton's commitment to industrial education. But discrimination, sanctioned by Jim Crow legislation in 1896, mob hatred and lynchings, was defining race relations in the South, and the great migration of Southern blacks to Northern cities had begun. By 1899, the bloom had faded from the first phase of Hampton's mission to inculcate in its students such Yankee values as the dignity of labor and the notion of industrial education as a stepping stone to academic learning. In addition, its buildings were aging. The officials, wishing to revitalize the school, believed that Johnston's highly respected photographs would help to promote and publicize it.

There are kinships between her famous Hampton Institute work and the Washington school photographs (figs. 8, 9). Both feature groups of proud students—the former of color, the latter predominantly white—learning by doing in and out of the classroom. Crisp focus and pleasingly balanced compositions distinguished those moments

which Johnston chose to arrange and capture for all time. Most of her 150 Hampton photographs were group studies of older students at the Institute or younger children at the associated Whittier Training School for elementary teachers. Hampton emphasized conformism to Anglo-Saxon values and upward economic mobility, and the general picture Johnston produced was of an isolated environment in which the student population was being purposefully acculturated into middle-class society as newly educated Negroes. Today, her reputation rests largely on the Hampton work. The careful arrangements of students of color in content-laden scenes can be used to deconstruct the past. Johnston's idealized view, expressed in a realist style with great attention to detail, provides ample opportunity for cultural interpretation.[36]

Advantageous as they were as a tool for the Hampton officials, Johnston's photographs also served the African-American organizers of the Negro section within America's "sociology" exhi-

FIG. 7. Cover of *The New Education Illustrated (Primary)*, Number 1. Washington, D.C., L. C., P & P Div., LC-DIGID-ppmsc-04828

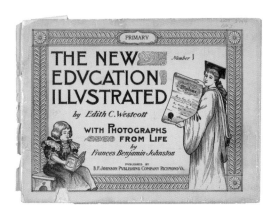

FIG. 10. *Exhibit of American Negroes at the Paris Exposition*, in *The American Monthly Review of Reviews*, 22 (November 1900), p. 576. Washington, D.C., L. C., General Collections, LC-DIGID-ppmsc-04826

bitions at the Universal Exposition. These were housed in the Palace of Congress and Social Economy, a simple white building on the right bank of the Seine opposite the Street of Foreign Nations on the left bank. The American displays were relatively small, sharing space with the mutual aid societies of France, workingman's circles of Belgium, the Red Cross Society, German state insurance, and others. Thomas J. Calloway, Special Negro Agent for the United States Commission to the Universal Exposition from the War Department, worked on the American Negro Exhibit with W. E. B. Du Bois, the great African-American leader and a former classmate at Fisk University. Impressed with Johnston's Hampton photographs, Calloway purchased special prints for the Paris display.

A sculpture of the abolitionist and scholar Frederick Douglass—depicted with arms outstretched as if speaking—greeted visitors to the American Negro Exhibit. The figure symbolized the social progress of America's ex-slaves and their descendants. The exhibit itself consisted of photographs and other pictures, as well as work samples, models and charts to describe the American Negro's history, condition, education and literature (fig. 10). Du Bois wrote that it was "an honest, straightforward exhibit of a small nation of people, picturing their life and development with-

out apology or gloss, and above all made by themselves". An "especially excellent series of photographs illustrating the Hampton idea of 'teaching by doing'" was situated with materials from similar institutions of higher learning.[37]

This feature was already very popular when Calloway wrote Johnston: "I am happy to inform you that the exhibit of the Hampton Institute is attracting considerable attention and has had many favorable comments."[38] The American Negro Exhibit as a whole, and Johnston's photographs in particular, were singled out by Universal Exposition judges for grand prizes. Dr. Du Bois received a gold medal for his role of "Collaborator as Compiler of Georgia Negro Exhibit."[39]

Europe and the "New School of American Photography"

Late at night on July 21, after four days of sightseeing in Holland, Johnston and her entourage arrived in Paris, more than a day ahead of the scheduled International Congress of Photography. She was the sole female and one of only two formally appointed Americans among the eighty delegates (fig. 11).[40] According to two official reports, Johnston did not attend the first meetings in the Palace of Congress and Social Economy (where her Hampton prints were on view) on the opening day, July 23. But her crate containing the women's photographs was on hand, and in their excitement, the attendees opened it and avidly examined its contents.[41]

Two days later, Johnston personally showed the approximately 150 photographs and spoke enthusiastically on behalf of the American women. Her presentation captivated the international audience. W. I. Sreznewsky of St. Petersburg "considered the work of our American women of such excellence that he asked … to be allowed to carry it from Paris to Russia."[42] Better known today as a philologist and editor of old and medieval Russian texts, Sreznewsky had written a popular photographer's handbook for Russians. At the congress, he described a process of layering exposures made with little light and also successfully transported delicate, photo-sensitized tissue paper to show his colleagues. In an article published in *Fotograficheskoe obozrienie*, he wrote that his request "to allow

FIG. 11. Identification tag,
Congrès International de Photographie,
Universal Exposition, Paris, July 1900.
Washington, D.C., L. C., P & P Div.,
LC-DIGID-ppmsc-04827

FIG. 12. Frances B. Johnston with her
camera after leaving Paris, Cadenabbia,
Lake Como, Italy, 1900.
Gelatin silver print, printed out
[postcard].
Washington, D.C., L. C., P & P Div.,
LC-DIGID-ppmsc-04840

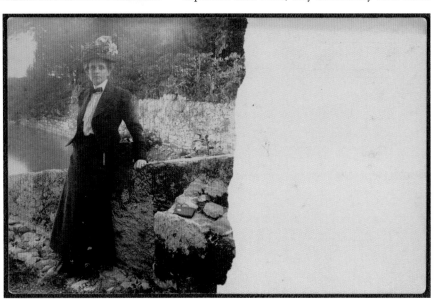

the collection [of women photographers] to stay for a while in Russia was graciously fulfilled by Miss Frances Benjamin Johnston," and "in detail" did he analyze "the collection, note its particulars, and assess its value." His short descriptive phrases are filled with enthusiasm. The Russian acknowledged the women's technical mastery, artistic design and composition, choice of models, faithful transmission of chiaroscuro and "the attempt to cross over into the world of ideas."[43] The intent of his effusive article was to inspire his countrymen to try artistic photography.

After the congress, Johnston met with government officials and a publisher, and probably arranged for work to be considered by the jury. With the help of her mother and aunt, she framed an unknown number of photographs and took them to the Photographic Section, in the Palace of Letters, Science and Art (Palais des Lettres, Sciences et Arts) where most of the photography, including that of the Americans, was on view.[44] The photographs by American women were then exhibited there, along with a group of her own works, including portraits of famous people.[45] From her agent Bain's postcard to the Commissioner General in April, it seemed it had been too late for her own work to be submitted for official adjudication by the jury,[46] but once again her persistence prevailed and her participation officially noted in a supplement to the official catalogue. According to Mrs. Johnston, when she and others went to retrieve the photographs in the Photographic Section two days before their scheduled departure from Paris, they had already been taken away by a member of the jury.[47] Mrs. Johnston did not record whether her daughter was able to pick them up and take them to the Photo-Club de Paris, her next stop where she needed to arrange for corresponding membership. Mrs. Johnston and Aunt "Nin" simply left her there to "transact her business."[48] Sreznewsky's comments which suggest that the collection of women's work shown at the photographic congress (not including Johnston's own) was probably "intended for the Paris Universal Exposition, but did not in fact end up there, either for missing the deadline, or overall lack of space" are misleading.[49]

Mrs. Johnston's diary contains a tally of the women's photographs, listed alphabetically by creator with numbers instead of titles. Her description relates how she "made a card catalogue [now unlocated] & a numbered list of the Photographic Exhibit to prepare them for their Russian tour... I also pasted labels on the photographs, numbering them to correspond with the catalogue".[50] This "List of Exhibitors & No. of Prints" at the end of her diary (see p. 9) and the surviving labels on the backs of the mounted photographs in the collections of the Library of Congress and the Smithsonian Institution help to reconstitute what was in the "exhibitions" at the congress, in St. Petersburg and Moscow, and at the Photo-Club in 1901. How the photographs got to Russia, exactly where they were shown, and how they returned to Paris remains a mystery.[51]

During the summer of 1900, Frances B. Johnston's offerings were the only significant representations in Paris of artistic photography from the United States. American photography had its official place in the Palace of Letters, Science and Art, but the displays were primarily by suppliers with a mélange of commercial photographs arranged in crowded, poorly lit spaces. The international Pictorial movement was incompletely represented at the Universal Exposition, with works mostly by the English, French, Austrians and Germans (in their national building) receiving commentary in the press.[52]

Anticipating such an unfavorable situation, Stieglitz, on behalf of the New York Camera Club, had boycotted the Universal Exposition. Appointed by officials in February to put together a broad representation of the American Pictorialists for shipment in eight weeks, he complained of insufficient time and protested as a "test case" for future Universal Expositions. He firmly believed that the American Pictorialists should only be seen with other art, not in isolation; photography should be included in the art palaces. Robert Demachy, the French leader and staunch defender of the Americans, took exception to Stieglitz's reasoning. He knew how crowded the fine arts halls were and thought artistic photography would get lost in them.[53]

Unfortunately, there was no coordination among the leading American art photographers with regard to exhibiting at the 1900 Universal Exposition. Though the First and Second Philadelphia Salons in 1898 and 1899 had increased contacts among artistically inclined camera workers in the United States and had sorted out leaders in the field, a formal school or movement had not yet jelled. Ever since he had served on the Second Philadelphia Salon jury with Johnston and others, F. Holland Day had been endeavoring to make the Americans' work better known in Europe. In the spring of 1898, he and Sarah Sears proposed a plan to Stieglitz for an American Association of Artistic Photography with a salon at the Museum of Fine Arts in Boston, but Stieglitz thwarted it. Despite this rebuff, in February 1900, when Day learned of Stieglitz's appointment to represent the Americans at the Universal Exposition, he offered to recall the circular he had sent a week earlier and meet with him. Notwithstanding a meeting and correspondence in March, they failed to resolve their differences. On April 14, just before Johnston received her invitation to attend the photographic congress, Day set sail for England in the company of his cousin Alvin Langdon Coburn and Coburn's mother, taking 400 photographs by Americans—including work by eighteen women, forty-two men, a large display of his own works, but none by Stieglitz (fig. 13).[54] Day and Johnston felt the time was ripe to organize the Americans for presentation on the European stage, while Stieglitz decided not to take any steps toward forming a national school for American art photographers until 1902, when he organized the

FIG. 13. "The New American School of Photography" exhibition (London, The Royal Photographic Society, October 10, 1900–November 8, 1900): Photographs by Sarah C. Sears, Alice Austin, Zaida Ben-Yusuf, in Photo-Era, 6:1 (January 1901), p. 213. Washington, D.C., L. C., Gen. Colls. LC-DIGID-ppmsc-04887

Photo-Secession.[55] Yet today, the Photo-Secession and not Johnston's nor Day's successes for American art photography in 1900 and 1901 is the only American movement that is recognized in photographic histories. It is important, therefore, to underscore the fact that, at the same time as Stieglitz was rejecting a showing for Americans in Paris, Johnston decided to represent the work of American women and Day was preparing to take the work of American art photographers to England on his own initiative.

In the first months of 1901, the Americans got their due in Paris, the art capital of Europe. Back-to-back exhibitions were displayed at the Photo-Club, 44 rue des Mathurins, the most exclusive society in Paris. Johnston's exhibit of the artistic women photographers ("Les Artistes Américaines") was on view from January 24 through February 13, and was followed by Day's "The New American School of Photography" from February 22 through March 10. (The latter had been shown the previous fall at the new headquarters of the Royal Photographic Society at 66 Russell Street, London.) This was nothing short of an unprecedented explosion of American talent in artistic photography in France. Although critics conflated the two exhibitions, which made it difficult for future historians to distinguish between them, they greatly admired the American camera workers.

Women photographers were praiseworthy in both shows. While Day's exhibition offered stylistic cohesiveness and subject matter common to painting, Johnston's show had broadened the playing field to include botanical subjects and a range of styles, from the idealism of Pictorialists like Farnsworth, Weil, Watson and Van Buren to the realism of Schäffer and Paschall. Johnston's "pet theory" about women's work and Day's "personal hobby… the theoretical differentiation of schools" resulted in American photographers showing together for the first time in Europe. Johnston and Day had allowed their passions, not politics, to determine their actions. Separately, they had seen to it that their compatriots garnered praise for their artistic progress from the Old World whose art history they so greatly admired.[56]

After returning from Europe and the showing at the Universal Exposition in Paris, Johnston returned immediately to her own work. In step with the strong women in her family, her professional achievements continued unabated. The District of Columbia Committee for the National Suffrage Bazar [sic] to be held in New York City's Madison Square Garden in November had commissioned her to make portraits for sale of veteran suffragist Susan B. Anthony at her home in Rochester, New York, and a calendar featuring

these pictures was in the works. Johnston's proposal to editor Edward Bok of the *Ladies' Home Journal* for several articles on "The Foremost Women Photographers in America"—ultimately, Gertrude Käsebier, Mathilde Weil, the Allen sisters, Emma Farnsworth, Eva Watson-Schütze, Zaida Ben-Yusuf, and Elizabeth Brownell—was accepted and well underway.[57]

Frances Benjamin Johnston's advocacy of women photographers and their work, which she brought to Paris collectively for the first time, offers a window into the art movement in photography during 1900 and 1901. The artful professional and the artist-amateur were beginning to find their own voices and were gaining confidence from public exposure. As predicted, the independence and originality of women photographers—embodied by Johnston—had "startled the Old World." Through her own photography and in the role of ambassador for other American women, Johnston had stepped adroitly over aesthetic, social and political thresholds in her own country to forge uncommon alliances abroad (figs. 14 and 15).[58]

FIG. 14. Frances B. Johnston
in her basement office, 1890s.
Cyanotype.
Washington, D.C., L. C., P & P Div.,
LC-DIGID-ppmsc-04834

FIG. 15. Portrait place and designed
by Mills Thompson, 1896. Cyanotype.
Washington, D.C., L. C., P & P Div.,
LC-DIGID-ppmsc-04898

I wish to thank Jeremy Adamson, Beverly Brannan, Robert Curtis, Judith Nash LeBon and Barbara L. Michaels for their help on my essay.

1. Frances Benjamin Johnston Papers, Manuscripts Division, Library of Congress, Washington, D.C. [hereafter Johnston Papers].

2. Although four American delegates are listed in S. Pector, *Congrès International de Photographie tenu à Paris du 23 au 28 juillet 1900, Procès-Verbaux Sommaires* (Paris: Imprimerie Nationale, 1900), p. 5 [hereafter Pector, 1900], neither Beatrice Tonnesen nor Alfred Stieglitz attended for reasons cited later in this essay.

3. "Progress in Photography; collection of specimens for the Paris Universal Exposition, All the work of American Women A proposed exhibit in this city," *The Evening Star* (July 6, 1900), p. 11. See also, "The Social World," *The Evening Star* (June 30, 1900), p. 7.

4. See Chapter 1, "What a Woman Can Do with a Camera," in Laura Wexler, *Tender Violence; Domestic Visions in an Age of U.S. Imperialism* (Chapel Hill and London: The University of North Carolina Press, 2000), pp. 13–51, for an engrossing discussion of Johnston's photographs aboard the *Olympia* in the context of a cult of domesticity.

5. Johnston would serve on the Philadelphia jury a second time in 1901, gaining further distinction as the only woman to serve twice. For more on Johnston's early life, see Pete Daniel and Raymond Smock, *A Talent for Detail: The Photographs of Miss Francis Benjamin Johnston, 1889–1910* (New York: Harmony Books, 1974), and Anne E. Peterson, "Frances Benjamin Johnston: the early years, 1888-1908," *Nineteenth Century*, 6:1 (spring 1980), pp. 58–61.

6. F. B. Johnston to "Faddie" [Anderson D. Johnston], July 7, 1900, Johnston Papers. The first thing she cited was a check for $400 that publisher B. F. Johnson owed her, presumably for her Washington school photographs.

7. Mrs. Anderson D. Johnston, *The Wanamaker Diary for 1900* [hereafter *Wanamaker Diary*], Johnston Papers, entries for July 7, 11 and 17.

8. Ellen Henrotin to F. B. Johnston, April 12 and May 25, 1900, Johnston Papers.

9. Ellen Henrotin to F. B. Johnston, May 25, 1900, Johnston Papers.

10. Thomas Calloway to F. B. Johnston, April 18, 1900, Johnston Papers.

11. George Grantham Bain to F. B. Johnston, postcard, April 25, 1900, Johnston Papers.

12. Ellen Henrotin to F. B. Johnston, May 25, 1900, Johnston Papers.

13. Ellen Henrotin to F. B. Johnston, July 2, 1900, Johnston Papers.

14. Beatrice Tonnesen to F. B. Johnston, June 21, 1900, Johnston Papers. Not mentioned in official reports.

15. F. B. Johnston, undated copy, Johnston Papers. Some women worked in partnerships. Thirty responses survive.

16. This list comes from a sheet in F. B. Johnston's hand, Johnston Papers.

17. *Wanamaker Diary*, entry for August 6 continued under May 25. Ward's photographs had to be packed to be returned to her.

18. Henry Troth to F. B. Johnston, June 7, 1900, Johnston Papers.

19. F. Holland Day to F. B. Johnston, undated (end of June), Johnston Papers.

20. Alfred Stieglitz to F. B. Johnston, June 8, 1900, Johnston Papers.

21. Zaida Ben-Yusuf to F. B. Johnston, May 31, 1900, Johnston Papers.

22. Joseph Keiley to F. B. Johnston, July 24, 1900, The Alfred Stieglitz Collection, Yale University, as cited in Barbara L. Michaels, *Gertrude Käsebier: The Photographer and Her Photographs* (New York: Harry N. Abrams, Inc., 1992), p. 171. Special thanks to Barbara Michaels for clarifying the information about Käsebier. When the work was shown at the Photo-Club in 1901, the review of Käsebier's work by French photographer and critic Robert Demachy demonstrated that Johnston's efforts paid off. See the essay by Michel Poivert in this book.

23. Nettie Boyce to F. B. Johnston, n.d., Johnston Collection indicated that she was sending prints, but no other evidence about this exists. Constance Parsons from Massachusetts wrote that she had no time to send anything. See Constance Parsons to F. B. Johnston, n.d., Johnston Papers.

24. "A commentary about the Paris Universal Exposition, Editorial Notes," *The Photogram*, 32 (August 1900), p. 377, followed the journal's description of Johnston's presentation about the women's work at the congress: "Miss Johnston rounds out the list of Washington exhibitors. She is undecided yet as to what class of work she will enter ... Miss Johnston is already represented in Paris by about 500 photographs, including the Washington public school views and a like series from the Hampton, Va. Normal Institute." The Wards, who edited this journal, were in close touch with Johnston.

25. Mary Paschall to F. B. Johnston, June 22, 1900, Johnston Papers.

26. Fannie Elton to F. B. Johnston, June 23, 1900, Johnston Papers.

27. Alta Belle Sniff to F. B. Johnston, June 23, 1900, Johnston Papers.

28. Eva Watson to Johnston, June 10, 1900, Johnston Papers.

29. Myra Wiggins, who was in Europe during the period of the Universal Exposition, chose to travel with her "camera and wheel" to Holland, a country she had "longed to visit." See Myra Albert Wiggins, "Alone in Holland," *The American Annual of Photography and Photographic Times Almanac for 1902* (1903), pp. 227–31.

30. Frederick Noble, "Science Has Made a Philosopher of Me. Declares a Famous Washington Woman Within Whose Photographic Focus Have Come the Notables of Many Lands," *Washington Times* (February 16, 1902), p. 3.

31. Mary L. Bisland, "Women," *The Illustrated American*, 7:69 (June 13, 1891), p. 185.

32. "School Children, Pictures of Them to Be Exhibited at the Paris Exposition," *The Evening Star* (November 11, 1899), p. 14.

33. W. B. Powell, *Statement Made to the Board of School Trustees*, Washington, D.C., 1900, p. 5.

34. "School Children, Pictures of Them to be Exhibited at the Paris Exposition," *op. cit.*, p. 14.

35. Hollis B. Frissell to F. B. Johnston, November 15, 1900, Johnston Papers. Whether Johnston knew her photographs were destined for Paris in November is unclear. By the end of the year, though, Calloway and Frissell were collaborating on the American Negro Exhibit. See Lori Mirazita, "Frances Benjamin Johnston (1864–1952) Photographer," in Richard J. Powell and Jock Reynolds, eds. *To Conserve a Legacy: American Art from Historically Black Colleges and Universities* (Andover and New York: Addison Gallery of American Art and The Studio Museum in Harlem, 1999), p. 205. The school treasurer's report indicates payment for "exhibit at Paris Exposition." See *The Hampton Normal and Agricultural Institute Treasurer's Statement for the Year Ending June 30, 1900*. I am grateful to Vivian Patterson for bringing this source to my attention.

36. For critical discussions of the Hampton pictures, see Laura Wexler, "Black and White and Color: American Photographs at the Turn of the Century," *Prospects: An Annual of American Culture Studies* 13 (1988), pp. 356–57; James Guimond, *American Photography and the American Dream* (Chapel Hill and London: The University of North Carolina Press, 1991), pp. 21–53; Judith Fryer Davidov, *Women's Camera Work; Self/Body/Other in American Visual Culture* (Durham and London: Duke University Press, 1998), pp. 160–78; Jeannene M. Przyblyski, "American Visions at the Paris Exposition, 1900: Another Look at Frances Benjamin Johnston's Hampton Photographs," *Art Journal*, 57:3 (fall 1998), pp. 60–68; Deborah Willis-Kennedy, "Visualizing the 'New Negro,'" p. 67; Denise Ramzy and Katherine Fogg, "Interview: Carrie Mae Weems," in Vivian Patterson, *Carrie Mae Weems: The Hampton Project* (Williamstown, MA: Aperture and Williams College Museum of Art, 2000), pp. 78–80.

37. W. E. B. Du Bois, "The American Negro at Paris," *The American Monthly Review of Reviews*, 22 (November 1900), p. 577.

38. Thomas Calloway to F. B. Johnston, May 15, 1900, Johnston Papers.

39. David Levering Lewis, *W. E. B. Du Bois: Biography of a Race* (New York: Henry Holt and Co., 1993), p. 247.

40. Pector, 1900, p. 5, and S. Pector, *Congrès International de Photographie; procès-verbaux, rapports, notes et documents divers* (Paris: Gauthier-Villars, 1901) [hereafter Pector, 1901], p. 19, list Cameron, Johnston, Tonnesen and Stieglitz as official United States delegates; of the four, only E. (probably "Edgar," who was a photography juror at the Exposition) Cameron from Chicago and Johnston were in attendance. Max and Edward Levy of Philadelphia and S. L. Sheldon of Ithaca, New York, listed as members (Pector, 1901, pp. 26 and 33), may have been unofficial delegates. See S. L. Sheldon, "The International Congress of Photography at Paris," *The Photographic Times*, 32 (December 1900), p. 558.

41. Pector, 1900, p. 9, and Pector, 1901, p. 40.

42. "Three Gold Medals," [Rochester, New York] *Post Express* (February 21, 1901), p. 12.

43. W. I. Sreznewsky, "Kollektsiia fotograficheskikh kartin, ispolnennykh amerikanskimi liubitel'nitsami fotografii" [The collection of photographs taken by American women amateur photographers], trans. by Harry M. Leich, *Fotograficheskoe obozrienie*, 6:1 (November 1900), pp. 1–5.

44. *Wanamaker Diary*, entries for July 30 and 31, August 1 and 4.

45. Étienne Wallon, "F. Holland Day et la Nouvelle École Américaine au Photo-Club," *Photo-Gazette* (March 25, 1901), p. 81.

46. Bain, *op. cit.*

47. *Wanamaker Diary*, entry for August 4, 1900.

48. *Ibid.*

49. Sreznewsky, *op. cit.*, p. 2. This could be interpreted as corroboration for the statements in Mrs. Johnston's diary that discuss the removal of photographs by a member of the jury. See note 47.

50. *Wanamaker Diary*, entry for August 5, 1900, continued under May 22.

51. See "Three Gold Medals," p. 12 and Appendix.

52. For more information on photography as a subject at the Universal Exposition, see "Photography at the Paris Exhibition," *British Journal of Photography*, 12 (June 7, 1900), pp. 380–86.

53. Alfred Stieglitz, "American Photography at the Paris Exposition," *The American Photographer*, 12:4 (September 1900), pp. 411–14.

54. Jane Van Nimmen, "F. Holland Day and the Display of a New Art: 'Behold It Is I,'" *History of Photography*, 18:4 (winter 1994), pp. 373–77.

55. See Sarah Greenough, "'Of Charming Glens, Graceful Glades, and Frowning Cliffs': the Economic Incentives, Social Inducements, and Aesthetic Issues of American Pictorial Photography, 1880–1902," in Martha Sandweiss, *Photography in Nineteenth-Century America* (Fort Worth and New York: Amon Carter Museum and Harry N. Abrams, Inc., 1991), pp. 276–78.

56 Clarence B. Moore, "Women Experts in Photography," *Cosmopolitan*, 14 (March 1893), p. 586, and F. Holland Day, "Opening Address, The New School of American Photography," *Photographic Journal*, 25:2 (October 31, 1900), p. 74.

57 An in-depth study of this project is underway, see Gillian Green Hannum, *Coming to Light: Frances Benjamin Johnston and the Foremost Women Photographers in America*.

58 The French government decorated Frances B. Johnston with its *palmes académiques*, conferring upon her the title Officier for her participation in the Universal Exposition, her exhibits there and her service as United States delegate to the Third International Photographic Congress, as well as her promotion of France at the St. Louis Exposition in 1904. Undated clipping, hand-titled *The Evening Star* (February 11, 1905), Johnston Papers.

A TASTE OF THE AVANT-GARDE
THE RECEPTION OF AMERICAN WOMEN PHOTOGRAPHERS IN PARIS (1900–1901)

MICHEL POIVERT

On the opening day of the International Congress of Photography in 1900, in the prestigious setting of the Universal Exposition, the organizers were intrigued by the contents of the American entry. The representative, Frances Benjamin Johnston, was not due to arrive until the following day, but it would appear that the participants at the congress were curious to see what the mysterious crate she had sent contained. After deciding to open it, they discovered that there were nearly 150 "superb photographs representing the work of American women."[1] They waited a few days, with some impatience, for Frances B. Johnston's presentation. Their curiosity was understandable, firstly because the congress was hungry for new things, and secondly because this consignment of photographs from America would compensate for the absence of the Americans from the international exhibition organized by the Photo-Club de Paris for the Universal Exposition (fig. 1), which was on view for the duration of the exposition. The

FIG. 1. Paul Bergon. *À l'exposition*, in *La Revue de Photographie*, 2 (1903).

absence was not due to a lack of organization, rather, it was a boycott.

The organizing committee of the Universal Exposition had refused to allow photography to be exhibited among the other arts, and confined it to the Palace of Letters, Science and Art.[2] At the time, art photography was flourishing internationally, and the "foreign schools"—American, German, Belgian and Austrian—decided to boycott the event because they considered the classification of photography anywhere but among the other arts unacceptable. The first victims of this boycott were the members of the Photo-Club de Paris who, as representatives of French Pictorialism, were denigrated in their own country. Hence, when the pictures taken by American women photographers arrived in France, the atmosphere was one of disappointment and controversy, evident in the disillusioned comments made by the leader of the French pictorialists, Robert Demachy, saddened by the mediocre French entries: "We no longer surprise anyone," Demachy said to his fellow French photographers, "Pictorial photography is accepted... So progress over here must be individual."[3] Tired of the amateurism of Pictorialism in France, Demachy dreamed of personal adventure and the avant-garde, but he could only watch as Paris fell behind London, Hamburg, Brussels and New York in the field of photography. Given these circumstances, the arrival of the American women's pictures was a kind of compensation, as well as a confirmation of the interest aroused by the American photographers glimpsed at the last Salon du Photo-Club in 1898. The American women's photographs thus seemed to embody the promise of a revival of the international movement which would be incarnated by the Photo-Secession two years later.

"The Avid Women"

The involvement of women in photography was a symbol of modernity around 1900. And yet the image of women in the commercial sector of photography was still a very conservative one. On posters, the front covers of publications and in advertisements, they were often used as a marketing device by the manufacturers of appliances—for example, a woman, with her legendary innocence in technical matters, was proof of how easy it was to use a new piece of photographic equipment. Alternatively, she sometimes appeared in the allegorical role of "Photography." Here the camera was a dream machine and a woman, in the form of an Art Nouveau muse, was used to represent the element of genius. These two figures seem very caricatured when compared with the militancy of the women involved in art photography. Nevertheless, this symbolic use of women was a fairly accurate reflection of prevailing attitudes in French photography, where they were either ignored or idealized. The almost total absence of women in the French Pictorialist movement before 1900 was nevertheless a little surprising, for right at the beginning of the movement, when photographers were taking an interest in developments in English Pictorialism, Julia Margaret Cameron was presented to them as a real role model. The English correspondents for the *Bulletin du Photo-Club de Paris*, impressed by the posthumous exhibition of Cameron's work in London (1890), as well as by her participation in the first English Pictorialist exhibitions (where this artist emerged as a veritable godmother for the new movement), mentioned her incessantly.[4] Furthermore, thanks to the English Pictorialists, some prints by Cameron were presented at the first Salon du Photo-Club de Paris in 1894, and attracted a lot of attention from critics.[5] Nevertheless, she does not seem to have played the same role in France that she played in England—not because of her qualities as a woman, but probably because the French Pictorialists wished, in a strategic national context, to make a clean break with the past, preferring to see themselves as the sole inventors of art photography.[6] Be that as it may, unlike the English Pictorialists, the French were not at all used to the idea that a woman could represent the highest levels of achievement when it came to photography. More generally, women were absent from the debate about photography, except perhaps as models or subjects.

Consequently, prior to 1900, no article of any substance attempted to examine the role of women in French photography in economic, artistic or scientific terms. However, after 1900 the place of women in the world of photography became an issue, as we shall see further on, and the American model—in addition to the British—had something to do with this. Should one believe then that French art photographers never heard or read anything about women photographers before 1900? As a matter of fact, their first contact with the works of women photographers began with the participation of a few women at the Salon du Photo-Club in 1895 (fig. 2). This participation nevertheless remained modest[7] and did not provoke much debate on the existence of a female form of art photography. And yet at this time a model of women's photography attracted the attention of the French—and this model came from America.

In June 1895, in the *Bulletin du Photo-Club de Paris*, Emmanuel Mathieu, vice president of the Photo-Club de Paris, published an original article entitled "L'Art photographique et les femmes américaines"[8] (fig. 3). The text was illustrated with pictures by "Madame N-G. Bartlett," "Miss

FIG.3. Emmanuel Mathieu,
"L'Art photographique et les femmes
américaines," *Bulletin du Photo-Club
de Paris* (June 1895).

Juin. — Mrs N.-G. Bartlett.

L'Art Photographique
ET LES FEMMES AMÉRICAINES

DANS ces dernières années, les procédés industriels tels que photogravure, typogravure, photocollographie, héliogravure, etc., sont parvenus à un tel degré de perfection que des journaux, même quotidiens, fournissent sans effort à leurs lecteurs, à côté de l'enseignement par la parole, l'enseignement par les yeux.

C'est là le succès le plus apparent, le plus matériellement saisissable de la photographie, qui, en révolutionnant la librairie, a permis aux populations qui jusqu'ici semblaient exclues du mouvement artistique, de se hausser jusqu'à la compréhension d'un idéal sans lequel leur vie continuerait à n'avoir qu'une fin et qu'un but, la satisfaction des intérêts purement matériels. Grâce à la photographie, l'exilé volontaire, dans les solitudes de l'Amérique ou de l'Afrique se rattache aux foyers intellectuels créés par nos artistes. Grâce à elle encore l'ouvrier, courbé tout le jour sur son établi, l'agriculteur, luttant

E.-V. Clarkson," "Miss E.-J. Farnsworth," "Miss E.-N. Slade," "Mrs. Wright" and "Miss Frances Benjamin Johnston," thereby offering for the first time in France an overview of the work of American women photographers. Attempting to explain the sudden craze for photography among women, Mathieu suggested that "women eager... to show that they can in all areas occupy an honorable place next to their husbands or their brothers" had been prevented from doing so in the field of photography basically because of the unpleasantness of handling chemicals and the stains that they left on the photographer's hands. But from now on, he went on to say, things had changed and it was possible to work in clean conditions, thus enabling women amateur photographers to retain their elegance. Although this argument might seem preposterous today, it was nevertheless symptomatic of a very male outlook that belonged to someone who inhabited an amateur (and bourgeois) world which preferred, to any social consideration of the place of women in artistic practice, an interpretation which reduced female ambitions to the contingencies of physical appearance. Nevertheless, Mathieu then emphasized the fact that France had fallen behind in the field of women's photography, an argument which would reappear continually in the writings of commentators, who pointed to foreign photography as a model which should inspire

French women to embark on the adventure of artistic photography. Drawing on the March issue of the New York magazine *The Cosmopolitan*, Mathieu briefly presented the six different photographers, emphasizing their training, their honors, their high aesthetic standards and their knowledge of technical matters. He concluded by expressing a wish to see a rivalry between American women and French women. Incidentally, this first list of American women photographers included not only Frances Benjamin Johnston but also three artists who would be present in the exhibition organized in Paris in 1900: Emma Farnsworth, Mabel Wright and Mary Bartlett. Although at the time Mathieu's article seemed to be of only passing interest, it nevertheless contributed to the discovery of the originality of the American school, a school which previously had been largely unknown to the French.

Indeed, the American presence at the first Salons du Photo-Club de Paris—beginning in 1894—had been relatively modest. Each year, about ten amateurs presented their prints and the majority of them came from the northeast of the United States: from New York, Philadelphia and Washington. Those who sent their pictures most regularly were Alfred Stieglitz, Rudolf Eickemeyer, W.-B. Post, Charles I. Berg, Emma Farnsworth and Eugene Lee Ferguson. Most of them were well known in America and were given solo exhibitions by the Camera Club in New York. Nevertheless, in the early years the critical reception of their work in Paris was rather condescending.[9] The American school, according to Frédéric Dillaye, could best be summed up as a judicious mixture of the different particularities of the European schools. Although he praised the work of Eickmeyer, he bemoaned a certain "hint of affectation and pretentiousness."[10] In 1896, more Americans exhibited at the Salon de Lille than in Paris. The Société Photographique de Lille presented eighteen photographers and fifty-three prints from across the Atlantic, notably the first pictures of F. Holland Day,[11] an artist Parisians would discover a few years later at the head of the "new American school." But for the time being, the Americans formed a rather heterogeneous group. All the same, in 1897 critics recognized a certain coherence in the fifteen American exhibitors at the Salon.[12] It was in 1898, however, that the French really identified the existence of a more homogeneous type of American photography. The role of Stieglitz in this trend was by this time fully understood, as the anonymous chronicler of the *Bulletin du Photo-Club de Paris* demonstrated in his description of the American photographer "whom we regard as a leader whose example has not been adequately followed and whose delightfully varied exhibition provides relief from a certain monotony of subject and treatment that we had observed among his compatriots."[13] For the Americans were criticized for their rather cold tones. "It's dull," regretted Étienne Wallon in the *Photo-Gazette*, but he too went on to praise the works of Stieglitz. But, Stieglitz aside, it was a woman who received the critics' plaudits, and that woman was none other than Frances B. Johnston.[14] This group of photographers that the French were discovering, dubbed "the generation of 1898" by the photography historian Weston Naef, were mostly centered around the Camera Club of New York.[15] It is this group that, at the turn of the century, would energize a Europe affected by a certain "malaise."

This dynamism was not merely the result of an expansionist desire and one must not forget that American Pictorialism was being consumed by internal crisis, the Camera Club in particular. In 1900, Stieglitz and the new generation attempted to take power within the jury of the Philadelphia Photographic Salon, but the latter was taken over by the Fine Arts Academy, who refused to let the Pictorialists take part in the Salon. Stieglitz reacted immediately by leaving the Camera Club in the summer.[16] This split happened at the same time as the boycott of the French exhibition and provided further confirmation of the Americans' desire to be recognized as artists, something which the classification of the Universal Exposition had denied them. The attitude of the organizers of the Philadelphia Photographic Salon who resisted the "new photography" and the extraordinary enthusiasm of the adherents of the future Photo-Secession explained by and large the American photographers' desire to take part more often in European exhibitions. From 1900, many of them decided to send their prints to the two London

salons: the Salon of the Royal Society of Photography and the Photographic Salon organized by the Linked Ring, the society most committed to Pictorialism. Indeed, more and more Americans joined this British society—between 1900 and 1901, there were no less than ten new American members. At the 1900 Photographic Salon, 28 of the 105 exhibitors were American, and they provided 70 of the 239 prints displayed.[17] The English photographer Alfred Horsley Hinton reported in the *Bulletin du Photo-Club* that the event constituted a veritable American invasion.[18]

"Friends of Progress"

One must realize that the presentation of nearly 200 prints by thirty-one American women at the congress,[19] exhibited a few months later at the Photo-Club de Paris, was the first manifestation in France of the new American photography that had caused such a stir in England. Nevertheless, the American women's contribution to the congress had a modest reception, with commentators emphasizing the professional status of the photographers. They had found "in photography a remunerative profession or a pleasant means of artistic expression; they are educated in their art and are friends of progress."[20]

It was above all on the occasion of the American women's exhibition at the Photo-Club de Paris from January 24 to February 13, 1901, that the French photographers fully appreciated the highly original contribution in the context of French Pictorialism (fig. 4). Due to the lack of archives and a catalogue, it is impossible to firmly establish a list of the photographers whose work appeared at this event, though the following photographers were mentioned in French critical reviews: Alice Austin, Zaida Ben-Yusuf, Rose Clark, Mary Devens, Sarah Jane Eddy, Floride Green, Gertrude Käsebier, Edith Lounsbery, Emily Mew, Anne Pilsbury, Sarah Sears, Emily and Lillian Selby, Amelia Van Buren, Eva Walborn and Mathilde Weil.

As the leader of the French movement, Robert Demachy offered the most complete analysis of the event in the *Bulletin du Photo-Club de Paris*. In his discussion of this foreign work produced by women, Demachy tried not to adopt an indulgent

M. A. Wiggins.   Effet de Brouillard.

L'Exposition des Artistes américaines

ÉCRIRE un article critique, ou même un simple compte rendu, sur une exposition d'œuvres exclusivement féminines est chose délicate. Le Français est supposé galant, légende qu'il s'applique du reste à détruire, et nous serions désolés si les artistes américaines, dont nous avons vu les œuvres, pouvaient croire que l'intérêt et l'admiration universels qu'elles ont provoqués ont été dus plutôt à un restant de la vieille galanterie française qu'à une appréciation de leur valeur véritable, sans le moindre parti pris d'indulgence.

Cette exposition, du reste, n'a pas grand caractère féminin, à l'encontre des expositions de peinture du même genre qui ne laissent aucun doute sur la parenté de la plupart des œuvres, soit à cause d'une certaine mièvrerie de sujets et de pose ou d'une facture un peu ronde, j'oserai même dire quelquefois « rondouillarde », où l'on semble retrouver, inconsciente, la courbe sinueuse de la ligne féminine. Ici nous ne pouvions nous attendre à un dessin différent de celui du sexe anguleux, l'objectif banal étant du genre neutre, mais nous croyions y trouver quelque caractère spécial. Il n'en a rien été et ce

attitude based on diplomacy and gallantry. Instead, he stated that the exhibition did not display a "feminine character," but that it was above all a show of "original work," even though some of the women had "still not been crowned with success." In this same spirit of fairness, he nevertheless acknowledged that their style was based on "simplicity," but that they were practitioners endowed with "an artistic education that was already advanced." Drawing on criticisms already expressed in England regarding the collective show that the American F. Holland Day was presenting in London at the time, he identified the stylistic characteristics which he felt were sufficiently coherent as to demonstrate the existence of a "new American school." Demachy's intuitive critical assessment came even before the French had had a chance to see the exhibition of the "new American school" that traveled from London to Paris a few weeks later. In this respect, the women's exhibition acted as a sort of harbinger of the fashion for American photography. In his discussion of the American women photographers, Demachy singled out Gertrude Käsebier for particular praise: "Her compositions reveal an artist's nature, a very lively sense of volume and a very special preoccupation with harmonious and decorative line."[21] But Demachy also observed the reactions of the public and sought to forestall certain critics who criticized all of the exhibitors for their predilection for "the somber note"—a some-

times radical use of chiaroscuro. Demachy, on the contrary, saw this as a facet of their free approach to technique and their disregard for existing rules: "If we are talking about the laboratory, then we are in agreement," he wrote, "the prints in question are bad... But if we restrict ourselves to art, that is something else. That which is dark and indistinct is not necessarily bad, any more than that which is light and brilliant is not necessarily admirable. Every effect attempted is interesting and worthy of being examined seriously and without prejudice."[22] Demachy thus attempted to dismiss the critical viewpoint of the partisans of technical perfection, lending his support to those fighting for an art freed from technical conventions. It is true that he was simply repeating arguments that he had been using against the professionals for the past ten years, but the context here was sufficiently new for him to take the opportunity of hardening a stance that the French failure in the Universal Exposition had weakened. Moreover, Demachy feared, and rightly so, that the American women's exhibition was merely a pretext for his detractors to ridicule what seemed to him to already form a characteristic of the American avant-garde.

His fears were to a degree borne out if we consider the views expressed in *Le Moniteur de la photographie* by Léon Vidal. Although Vidal, as we shall see, regarded the exhibition as a model for French women photographers, he couldn't resist ridiculing the stylistic effects: "As for the 'Artistic School,' we will not say that we would prefer something else, but we cannot discuss matters of taste; the portraits, appearing in the corner of the print, seem to constitute the 'nec plus ultra' of the current American fashion. Perhaps they would be better in the middle, and we find it hard to understand the charm of this offsetting."[23] These harsh criticisms clearly demonstrate how difficult it was to appreciate daring innovations, but the author nonetheless hailed the worthiness of the women's work. A few weeks before, Étienne Wallon, in the magazine *Photo-Gazette*, had been both respectful and severe. Although this critic, otherwise close to the Pictorialists, acknowledged the presence of "very remarkable pieces," he admits to having found "some very bad things, and others that were quite simply ordinary," but like Demachy, Wallon noticed under the differences a "tendency" common to all these artists. The reception given to the American women's exhibition was thus mixed, doubtless due to the difficulty of evaluating the exact nature of the innovations and the critics' propensity for rejecting the excesses. Nevertheless, this reception was also marked by an acknowledgement of the stylistic homogeneity that Demachy identified as a distinguishing feature of an "American school."

"Modern" Women Photographers

But despite the difficulty they experienced in formulating a judgement, the critics were all unanimous on one point: American women's photography here represented a model for French women. According to Vidal, this event "constituted a fact likely to exert an influence on the expansion of photography among women amateurs, more extensive than it is at the moment, that is to say with artistic aims that most of them lack."[24] But more than an artistic model, the American example was especially valuable as a new vision of professional practice. Indeed, it was a novelty within a novelty: not only were the artists women, but most of them were *professional* photographers who were thus presenting the fruits of artistic work and not simply the results of a hobby. This realization was received in two different ways in France. On the one hand, the professionalization of women's photography was seen as a sign of modernity, but also—on an artistic level—it testified to the high standards demanded by American clients. "These works," explained Demachy, "commissioned and executed for sale, are totally different from those that are delivered to us in Paris in the same conditions, and they are sought after, praised and expensive. The question is: are Americans more artistic than the French, or is it that photographers over there are more artistic than ours? [American women] whose original and professional artistic works we have frankly admired are photographers by profession, and their behavior toward the public, relatively speaking, is comparable to that of a painter or illustrator and not that of a simple manufacturer."[25] The astonishment and interest aroused by the Ameri-

can women's exhibition thus went beyond the originality of their photography. The very sharp distinction between amateurism and professionalism was consistent with the distinction in France between art and commerce. In France, only the disinterested amateur was deemed capable of producing art photography, while the professional photographer was regarded above all as a vulgar salesman. In the context of the work of the American women, who combined business and artistic talent, this very French distinction appeared odd to say the least. An identical analysis was put forward by Étienne Wallon: "They have succeeded in their enterprise and their success shows that on the other side of the ocean—and certainly on this side as well—there is an intelligent clientele which is ready to pay a remunerative price for a single print."[26]

This situation astonished French commentators struggling to come to terms with this new figure of the "woman photographer" (fig. 5). Under this title, Louis Gastine supplied an analysis in 1902 in the *Bulletin du Photo-Club de Paris* which revealed the gap between women's photography in the United States (and England) and in France. "The woman photographer does not exist yet in France, except simply as an amateur, but she already exists in England and America," was how Gastine began his remarks, which he wrote after seeing the Photo-Club de Paris exhibition the previous year.[27] The author emphasizes the

Ch. Labouret.

La Femme Photographe

L A Femme photographe n'existe pas encore positivement en France, — sinon à titre de simple amateur, mais elle existe déjà en Angleterre et en Amérique.

Nous avons pu voir des manifestations de son art aux dernières expositions du Photo-Club de Paris. Tout porte à penser qu'un jour ou l'autre, bientôt peut-être, Paris aura des professionnelles de la photographie, comme Londres et New-York.

Chez nos voisins et de l'autre côté de l'Atlantique, les premières femmes photographes « établies » ont été des artistes des arts du dessin abandonnant peu ou prou le pinceau, le crayon ou l'ébauchoir pour se consacrer à la portraiture photographique.

Leur façon de procéder diffère profondément de celle de nos professionnels parisiens. Tandis que ceux-ci opèrent dans des ateliers aménagés en vue de leur industrie artistique et attenant à des locaux plus ou moins luxueux, la professionnelle anglaise ou américaine ne s'embarrasse d'aucune installation.

Au lieu d'appeler le client à poser dans son atelier, elle se transporte à domicile avec ses appareils, et le photographie chez lui, ou du moins dans son milieu habituel.

C'est moins dispendieux, mais c'est beaucoup plus difficile... et c'est, en somme, plus normal, plus juste, plus rationnel à tous les points de vue.

FIG. 5. Louis Gastine, "La Femme Photographe," *Bulletin du Photo-Club de Paris* (August 1902).

two distinctive characteristics of the Anglo-American women photographers: first their professional status and secondly their artistic training. It was this link between the artistic and the commercial in their work that interested Gastine, and particularly the unusual relationship between the photographer and her client. Indeed, in contrast to French studio protocol, women photographers in New York and London would also go to their clients to photograph them in an everyday setting. After adopting this unusual approach in order to take their photographs, the women then did something even more extraordinary which affected the quality and originality of their negatives and prints. These "Modern" women photographers would select a single image, make a print from it using luxurious techniques with pigments (such as coal) then destroy all the negatives, leaving the client with a unique image just as if he had had his portrait painted by a painter. A miraculous association of art and money, women's photography thus embodied a modern vision of portraiture which marked a return to the great pictorial tradition. Gastine contrasted the Anglo-American model with the very different situation in France, where women were still restricted to the secondary tasks of the studio, such as developing the negatives, and making and touching up prints. There was no question of women being involved in the most important part of photography—the taking of pictures. Nevertheless, Gastine underscored the merits and the profitability of these professions, but he also emphasized that only a rethinking of the way girls were taught would turn them into real professionals, and consequently autonomous women.

The aesthetic and sociological curiosity aroused by the American women was comparable to the example that English women photographers offered to the French public. From 1906, an anonymous article circulated in the French photographic press under the title "La photographie comme profession féminine" (Photography as a Women's Profession).[28] It was a presentation of three English women photographers: Miss Alice Hughes, Mrs. Garet-Charles and Miss Kate Pragnell. The author was nevertheless keen to remind readers that "America, it goes without saying, was

in the lead in everything relating to female emancipation [but] England is close behind its young overseas sister and several ladies, even in high society, have put to one side the class pride and disdain for manual work so common in England, in order to direct commercial businesses in which they have been totally successful."[29] These London businesswomen could thus be seen as an extension of the image forged in 1900 by the American women. After the Photo-Club de Paris exhibition, a second show established even more firmly the central role played by American women in modern photography.

The exhibition organized in London by F. Holland Day arrived in Paris in 1901 and competed directly with the ambitions of Alfred Stieglitz on European territory. It took place on the premises of the Photo-Club de Paris from February 22 to March 10, following the exhibition of work by American women. As was to be expected, Stieglitz did not take part, and Frances B. Johnston presented only three studies—a poor showing that Constant Puyo, one of the central figures in the French Pictorialist movement, openly regretted in the account that he wrote for the *Bulletin du Photo-Club de Paris*.[30] This is not to say that women played a small role in the show. Indeed, among the thirty or so participants there were no less than eighteen women, including some who would shortly after join the ranks of the Photo-Secession, notably Zaida Ben-Yusuf, Eva Watson and the most famous of them all, Gertrude Käsebier. The two thousand or so visitors who had come to admire the three hundred examples of modern American photography had probably been made aware of the presence of the women—Puyo's report devoted much space to illustrate their works. The author's generally positive comments were accompanied by no less than nine reproductions of photographs by women. Zaida Ben-Yusuf, Elise Cabot, Mary Devens, Frances Benjamin Johnston, Margaret Russell, Sarah Sears, Ema Spencer, Mathilde Weil, Mary Stanbery, Eva Watson and Gertrude Käsebier were each in turn congratulated. None of them, in any case, were the target of the sort of criticism that Puyo directed at Steichen and, above all, Day—"avant-garde artists" and artists "at the forefront of the avant-garde." The French photographer felt that the methods and the mystical style they expressed, and Day in particular, clashed with the conventions of art photography. Nevertheless, the women did not escape criticism completely. Concluding his article, Puyo wrote: "Emerging from all this is an aesthetic of little ambition, but all in all well thought out and with solid foundations, and of which the works of Mme. Käsebier are, it seems to me, the highest and most brilliant expression; the freest as well, for the work of Mme. Käsebier is not enslaved to any formula, being perfectly original."[31]

These last comments by Puyo sum up the attitude of French critics in general: the large number of American women photographers presented in France in the space of less than ten months, from the exhibition at the Congress to the one held at the Photo-Club de Paris, followed by the exhibition of the "Nouvelle École Américaine," seem to have overwhelmed the French commentators. The women's strong presence in 1901, which was indicative of American society in general and of their art school training in particular, could not be passed off as a simple curiosity. That is probably why the French needed to isolate a single, perhaps symbolic, figure who would help make the American model easier to understand, more familiar even. Without a doubt, French critics cast Gertrude Käsebier in this role. But before describing this emblematic figure in American women's photography, we should examine the very mixed reception given to the Americans at the Salon du Photo-Club de Paris in 1901, which concluded this very "American" year for the world of French photography.

Reactions to the Avant-Garde

The surprise and the curiosity generated by the American photographers among French critics stemmed from a feeling that their work was simply the result of some admittedly daring experimentation, but that their future seemed at best uncertain. The reason for the extraordinary outcry that greeted the opening of the Salon in 1901 became clear: this was not an experiment, and what had been seen as new exaggerations were the basis of a new aesthetic. This time, Alfred Stieglitz was present, and with him Steichen,

Käsebier, White and Coburn—all but Day future members of the Photo-Secession. Furthermore, Stieglitz was acknowledged by Demachy, and through him by the Photo-Club de Paris, as being the one who "has always been loyal to our Salons" and who is "the founder of the American pictorial school."[32] Nevertheless, Étienne Wallon "didn't believe in it anymore," Georges Lanquest railed against the experimentation proudly presented to the public, Albert Reyner deplored the taste for the bizarre which led to incoherence and Rainbow denounced the snobbery of all the exaggerations: "Thus," concluded the chronicler of *Arc en Ciel*, "we will not follow the impulse of the so-called American school, although it has already found imitators, and we save our praises for works more in keeping with our French tastes."[33] Albert Reyner, for his part, pointed out that some French people had remained under the spell of the American prints: "Abandoning the old French school, reputed for its clarity and the good taste of its works, they rushed to imitate... the 'pictures' exhibited by their colleagues from the New World."[34] This nationalistic reflex was shared by many, and even in the Photo-Club bulletin people were predicting that "pictorial" photography would progress, but "on condition all the same that our artists follow their own path, that they do not stray onto the German or American paths and that they preserve the French character of our art."[35]

Thus, Robert Demachy remained alone in his defense of American photography (fig. 7). Indeed, he seemed to be the only person in the field of photography who was fighting for the new American aesthetic. In his report on the Salon, the Frenchman sang the praises of Clarence H. White's prints. In the latter's *Ring Toss*, he admired "the suppression of detail which has been taken to the highest degree without creating the least vagueness in the design." In the work of the young Alvin Langdon Coburn he detected

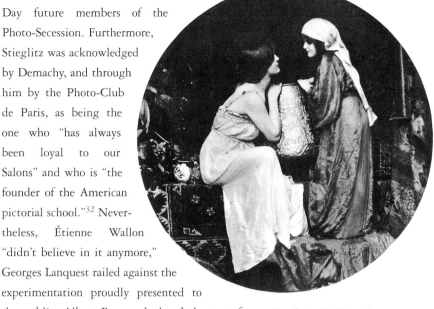

FIG. 6. René Le Bègue. *Sœurs*, in *L'Art photographique* (September 1899).

FIG. 7. Robert Demachy.
Femme lisant, ca. 1900.
Paris, Société Française de Photographie.

"remarkable beginnings," and when discussing Gertrude Käsebier he stated that she had acquired "a reputation that is difficult to sustain."[36] In addition, the French photographer felt that his compatriots' progress should no longer be driven by their own ambition, but should be inspired by the American example. "The American exhibitors have enabled us to understand," suggested Demachy, "that the cessation of French progress was due to the lack of enthusiasm and faith in the future."[37] Less than two years later, when French Pictorialism was going through a period of stagnation, Constant Puyo gradually began to share Robert Demachy's opinion, and sought to understand the reasons for the American success: "It is doubtless that, historically, thanks to their training, they have not been vaccinated against originality as successfully as the Latin peoples, they are not afraid to challenge the rules and firmly believe that the ends justify the means; a detestable maxim in morals but an excellent one when it comes to aesthetics."[38]

In the years following the American exhibitions of 1901, Paris was able to discover the "triumphant" Pictorialism of the Photo-Secession led by Alfred Stieglitz. But as the group was still young, the Americans taking part in the Parisian Salon of 1902 did not appear under this new banner. However, the leader was present, with only two prints, together with Steichen, Käsebier and Abbott. Their pictures, however, were once again given a hostile reception by the critics: "These prints are horrible," exclaimed Albert Reyner, "American amateurs have lost their way and now

they are floundering, getting bogged down, unaware perhaps of the danger that stalks them."[39] All the same, their participation in the Photo-Club exhibition devoted to gum bichromate some weeks before gave Robert Demachy the chance to defend the work of the Americans. It was his enthusiasm in particular for the pictures of Steichen, "who is like no one else [and who] continues to exasperate a section of the public,"[40] which irritated critics like Louis Bordat, who saw in them nothing but aberrations. For others, Steichen "seems very strange [and] we are forced to admit that we do not understand his style at all."[41]

In Demachy's on-going attempt to defend American innovation, the figure of the woman photographer in the form of Gertrude Käsebier became a sort of ambassador of the Secessionist modernity. If Steichen and above all Coburn (whom Demachy himself criticized strongly at the 1903 Salon) were the focus of the critics' attacks, Käsebier succeeded in creating the image of a more sensitive and less scandalous modernity.

Gertrude Käsebier: The Incarnation of a Model

Frances B. Johnston had asked Käsebier to contribute to the collection of works to be sent to the congress in 1900, but unfortunately Käsebier was reluctant to participate in this event. However, Käsebier's works were noticed by French critics during the two American exhibitions organized on the premises of the Photo-Club de Paris. And she participated regularly in the Salon du Photo-Club de Paris in the following years (with the exception of 1905). In general her work was regularly well received by critics, even if she occasionally shocked, and gradually she emerged as the American artist who was closest to the French Pictorialist community. We know that Edward Steichen was a regular visitor to Paris at the beginning of the century. He frequented the circle around Auguste Rodin that Käsebier was also part of, but he had only distant links with the Parisian photography world, preferring the more prestigious art circles. As for Käsebier, it would appear that her close links with Robert Demachy facilitated her adoption by the French critics. Also, the fact that she studied art in France, at the Académie

Julian, made Gertrude Käsebier the most "French" of American photographers. We can get an idea of the special reception she received by looking at two major texts written on her by French critics in 1906, the first in the *Revue de Photographie* (which succeeded the *Bulletin du Photo-Club de Paris*; fig. 8), the second in 1909 in *Photo-Magazine*, where Cyrille Ménard devoted a chapter of his "Maîtres de la photographie" to her.[42] The first, not surprisingly, was written by Robert Demachy. He presented her, in keeping with the general view of American women photographers in France, in terms of having a "double personality as artist and professional,"[43] a view that Cyrille Ménard would reiterate later, albeit in a slightly different way. A symbol of the "totally modern professional," Käsebier exemplified the type of photographer who could produce work for art salons as well as portraits to commission in the manner of a "painter." The reference to the art of portraiture was explained by mention of Käsebier's artistic training in Paris and of her ten-year career as a painter—a career that was followed by a veritable conversion to photography. Nevertheless, Demachy commented on the artist's odd style (an oddness that the French photographer had already emphasized in his account of the exhibition of work by American women in 1901 and which at the time provoked a mixed reaction), namely a taste for dark tones and her propensity for taking great liberties with technical rules. It was from this angle that Demachy intended to defend the originality of American photography, an originality based on the importance accorded to expression of feeling above and beyond adherence to technical rules: "I would cite, for example, a dull picture whose blacks are distorted by the dryness of the platinum. It is a gloomy avenue whose trees stand out against the dying light of dusk… But it is a memory, it is nothing but a personal memory full of poetry. The story behind it is touching, and I am affected by the totally new charm of this imperfect picture."[44] Going beyond technical perfection, Käsebier's art is thus presented as that of an inspired, "mystical, almost visionary" photographer. Quoting at length the American artist's remarks, Demachy continually emphasized the distinction in her conception of

Mme KÄSEBIER ET SON ŒUVRE

LES œuvres de Mᵐᵉ Gertrude Käsebier sont depuis longtemps connues par nos lecteurs. Sa personnalité l'est moins, surtout sa double personnalité d'artiste et de professionnelle, car si Mᵐᵉ Käsebier représente pour le public européen un des éléments les plus avancés de l'école américaine, elle incarne aussi, pour ses compatriotes, le type de la professionnelle toute moderne, qui ne réserve pas ses qualités d'artiste pour les *tableaux* qu'elle envoie aux divers Salons, mais qui les prodigue avec tout autant de conscience en faveur de l'inconnu qui s'asseoit devant son objectif et lui demande comme à un peintre un portrait d'art.

La comparaison est juste, car les débuts de Mᵐᵉ Käsebier ont eu lieu à Paris à l'Académie Julian. Ce n'est qu'après dix ans de travail que le peintre abandonna ses pinceaux et profita de son éducation première pour tirer des moyens — plus restreints assurément — que lui octroya la photographie, des effets originaux qui n'ont pas été surpassés.

L'œuvre de Mᵐᵉ Käsebier n'est pas appréciée de tout le monde. Plusieurs de ses productions peuvent sembler obscures comme inten-

photography between technical conventions and personal expression, which he made the *sine qua non* of a photograph. Demachy's insistence on this point must be understood in the context of the stagnation of French Pictorialism. Indeed, from the boycott of the 1900 exhibition up until 1905, the French struggled to catch up with American, German or even English innovations. French innovation was essentially based on thick inks (Rawlins technique) that took the print further and further away from photographic similitude. Demachy and Puyo regularly attempted to justify the use of such techniques by emphasizing the necessity of interpreting the subject, of expressing emotions, rather than merely creating crude documents. Thus, even before the great debate between Demachy and the English photographer Frederick Evans about "pure" (or "straight") photography had begun, a debate that Stieglitz's *Camera Work* would cover, what Demachy drew attention to in Käsebier's work was the rejection of technical norms in favor of the artist's desire for expressiveness. And even if the means used by Käsebier were very different from those which the French resorted to, Robert Demachy was intent on promoting this conception of photography as an art of expression through the work of Käsebier.

When, three years later, Cyrille Ménard penned a portrait of Gertrude Käsebier (fig. 9), he reiterated the main traits that Demachy had emphasized. "This incomparable magician of feeling

FIG. 9. Cyrille Ménard,
"Les Maîtres de la photographie :
Gertrude Käsebier," *Photo-Magazine*, 23
(1909).

FIG. 10. Louise Binder-Mestro.
Jeux d'adolescents, in *L'Art photographique*
(May 1900).

Gertrude KÄSEBIER

Tout là-bas, au delà de l'Atlantique, dans la cinquième avenue de la frémissante et populeuse cité assise au bord de l'Hudson, se dresse, sous la grande lumière du ciel et tout en haut d'une immense ruche où bourdonnent les innombrables employés d'une grosse maison d'affaires, un petit atelier d'apparence tranquille et modeste et qui est pourtant connu et fréquenté de tout New-York. C'est là, dans le calme d'une atmosphère reposante, au milieu des fleurs et des sourires qui vous accueillent dès l'abord, qu'ont été tissées par la main d'une fée les ailes fines et délicates de jolis papillons qui se sont envolés depuis douze ans, sous forme de délicieuses images, vers les quatre points cardinaux, pour aller se piquer aux murs des salons les plus aristocratiques ou sur la cimaise des expositions photographiques les plus renommées.

Entrez sans crainte et vous allez voir paraître, dans un instant, la main tendue et le sourire aux lèvres, la gracieuse maîtresse de céans, que tout le monde connaît ou, pour mieux dire, aime à New-York : *Gertrude Käsebier, photographe.* C'est une femme, jeune encore, malgré la longue carrière de travail et de succès qu'elle a déjà à son actif, simple de mise et d'allure, mais, par-dessus tout, gaie et charmante, à la figure ouverte et empreinte d'une franchise qui vous met tout de suite à l'aise ; ses yeux profonds et très doux rencontrent les vôtres avec un regard pénétrant, un peu gênant d'abord, tant il est profond, mais qui vous remplit bientôt des effluves d'une extraordinaire séduction. L'impression dominante que vous ressentez après un moment de trouble, qui n'est d'ailleurs que passager, est celle d'une vitalité intense qui se dégage d'une âme d'élite et d'une personnalité très nettement accusée ; elle vous séduit immédiatement et vous captive définitivement par un air de suprême bonté, de pondération et d'intelligence fine et délicate.

Cette artiste distinguée, d'une politesse exquise et d'une affabilité extrême, qui joint au charme naturel de la femme le prestige d'un talent qui a su s'imposer en quelques années au monde entier, est connue chez nous depuis longtemps dans son œuvre, mais très peu dans sa double personnalité d'artiste et de professionnelle.

Écoutez : la voici qui parle, et, dès les premiers mots, vous êtes gagné par le

Gertrude Käsebier, par M. Demachy.

has on more than one occasion violated the rules of aesthetics and photographic technique, but I do not think," wrote Ménard, "that she ever produced a single image where we do not feel under her hand the beating of the soul and the heart."[45] The image here is one of a woman who was keener to communicate her emotions sincerely than of an artist who believed strongly in conventions. Ménard also emphasized the daring formal innovations of Käsebier's compositions that occasionally angered French critics and "greatly shook up the poor European aesthetic." That was how Ménard concluded his article, nearly ten years after the congress of 1900, the American women's first show. Throughout this period, the critical reception had been a combination of astonishment and respect, cultural curiosity and aesthetic quarrels. To what extent, however, was the example set by the American women followed by women photographers in France?

The difference in status between American professionals and French amateurs sometimes makes comparison impossible. For what exactly was the place of women in the world of French Pictorialism? If, according to Louis Gastine, "the woman photographer did still not positively exist in France," it was because women were involved in the photographic industry, limited to the retouching of images and prints, and in the subsidiary profession of photographer, where you had to be "as you were required to be, discreet, skill-

ful; you have to know how to speak to high-ranking clients, to princes, to sovereigns in first-rate establishments."[46] As for taking photographs in the client's home as they did in the United States, there was no question of that. Pascaline, the only female "chronicler" of the French photography press, agreed with this: any woman who had a profession or had been an artist would have been regarded as a hybrid and would rapidly have become an object of curiosity more than of interest.[47] The photographic societies hardly had a more progressive position on the issue of women. In 1900, Albert Reyner counted only around fifty female members of photography clubs, of whom thirty-seven belonged to the very feminist Société Havraise de Photographie. Furthermore, the pleas to have women admitted to photographic societies were based on strange arguments: wouldn't it be a solution, some felt, for bringing together those couples where the husband is a photography enthusiast and is always away on meetings and excursions?[48] Only the Photo-Club de Paris could pride itself on being relatively open-minded on this subject. Louise Binder-Mestro (fig. 10), Madame Albert Huguet, Antoinette Bucquet and later Céline Laguarde formed the hardcore of this "women's school," and their careers were every bit as successful as those of their male counterparts. Moreover, in Cyrille Ménard they had a champion of the highest rank, and as a result *Photo-Magazine* welcomed them with open arms.

Of these women, Céline Laguarde is probably the one who best epitomizes the woman photographer who reached the highest level in her artistic career (fig. 11). This artist, who was born in the Basque region and lived in Aix-en-Provence and Paris, enjoyed considerable critical success. A major figure in the second generation of Pictorialists which emerged after 1900, she showed great mastery of bichromate gum and other pigment techniques. A member of the Photo-Club de Paris and a regular in international salons, her work typified the art photography produced in the South of France. Praised in Nice and Marseille, where critics hailed her with the name "maître des gommistes marseillais" (master of the Marseille gum bichromatists),[49] Céline Laguarde also exhibited at all the salons of the Photo-Club de Paris from 1901 (fig. 12). Her output, widely published in specialist reviews, was initially tinged with a certain mysticism reminiscent of Käsebier's work. But from 1910, she devoted herself to portraits of celebrities such as Maurice Ravel, Darius Milhaud, Francis Jammes, Maurice Barrès, Frédéric Mistral and Jules Chéret, creating a body of work as a portraitist which was unusual in the context

FIG. 11. Céline Laguarde. *Stella*, in *L'Épreuve photographique*, 3 (1904).

of French Pictorialism. In this respect, Céline Laguarde seems to be a unique example of an accomplished woman art photographer in the world of French Pictorialism and it is likely that the American women provided her with an example that she relished following.

FIG. 12. Céline Laguarde. *Étude en brun*, in *L'Épreuve photographique*, 6 (1904).

1. Sosthène Pector, *Congrès international de photographie, tenu à Paris du 23 au 28 juillet 1900. Procès-verbaux sommaires*. Ministère du Commerce, de l'Industrie des Postes et des Télégraphes. Exposition Universelle Internationale de 1900, Paris, Imprimerie Nationale, 1900, p. 9. (In a more detailed account of Johnston's presentation two days later, he places the number of works at 200, see introduction)

2. Michel Poivert, "Le Sacrifice du présent—pictorialisme et modernité," *Études photographiques*, 8 (November 2000), pp. 92–110.

3. Robert Demachy, "Conclusion," *Bulletin du Photo-Club de Paris* (December 1900), pp. 392–93.

4. See the articles by Dr. Phipson in *Le Moniteur de la photographie*.

5. Frédéric Dillaye, "Études critiques sur le premier Salon d'art photographique," *Bulletin du Photo-Club de Paris* (February 1894), pp. 33–43.

6. Poivert, *op. cit.*

7. Between 1895 and 1898, the first women's names began to appear in the catalogues of the Salon; some of these women photographers went on to have careers, notably Mme Binder-Mestro, Antoinette Bucquet and Mme Huguet.

8. Emmanuel Mathieu, "L'Art photographique et les femmes américaines," *Bulletin de Photo-Club de Paris* (June 1895), pp. 166–74.

9. Dillaye, *op. cit.*

10. Frédéric Dillaye, "Études critiques sur l'Exposition d'Art Photographique," *Bulletin du Photo-Club de Paris* (May 1895), pp. 129–40.

11. M. Nicolle, "À propos de l'Exposition d'art photographique," *Le Nord photographe*, 10 (1896), pp. 120–26.

12. R. T. D., "Le Salon de photographie: Angleterre, Amérique," *Bulletin du Photo-Club de Paris* (June 1897), pp. 174–91.

13. Déambulator, "Les Anglais et les Américains à l'exposition du Photo-Club," *Bulletin du Photo-Club de Paris* (June 1898), pp. 185–202.

14. Étienne Wallon, "L'Exposition des artistes américaines au Photo-Club," *Photo-Gazette* (February 25, 1901), pp. 61–64.

15. Weston Naef, *The Collection of Alfred Stieglitz: Fifty Pioneers of Modern Photography* (New York: The Viking Press, 1978), p. 71.

16. Alfred Stieglitz, "The Philadelphia Salon," *Camera Notes*, 2 (October 1901), pp. 121–22.

17. The French were represented by four artists and twenty-two prints, a modest contribution doubtless due to their participation in the Universal Exposition in Paris.

18. Alfred Horsley Hinton, "À l'Ètranger—Angleterre," *Bulletin du Photo-Club de Paris* (October 1900), pp. 330–37.

19. In other sources the number of participants and works exhibited vary. For an explanation, see the introduction.

20. Sosthène Pector, *Congrès international de photographie, procès-verbaux, rapports, notes et documents divers* (Paris: Gauthier-Villars, 1901), p. 44.

21. Robert Demachy, "L'Exposition des artistes américaines," *Bulletin du Photo-Club de Paris* (April 1901), pp. 107–13.

22. *Ibid.*, p. 112.

23. Léon Vidal, "L'Exposition des artistes américains [*sic*] au Photo-Club de Paris," *Le Moniteur de la photographie*, 4 (1901), pp. 49–51.

24. *Ibid.*, p. 49.

25. Robert Demachy, "L'Exposition des artistes américaines," *Bulletin du Photo-Club de Paris* (April 1901), note 20, see p. 113.

26. Wallon, *op. cit.*

27. Louis Gastine, "La Femme photographe," *Bulletin du Photo-Club de Paris* (August, 1902), pp. 268–71.

28. First in *Photo Pêle-Mêle* (March 3, 1906), then in *Photo-Magazine* (June 28, 1908).

29. Anonymous, "La Photographie comme profession féminine," *Photo Pêle-Mêle* (March 3, 1906), p. 66–69.

30. Constant Puyo, "L'Exposition de M. H. Day et de la 'nouvelle école américaine,'" *Bulletin du Photo-Club de Paris* (April 1901), pp. 114–38.

31. *Ibid.*, p. 119, by all evidence Cabot only participated in the "New School" exhibition and not Johnston's exhibition. See introduction.

32. Robert Demachy, "Le Salon de 1900," *Bulletin du Photo-Club de Paris* (June 1901), pp. 207–38.

33. Rainbow, "Le Salon de Photographie," *L'Arc en Ciel* (June 1901), pp. 57–61. See also Étienne Wallon, "Le Salon," *Photo-Gazette* (May 1901), pp. 121–34; G. Lanquest, "Le Salon de photographie," *Le Home* (June 1901), pp. 125–29; Albert Reyner, *L'Année photographique 1901*, Paris, C. Mendel, 1901.

34. Reyner, *op. cit.*, p. 70.

35. Georges Hamand, "Le Salon de 1901," *Bulletin du Photo-Club de Paris* (June 1901), pp. 238–54.

36. Demachy, "Le Salon de 1901," *op. cit.*

37. Robert Demachy, "Artistic Photography in France," *Photograms of the Year* (1901), pp. 8–12.

38. Constant Puyo, "L'Évolution photographique," *La Revue de Photographie*, 1 (1903), pp. 1–6.

39. Albert Reyner, "Le Salon du Photo-Club de Paris," *Photo-Revue*, 23 (1902), pp. 178–81. See also Albert Reyner, "Le Salon du Photo-Club," *La Photographie*, 6 (1902), pp. 84–88.

40. Robert Demachy, "L'Exposition des gommes bichromatées," *Bulletin du Photo-Club de Paris* (May 1902), pp. 141–53.

41. "Le Salon des gommistes," *Le Nord photographe* (April 1902), pp. 51–53.

42. Cyrille Ménard, "Les Maîtres de la photographie—Gertrude Käsebier," *Photo-Magazine*, 23 (1909), pp. 177–84; 24, pp. 185–92.

43. Robert Demachy, "Mme Käsebier et son œuvre," *La Revue de Photographie* (October 1906), pp. 289–95.

44. *Ibid.*, p. 290.

45. Cyrille Ménard, "Les Maîtres de la photographie—Gertrude Käsebier," *Photo-Magazine*, 23 (1909), p. 182.

46. G. Régnal, "La Photographie" in *Comment la femme peut gagner sa vie*, J. Tallandier ed. (Paris: Librairie illustrée, 1908), pp. 220–21.

47. Pascaline, "La Femme-photographe," *La Photographie*, 2 (1903), pp. 28–30.

48. A. Reyner, "La Femme et la photographie," *Le Nord photographe*, 7 (1907), no page numbers. See also J. B., "Chronique," *Photo-Midi*, 7 (1908), pp. 85–88.

49. Dr. Casteuil, "Concours-Exposition de photographie du Photo-Club de Marseille," *Photo-Midi* (January 1905), pp. 7–8.

PLATES

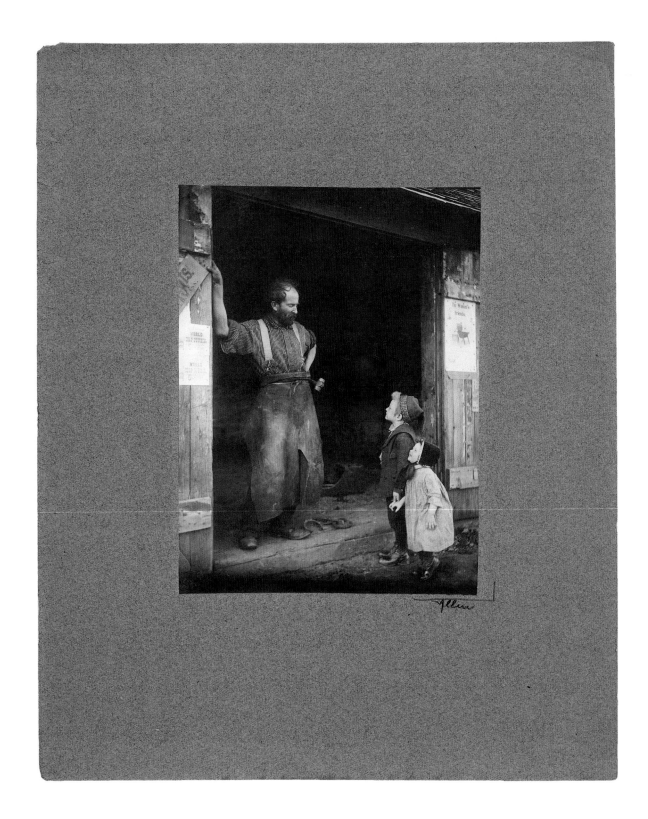

PLATE 1 (cat. 3)
Mary Electa Allen and Frances Stebbins Allen
A 'Crack' with the Blacksmith, ca. 1900

PLATE 2 (cat. 4)
Mary Electa Allen and Frances Stebbins Allen
A Holbein Woman, ca. 1890–92

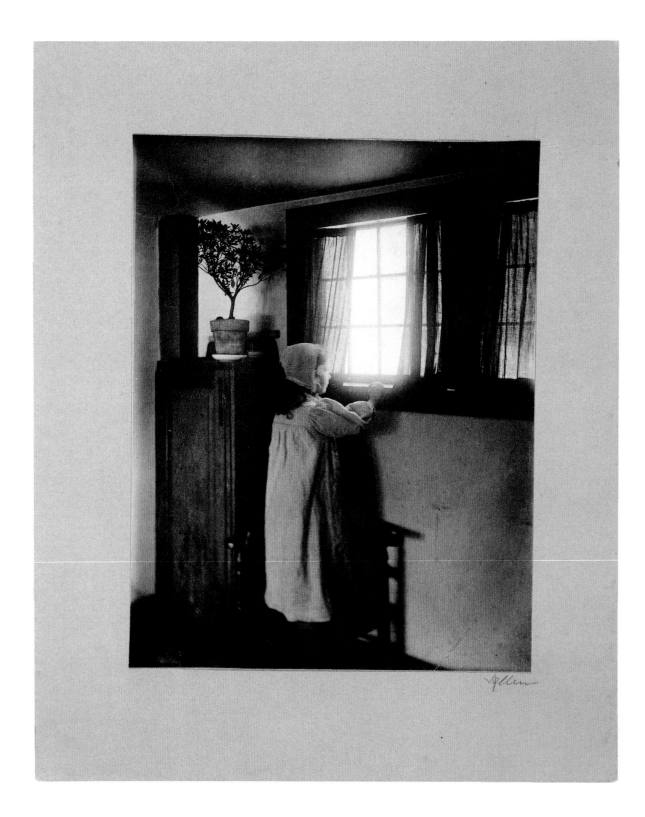

PLATE 3 (cat. 6)
Mary Electa Allen and Frances Stebbins Allen
Good Morning!, ca. 1900

Col. Joseph Stebbins house - built just before Revolution

PLATE 4 (cat. 10)
Mary Electa Allen and Frances Stebbins Allen
Old Deerfield, ca. 1900

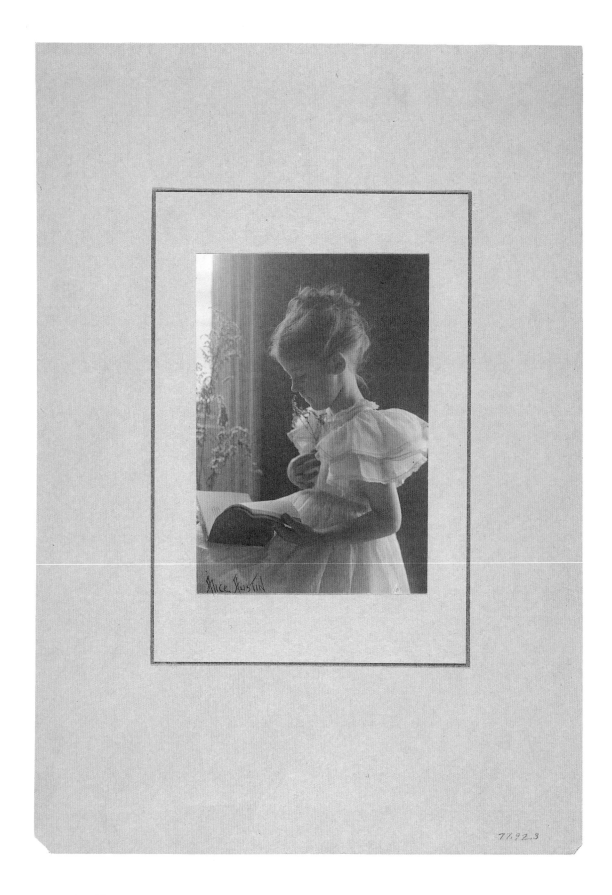

Plate 5 (cat. 28)
Alice Austin
[Young girl reading], ca. 1900

PLATE 6 (cat. 25)
Alice Austin
[Man holding an infant], ca. 1900

PLATE 7 (cat. 31)
Alice Austin
[Portrait of a bearded man], ca. 1900

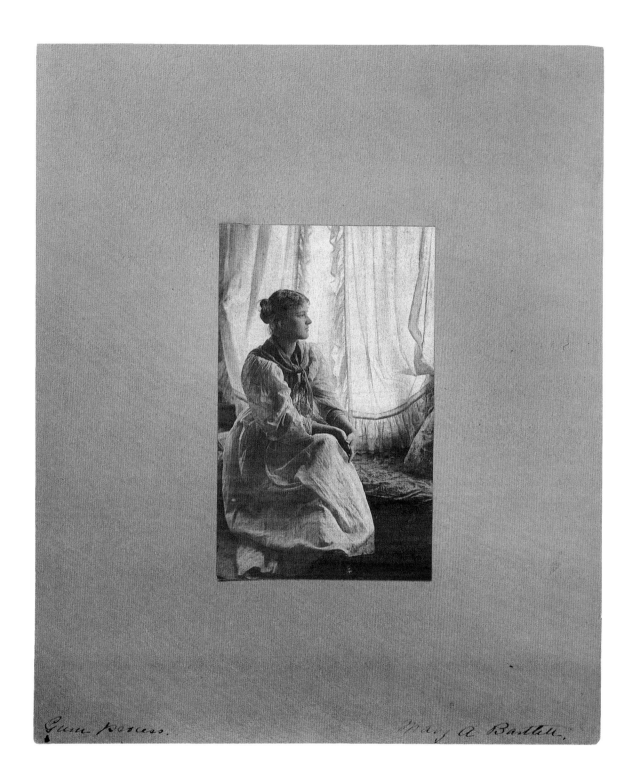

PLATE 8 (cat. 32)
Mary A. Bartlett
[Woman seated with crossed legs in front of sheer curtains], ca. 1900

PLATE 9 (cat. 33)
Mary A. Bartlett
[Young woman seated by a window with flowers in her lap], ca. 1900

PLATE 10 (cat. 34)
Mary A. Bartlett
[Woman on path in the woods], ca. 1900

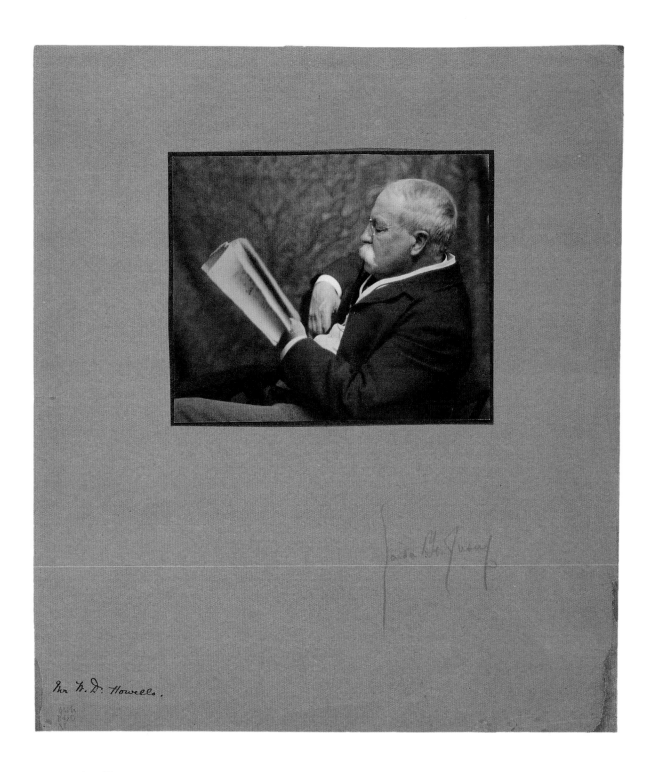

PLATE 11 (cat. 40)
Zaida Ben-Yusuf
Mr. W. D. Howells, ca. 1900

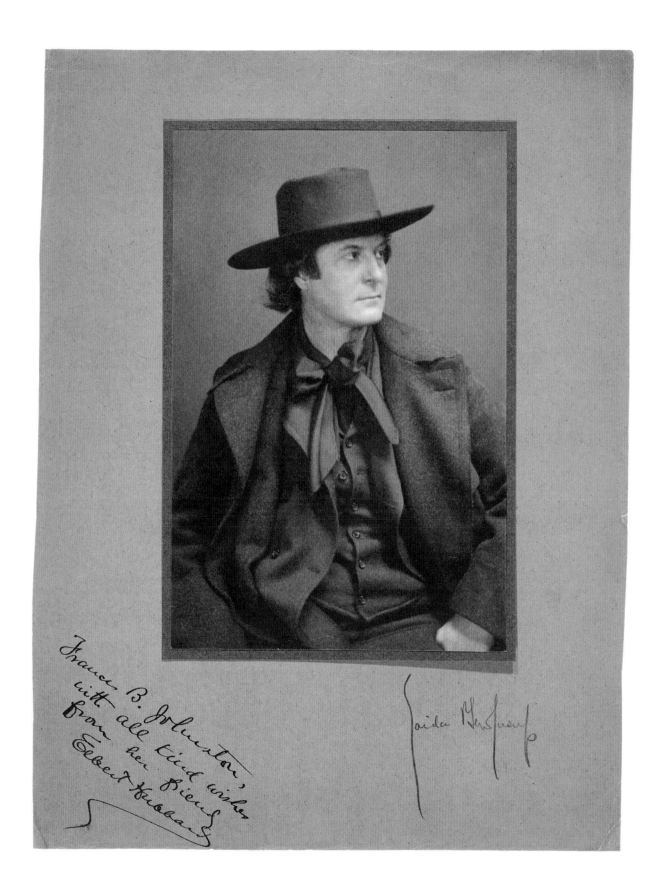

PLATE 12 (cat. 41)
Zaida Ben-Yusuf
Portrait of Elbert Hubbard, ca. 1900

Portrait of Miss K.

PLATE 13 (cat. 42)
Zaida Ben-Yusuf
Portrait of Miss K., ca. 1900

PLATE 14 (cat. 43)
Zaida Ben-Yusuf
The Odor of Pomegranates, ca. 1900

PLATE 15 (cat. 44)

Zaida Ben-Yusuf

Portrait of Miss Ben-Yusuf [self-portrait], ca. 1900

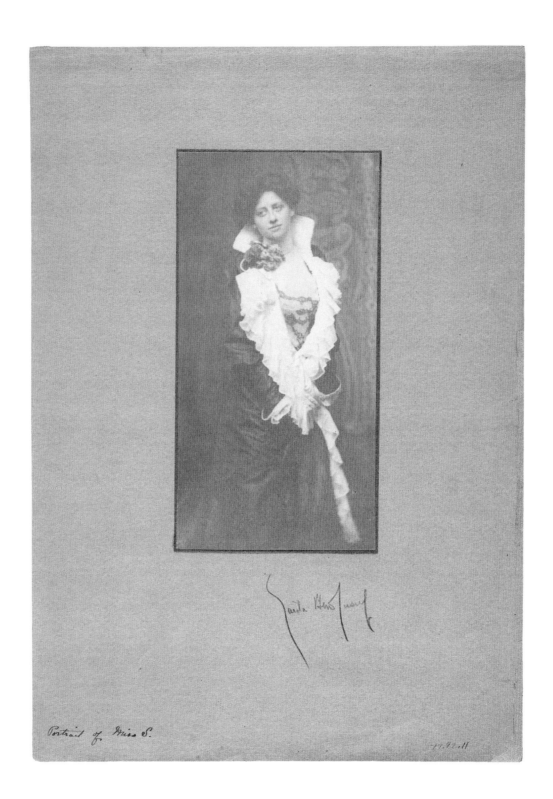

PLATE 16 (cat. 45)
Zaida Ben-Yusuf
Portrait of Miss S., ca. 1900

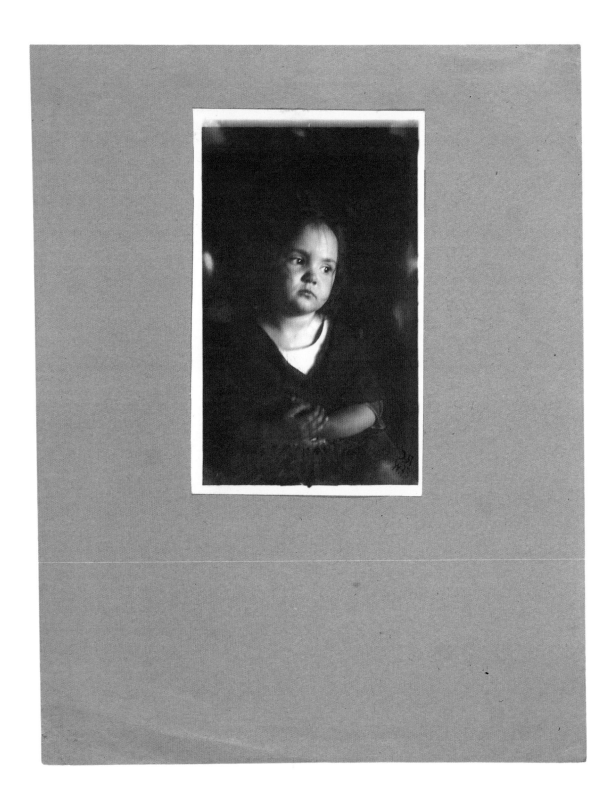

Rose Clark and Elizabeth Flint Wade
Annetje, 1898

PLATE 18 (cat. 56)
Sarah Jane Eddy
The Old Mill, ca. 1900

PLATE 19 (cat. 61)
Sarah Jane Eddy
The Fisherman's Home, ca. 1900

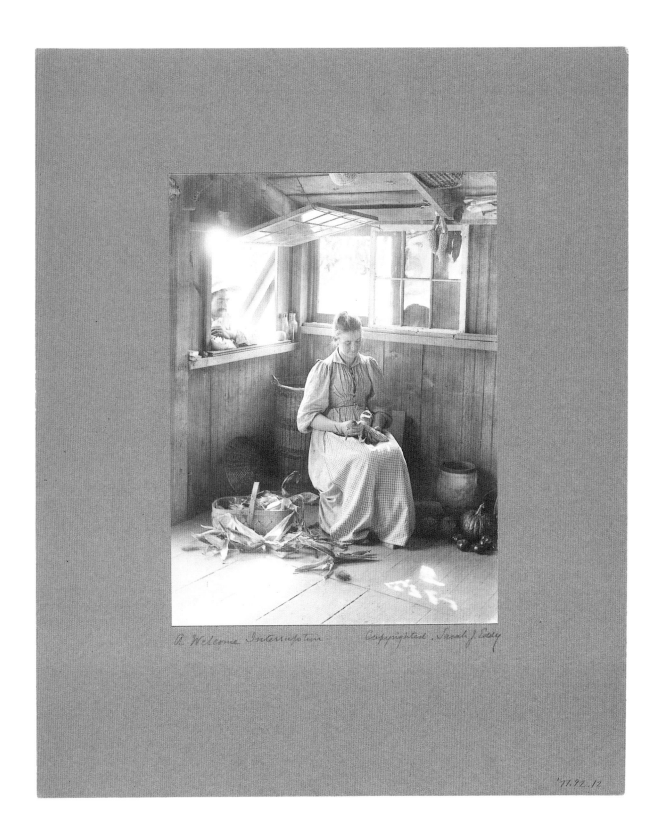

A Welcome Interruption   *Copyrighted . Sarah J. Eddy*

'77.92.17

PLATE 20 (cat. 62)

Sarah Jane Eddy

A Welcome Interruption, ca. 1896

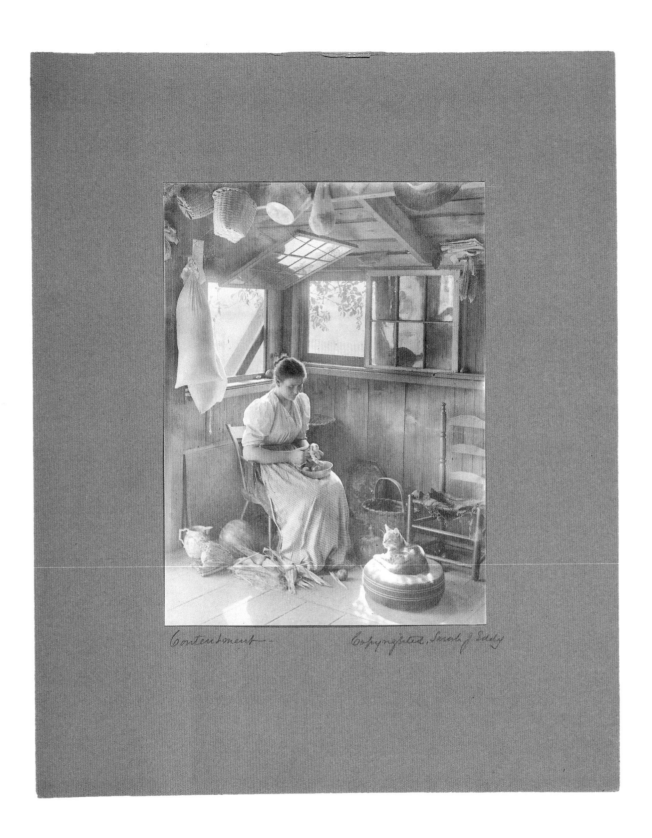

Contentment —   *Copyrighted, Sarah J. Eddy*

PLATE 21 (cat. 60)
Sarah Jane Eddy
Contentment, ca. 1900

PLATE 22 (cat. 70)
Sarah Jane Eddy
The Spirit of a Flower, ca. 1900

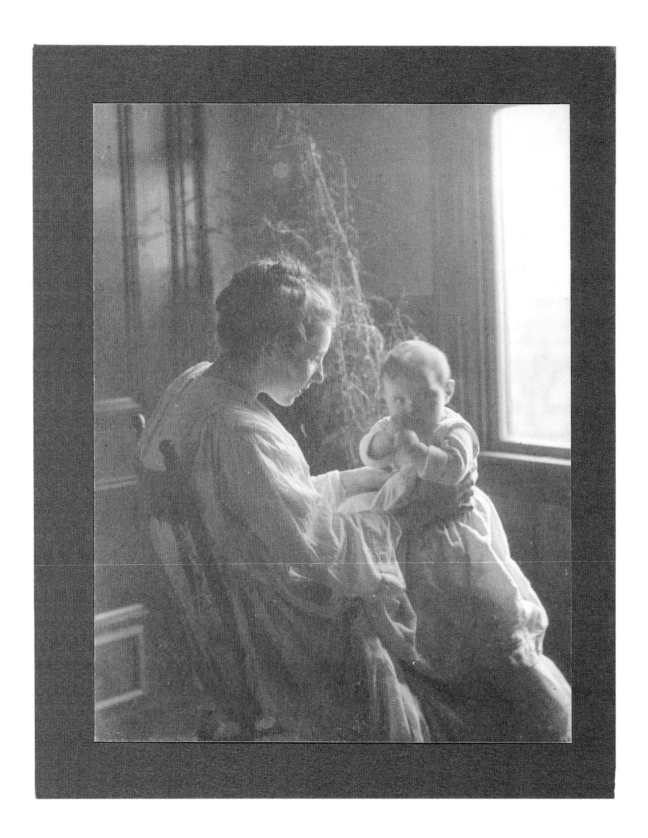

PLATE 23 (cat. 58)
Sarah Jane Eddy
Mother and Child, ca. 1900

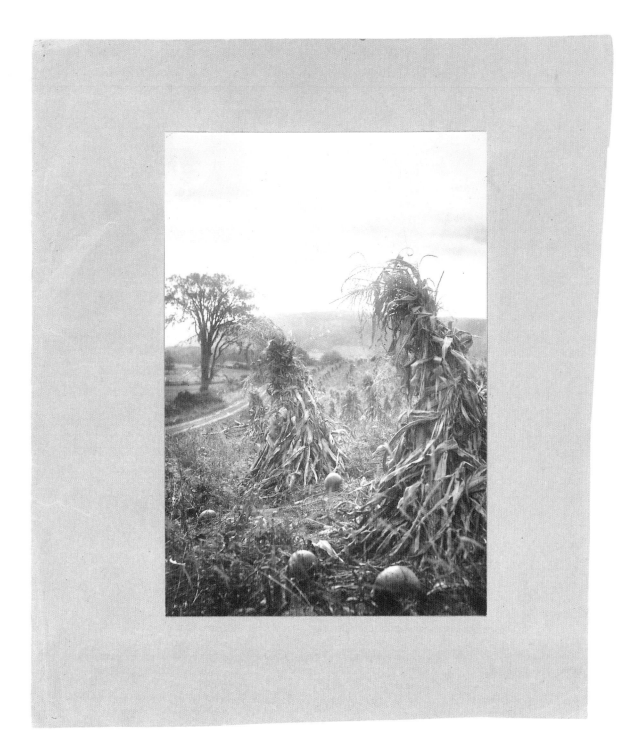

PLATE 24 (cat. 74)
Emma Justine Farnsworth
[Field with cornstalks twisted into bunches and pumpkins], ca. 1900

PLATE 25 (cat. 75)
Emma Justine Farnsworth
At Dusk, 1893

PLATE 26 (cat. 76)
Emma Justine Farnsworth
Diana, 1898

PLATE 27 (cat. 79)
Emma Justine Farnsworth
To A Greek Girl, 1873

PLATE 28 (cat. 86)
Emma Justine Farnsworth
When Spring Comes Laughing by Vale and Hill, ca. 1900

PLATE 29 (cat. 88)
Emma Justine Farnsworth
The Faggot Gatherers, ca. 1900

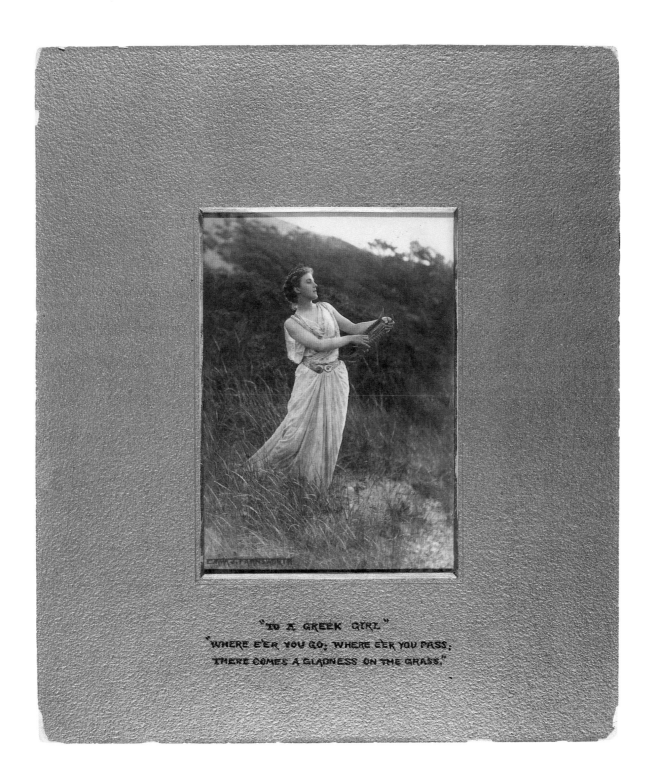

PLATE 30 (cat. 85)
Emma Justine Farnsworth
To A Greek Girl, ca. 1900

173 - 3

PLATE 31 (cat. 89)
Emma L. Fitz
The Village Politician, ca. 1900

PLATE 32 (cat. 94)
Gertrude Stanton Käsebier
Blessed Art Thou Among Women, 1899

PLATE 33 (cat. 95)
Gertrude Stanton Käsebier
The Manger, 1899

PLATE 34
Gertrude Stanton Käsebier
The Vision, ca. 1900

77.92.62

PLATE 35 (cat. 97)
Edith Haggin Lounsbery
Portrait Study, ca. 1900

Edith A. Lounsbery

PLATE 36 (cat. 96)
Edith Haggin Lounsbery
Portrait of John Lane, Publisher, ca. 1900

PLATE 37 (cat. 103)
Emily G. Mew
Prince Pierre Troubetskoy, Painter, ca. 1900

PLATE 38 (cat. 101)
Emily G. Mew
[Girl in period dress with headband], ca. 1900

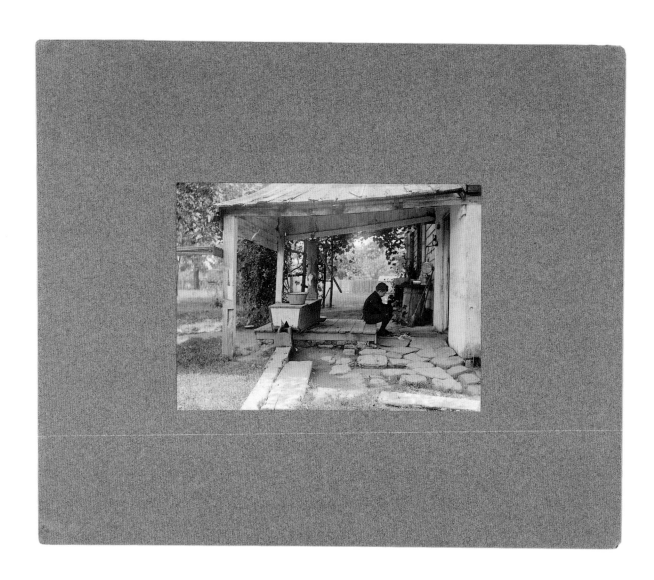

PLATE 39 (cat. 106)
Mary F. Carpenter Paschall
An Old Porch, ca. 1900

PLATE 40 (cat. 108)
Mary F. Carpenter Paschall
Milkweed, ca. 1900

PLATE 41 (cat. 109)
Mary F. Carpenter Paschall
Picking Geese, ca. 1900

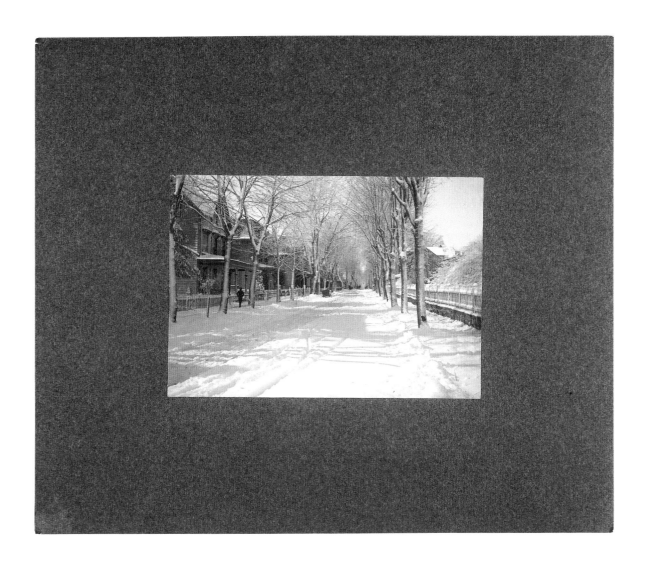

PLATE 42 (cat. 113)
Mary F. Carpenter Paschall
An April Snow, ca. 1900

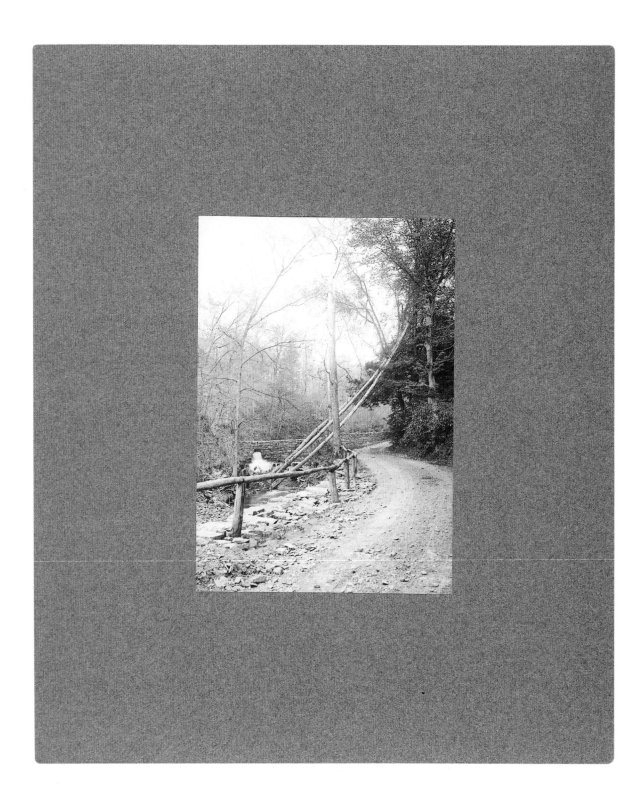

PLATE 43 (cat. 114)
Mary F. Carpenter Paschall
Along the Euttalossa, ca. 1900

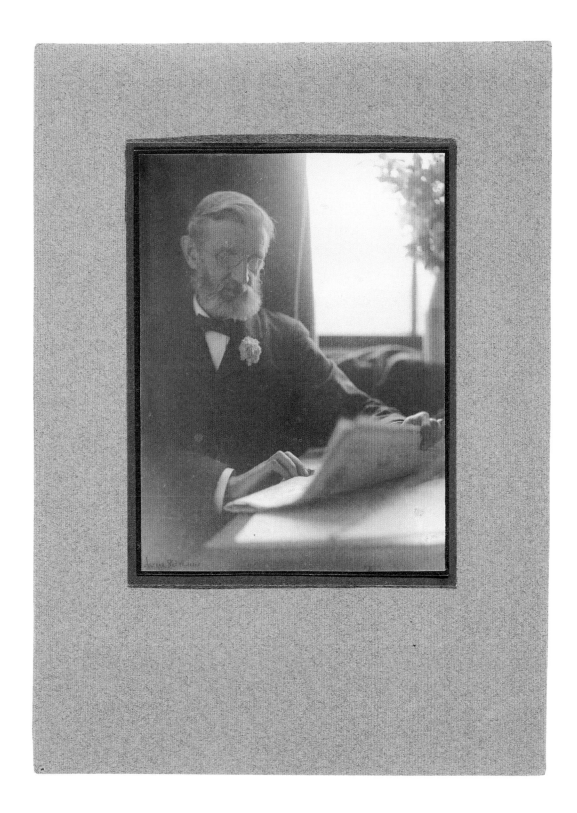

PLATE 44 (cat. 115)
Anne K. Pilsbury
[Bearded man in spectacles reading a newspaper], ca. 1900

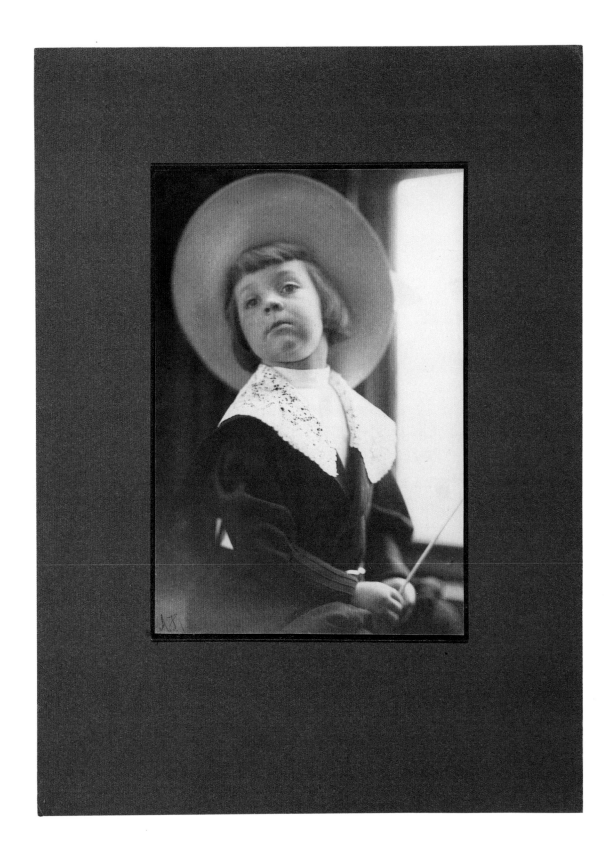

PLATE 45 (cat. 116)
Anne K. Pilsbury
[Portrait of a boy in a round hat], ca. 1900

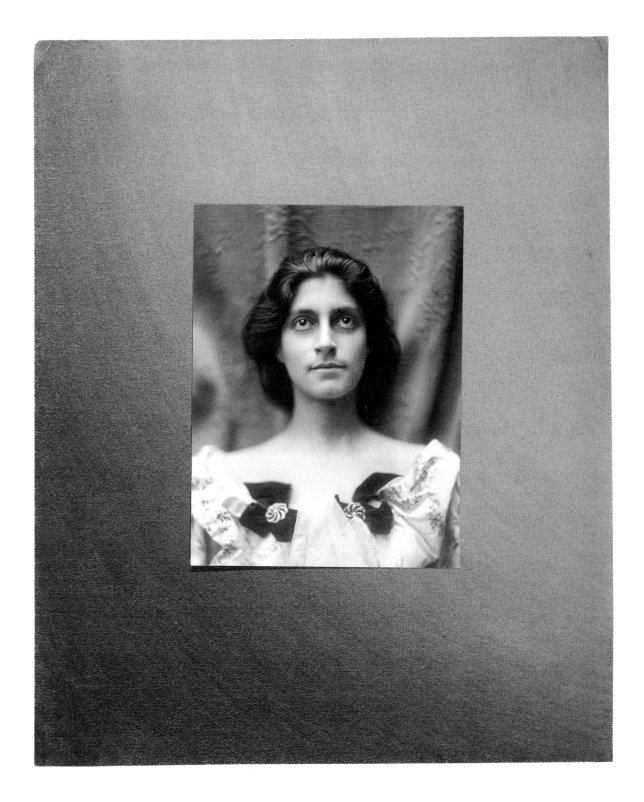

PLATE 46 (cat. 119)

Virginia M. Prall

[Portrait of a woman in a floral dress adorned with diamond brooches and bows], ca. 1900

PLATE 47 (cat. 120)
Virginia M. Prall
[Two girls wearing white dresses and dark stockings reading a book], ca. 1900

PLATE 48 (cat. 121)
Virginia M. Prall
From Old Virginia, ca. 1900

PLATE 49 (cat. 125)
Addie Kilburn Robinson
Geraldine Farrar, 1898

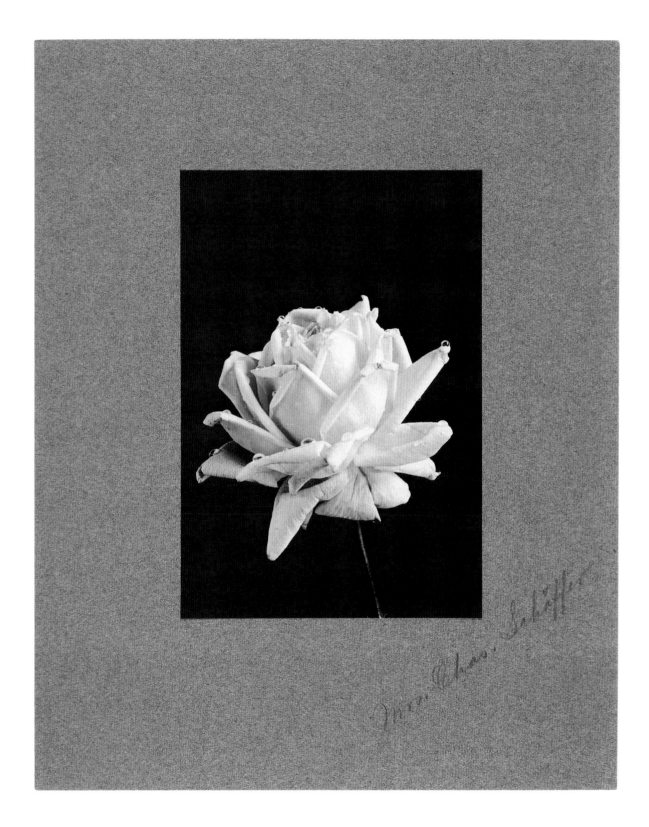

PLATE 50 (cat. 132)
Mary Townsend Sharples Schäffer
La France Rose, Sprinkled with Water, ca. 1900

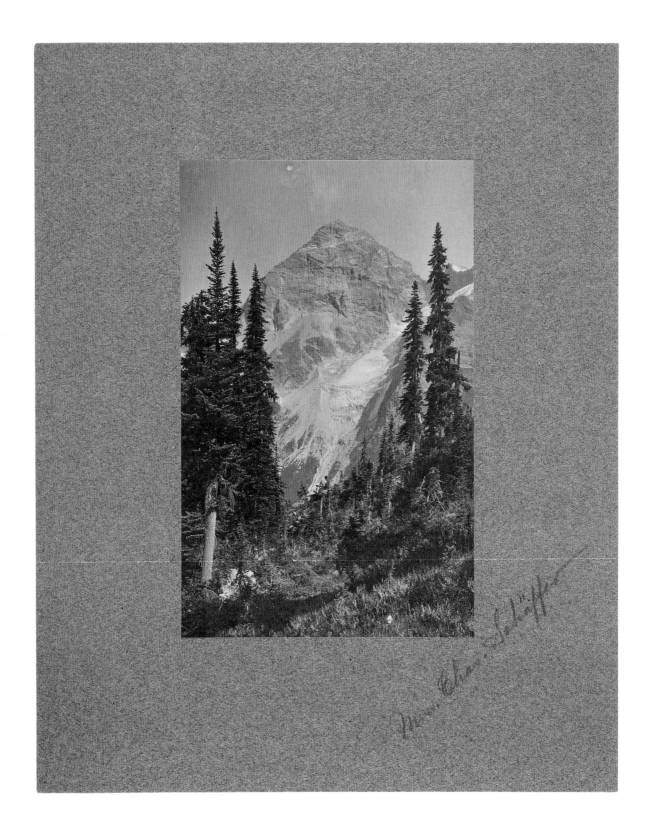

PLATE 51 (cat. 136)
Mary Townsend Sharples Schäffer
Mount Sir Ronald, ca. 1900

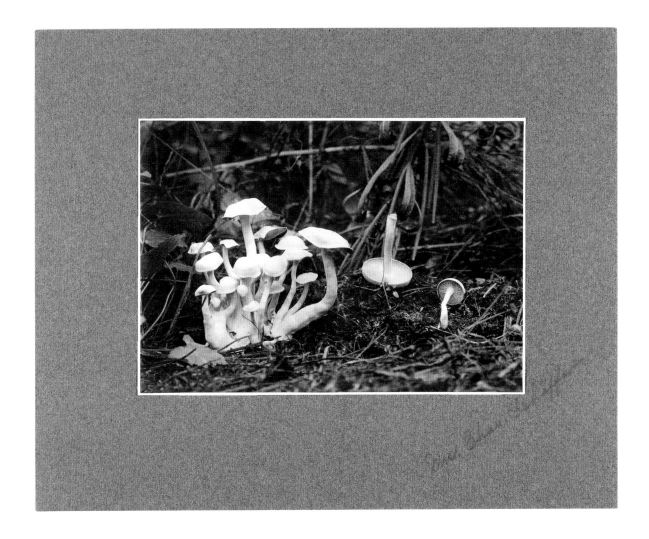

PLATE 52 (cat. 133)
Mary Townsend Sharples Schäffer
Chalk Mushroom from the Selkirk Mountains of Canada, ca. 1900

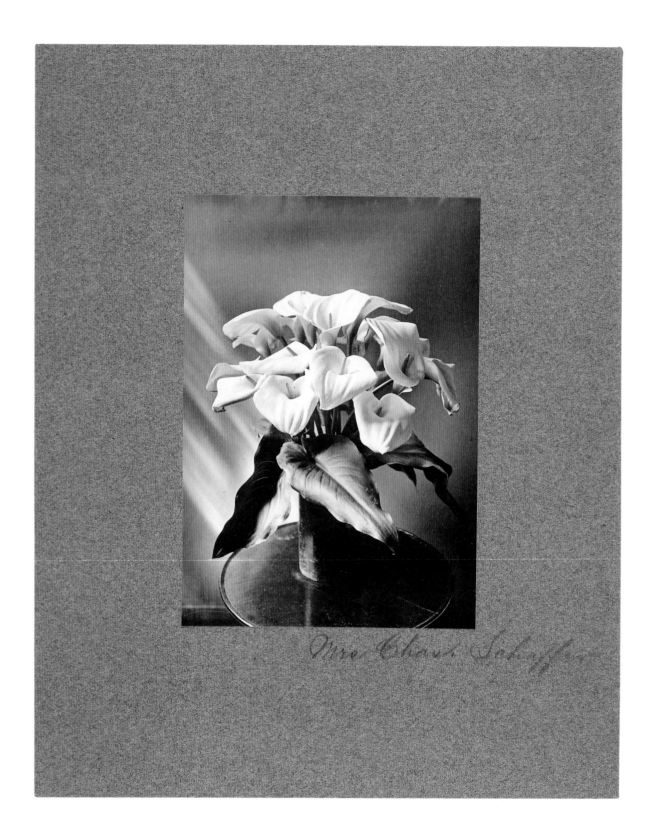

PLATE 53 (cat. 139)
Mary Townsend Sharples Schäffer
Easter Morning, ca. 1900

PLATE 54 (cat. 147)

Emily and Lillian Selby
[Portrait of woman in walking dress
holding a fur muffler], ca. 1900

PLATE 55 (cat. 150)
Emily and Lillian Selby
[Old woman reading a book], ca. 1900

PLATE 56 (cat. 149)
Emily and Lillian Selby
[Portrait of a young girl with tousled hair], ca. 1900

PLATE 57 (cat. 153)
Alta Belle Sniff
[Boy with suspenders], ca. 1900

PLATE 58 (cat. 168)
Amelia Van Buren
[Profile portrait of woman draped with a veil], ca. 1900

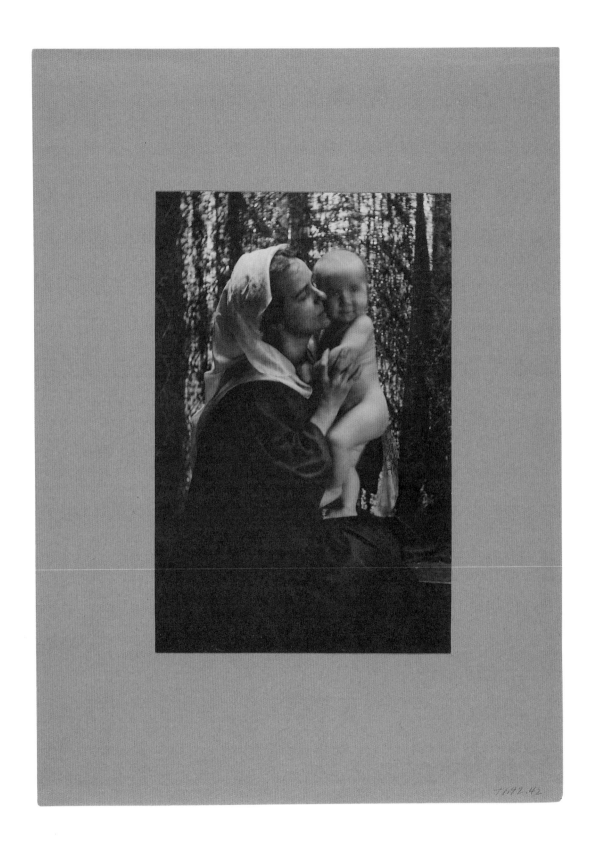

PLATE 59 (cat. 173)
Amelia Van Buren
Madonna, ca. 1900

PLATE 60 (cat. 176)
Eva Gamble Walborn
A Portrait, ca. 1900

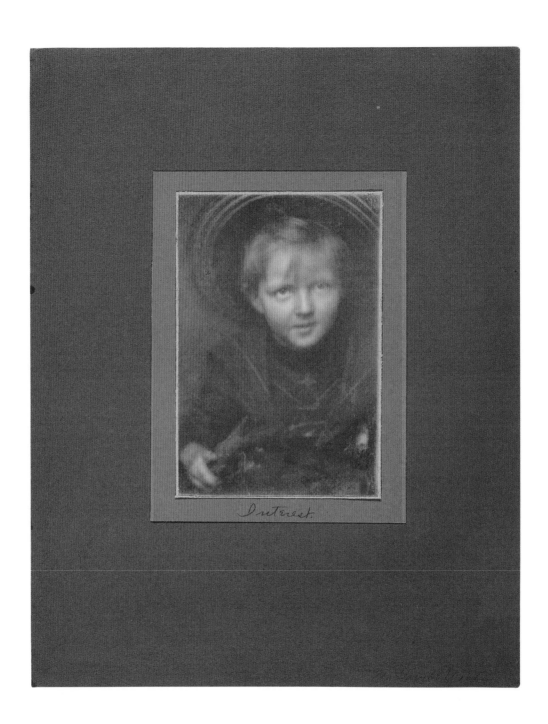

PLATE 61 (cat. 177)
Eva Gamble Walborn
Interest, ca. 1900

Sweet Peas.

PLATE 62 (cat. 178)
Eva Gamble Walborn
Sweet Peas, ca. 1900

PLATE 63 (cat. 179)
Eva Gamble Walborn
Zylpha, ca. 1900

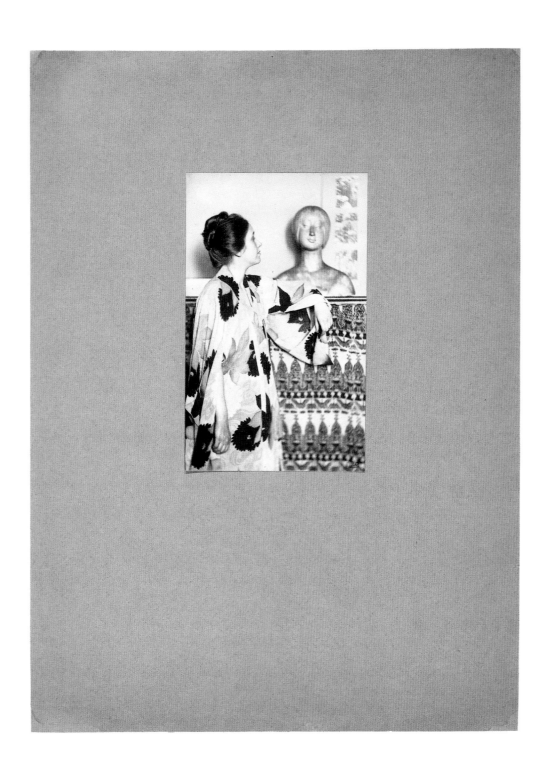

PLATE 64 (cat. 182)
Eva Lawrence Watson-Schütze
[Woman in a kimono standing looking at a sculpted bust], ca. 1900

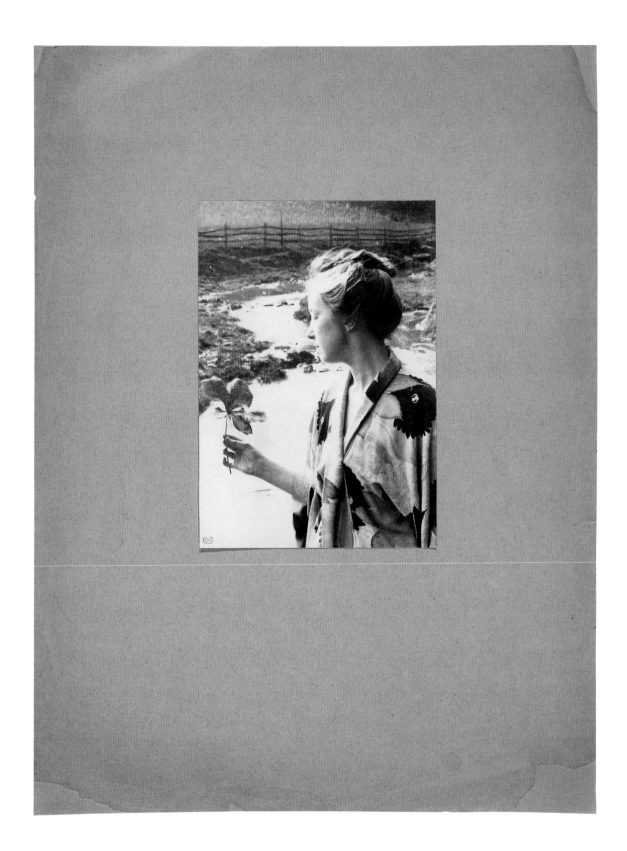

PLATE 65 (cat. 183)
Eva Lawrence Watson-Schütze
The May Apple Leaf, ca. 1900

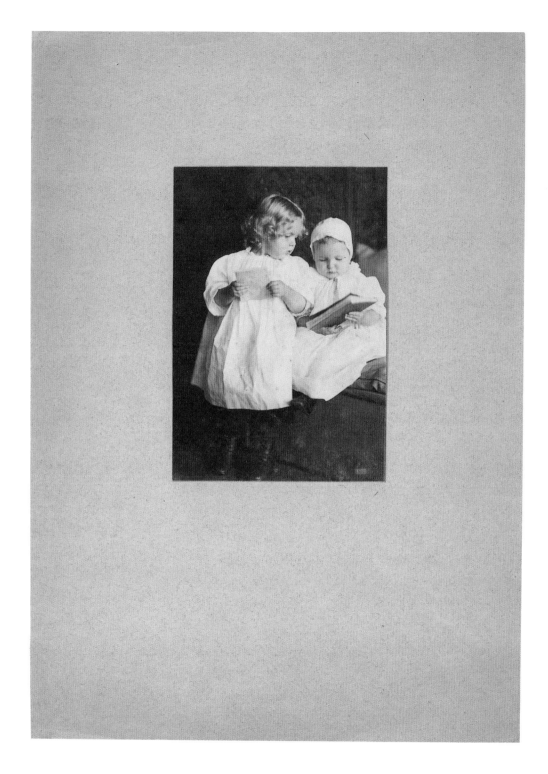

PLATE 66 (cat. 191)

Eva Lawrence Watson-Schütze

[Child standing with piece of paper looking at a book held by a seated infant], ca. 1900

PLATE 67 (cat. 197)

Eva Lawrence Watson-Schütze

[Portrait of William Rau leaning on sword], ca. 1900

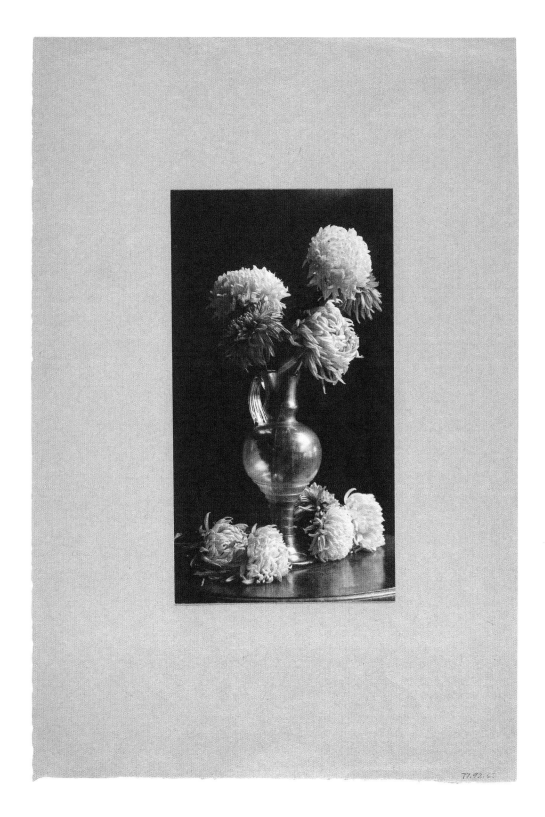

PLATE 68 (cat. 200)
Eva Lawrence Watson-Schütze
[Still life with chrysanthemums], ca. 1900

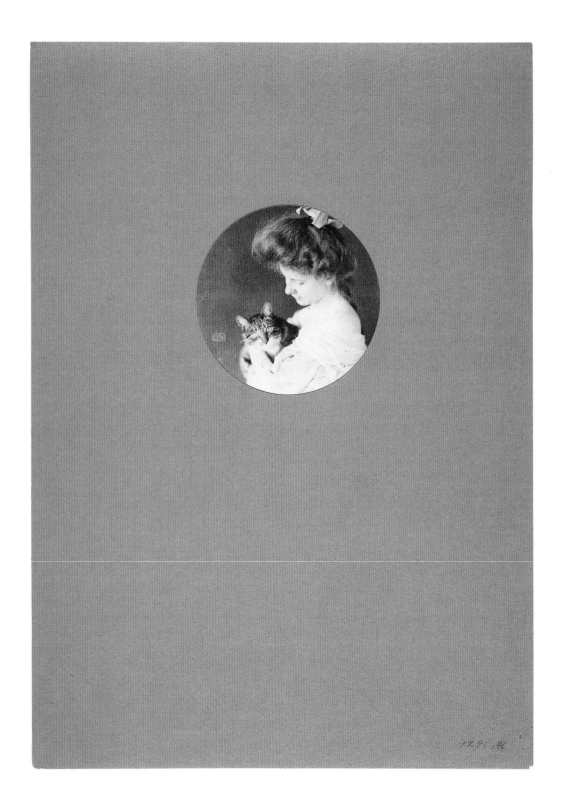

PLATE 69 (cat. 196)
Eva Lawrence Watson-Schütze
[Woman with cat], ca. 1900

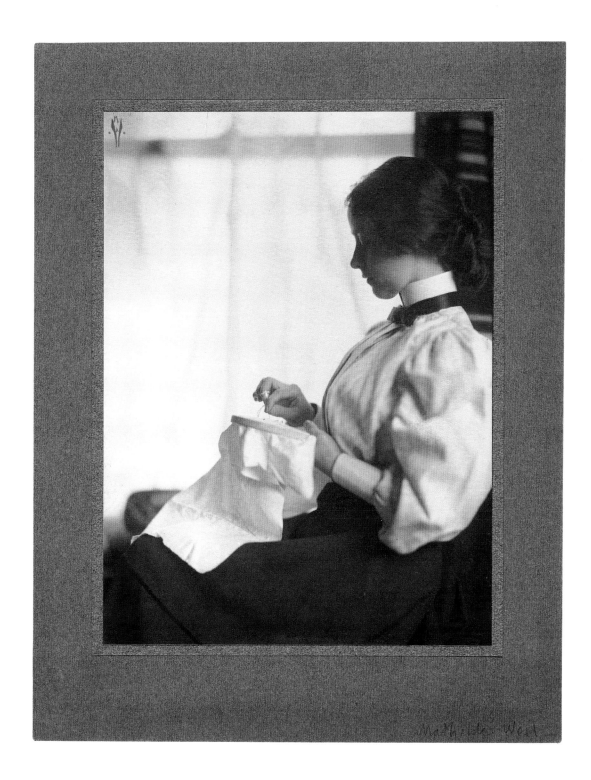

PLATE 70 (cat. 201)
Mathilde Weil
The Embroidery Frame, ca. 1900

PLATE 71 (cat. 202)
Mathilde Weil
Constance, ca. 1900

PLATE 72 (cat. 203)
Mathilde Weil
Il Penseroso, ca. 1900

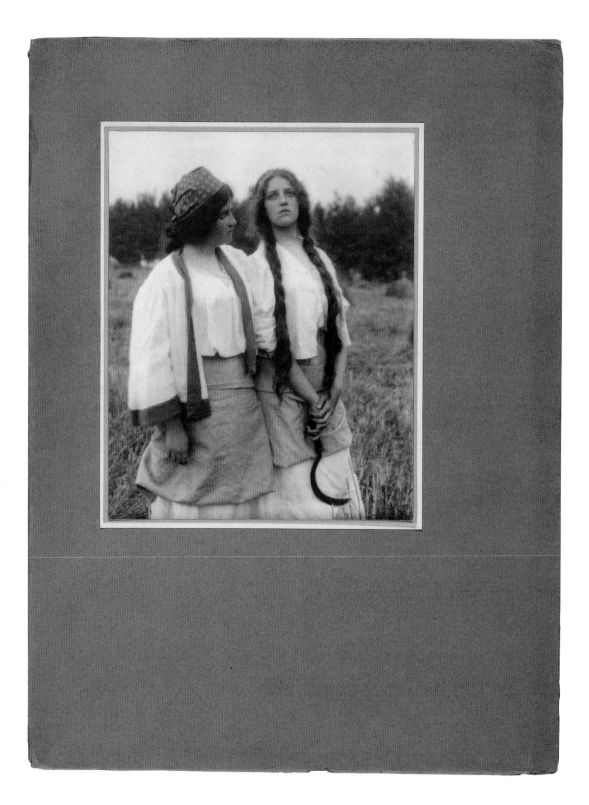

PLATE 73 (cat. 205)
Mathilde Weil
Song of the Meadow Lark, ca. 1900

PLATE 74 (cat. 208)
Mathilde Weil
[Old woman in an armchair with an open book in her lap], ca. 1900

PLATE 75 (cat. 211)
Myra Albert Wiggins
Hunger ist der Beste Koch [Hunger is the best cook], 1898

PLATE 76 (cat. 217)
Myra Albert Wiggins
Looking Seaward, 1889

PLATE 77 (cat. 218)
Mabel Osgood Wright
Feeding the Calves, ca. 1900

PICTORIAL PHOTOGRAPHS FROM THE FRANCES BENJAMIN JOHNSTON COLLECTION

A CONSERVATOR'S VIEW

ANDREW ROBB

In "What a Woman Can Do with a Camera," Frances Benjamin Johnston made a clarion call for the role of women in the field.[1] By the late 1890s many women had became involved in Pictorialist photography and produced work of high quality. Work of this period poses a challenge to the conservator who strives to understand the materials and historical context of a time quite different from those of today. Pictorialist photographers could choose from a wide range of materials and processing methods whose diversity we are only beginning to rediscover. The rejection of Pictorialist conventions by Modernist photographers and critics limited the study of Pictorial works and made full appreciation of these works difficult during much of the twentieth century. As part of the conservation of the collection, there has been a reexamination of the aesthetic goals of Pictorialism and the photographic materials and methods used at the turn of the last century. This has led to a better understanding of these works, the manner in which they were intended to be viewed, and the way they can best be preserved.

FIG. 1. Advertisement for mounting adhesive, in *American Amateur Photographer*, 1898.

Since the announcement of its invention in 1839, photography has consisted of three basic steps: the manufacture of light-sensitive photographic materials; the exposure of these materials to light; and the processing of the exposed photograph to develop and fix the captured image. In the early years of photography, the photographer completed all three of these steps. Manuals and journals described in detail each of these steps and how to perform them successfully.[2] During the 1850s and 1860s, the photography industry sought to expand its markets by simplifying the photographer's task. Rather than only supplying the materials needed to make photographs, the industry gradually began to sell ready-to-expose papers. During the 1860s and 1870s, sensitized albumen and collodion printing-out papers became available and greatly reduced the effort required to make photographic prints. These print materials led to a sharp rise in commercial photography studios, which produced vast numbers of *cartes de visite*, cabinet cards and stereocards.

However, it was still necessary to make negatives with the collodion wet-plate process and this remained an obstacle to many interested in photography—especially those that wished to work outside the studio. The collodion process required the photographer to coat the glass, take an exposure and then process the negative in a matter of a few minutes. For work outside the studio, not only did a photographer have to carry a view camera (often with a tripod), but also a portable darkroom. The time, skill, experience and resources required to successfully produce a negative limited photography to a relatively small number of professionals and a very small number of skilled amateurs. The invention of the gelatin dry-plate negative in 1873 by Dr. Richard L. Maddox radically changed the situation. The gelatin plate manufactured for the photographer did not require immediate processing upon exposure; thus the photographer could take the pre-sensitized negatives into the field and process them at their convenience upon return to the darkroom. The widespread availability of the dry plate by the late 1870s and 1880s allowed for the rise of amateur and art photography in the 1880s and 1890s.[3]

Many innovations in photographic printing papers coincided with the emergence of the dry-plate process and the rising number of amateur and professional photographers with artistic interests. The gelatin silver, platinum, kallitype, gum bichromate, and carbon processes were all popularized during the 1880s and 1890s. With the exception of the gelatin silver papers, the results were quite different from those obtained with the albumen and collodion papers commonly used during the 1860s and 1870s. They could have different tonalities, most could be more permanent, have less gloss and contrast, and they could be mounted onto flexible artist's papers instead of the stiff boards required for albumen and collodion prints. Those that sought to differentiate their work from that of the commercial studio photographer or conservative approaches to photography seized upon these qualities. As P. H. Emerson stated concerning the Photographic Society of Great Britain's annual exhibition at Pall Mall of 1889: "On entering the exhibition the first impression is one of joyful surprise. Purple and black gloss have given way to black and white and brown, in short the general appearance of the exhibition is more like an exhibition of etchings or engravings than any photographic exhibition we have ever seen. That at any rate is satisfactory and it is especially to me, for seven years ago I was one of the trio of men who exhibited platinotypes... The battle [within artistic photography] is completely won now."[4] The situation in photography at this time was similar to the expressive freedom that new artistic materials, such as prepared paints in tubes, had given painters in the late nineteenth century.

The technique of contact printing was used to make virtually all of the photographs in the Frances Benjamin Johnston Collection. Prints made by contact printing are the same size as the negative, so a large print requires either an equally large negative in size or that a negative be enlarged to the desired size. A camera able to hold such a relatively large negative is required as well. Contact printing begins by placing a negative in contact with the photographic paper in a printing frame and then exposing the printing frame to light. With some processes, such as a gelatin silver printing-out paper, a visible image will be formed by the action of light alone. The main disadvantage of this method is that exposure time can be very lengthy, and may take many minutes even on a sunny day. Other processes, such as the platinum, involve a shorter initial printing-out stage followed by development in a chemical bath. Upon formation of the image, the photograph is processed further or "fixed" to render it insensitive to light. Many processes can be modified by incorporating silver, gold, platinum, sulfur, mercury and even uranium in various possessing solutions to alter a photograph's tone or to make the image more resistant to fading.

For the typical Pictorial photographer, once processing was complete further steps were performed before the photograph was considered finished. In an article from 1894, Myra Albert Wiggins stated, "And so from the exposure to the mounting, trouble should not count, since experience has taught me that I cannot afford to be careless."[5] Another writer expressed it this way, "As the mounting of a print in all cases is the making of it, the amateur should pay much attention to it." This article goes on to describe in detail various mounting adhesives and procedures.[6] Photographs were adhered to the mount in a variety of ways: adhesive was tipped locally at each corner, along the top edge or applied to each corner. Typical adhesives used included starch paste, arrowroot, casein, mucilage, dextrin, India rubber (gum) solution, glue and gelatin.[7] Figures 1 and 2 show various products for mounting photographs.

FIG. 2. Advertisement for a mounting apparatus, in *American Amateur Photographer*, 1898.

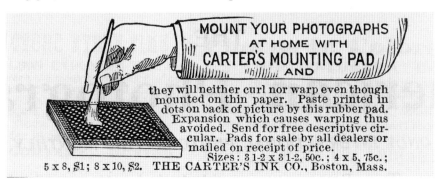

MOUNT YOUR PHOTOGRAPHS
AT HOME WITH
CARTER'S MOUNTING PAD
AND
they will neither curl nor warp even though mounted on thin paper. Paste printed in dots on back of picture by this rubber pad. Expansion which causes warping thus avoided. Send for free descriptive circular. Pads for sale by all dealers or mailed on receipt of price.
Sizes: 3 1-2 x 3 1-2, 50c.; 4 x 5, 75c.;
5 x 8, $1; 8 x 10, $2. THE CARTER'S INK CO., Boston, Mass.

As evidenced by the Frances Benjamin Johnston Collection, the mounts were considered an integral part of the finished photograph, especially in the manner that the color of the mount complemented the photograph. Some authors suggested not using the white mounts commonly used for drawings and etching and advocated using darker colors to accentuate the particular qualities of the photographic image.[8] Many photographers would make use of several mounting papers for a single work. The intermediate papers are typically 1 or 2 mm larger than the photograph and could be of similar or contrasting color to the photographs and mount. The tendency to use multiple mounts appears to be an especially American one, due largely to the influence of F. Holland Day,[9] referred to by one critic, "Here's one of those American prints."[10] This tradition persisted into the early twentieth century. For example, many of the photogravure reproductions in *Camera Work* not only match the image color of the original, but also replicated the original mount or mounts.

Photographic Materials in the Frances Benjamin Johnston Collection

Listed below are general descriptions of the process terms used to identify the photographs in the catalogue. During the period from 1870 to 1900, a great number of photographic print processes were invented or revitalized. In addition, within each process the photographer had a variety of options thanks to different sensitizing solutions, developers and development conditions (including local manipulation) and toners. Processes could also be used together, such as combination printing with gum bichromate and platinum. All of these factors make process identification complicated and identification by visual means alone difficult. Often only a general identification is possible. Recently, new analytical techniques using instruments such as X-ray fluorescence (XRF) have proved useful in distinguishing between visually similar processes.[11] It is hoped that such approaches will give us a better understanding of the marvelous variety of photographic materials from the late nineteenth and early twentieth centuries.

Iron Processes: Platinum, Cyanotype and Kallitype

The platinum print, cyanotype and kallitype together make up a group of processes that use iron salts as the light-sensitive material. Although various people had noted the light sensitivity of iron salts in the early part of the nineteenth century, it was not until 1842 that Sir John Hershel described how light-sensitive iron salts could be used to make photographic prints by brushing or coating the surface of paper with them and contact printing.[12] After exposure to light, the paper is then developed and the image becomes visible. The metallic salt used in the process (platinum, silver or iron) ultimately replaces, fully or partially, the iron salts that were exposed to light and determines the process of the photograph—platinum, kallitype or cyanotype respectively. The iron salt family of processes was quite accommodating. They could be easily manipulated by the photographer through changes in processing and papers could be made by the photographer or purchased from a manufacturer.

William Willis, Jr., patented the platinum print in 1873. He made further modifications and applied for additional patents in 1878 and 1880. In 1879 he formed The Platinotype Company in London and initially platinum papers were available exclusively through the company. The platinum process became more accessible in 1883 due to the English translation in *The Photographic Journal* of an article by Austrians Giuseppe Pizzighelli and Baron Arthur von Hügl that described the process in detail.[13] The platinum process became quite popular during the 1890s and was used in a large number of the pictures in the Frances Benjamin Johnston Collection.

The image tone can vary from neutral black to warm brown in color due to variations in processing such as sensitizing solution, developer composition, developer temperature and toning. The platinum process allows for great tonal variation, although shadow areas are lighter in comparison to other processes. To achieve sufficiently satisfying dark tones, the platinum print and gum processes may be combined by first making the platinum print and then printing the same image over it using gum bichromate. The high cost and scarcity of platinum during World War I caused its decline in use until the process was repopularized in the 1970s.

The cyanotype takes its name from its distinctive cyan image tone. The image material formed during development is the compound commonly known as Prussian blue. Unlike other iron processes, the platinum print and the kallitype, the cyanotype was used throughout the nineteenth century. Popular for reproducing architectural drawings (known as blueprints), some photographers used the process, especially as a proofing paper for the more expensive platinum print or to serve as reference prints.

Dr. W. W. J. Nicol invented the kallitype in 1889.[14] Because it was less expensive than platinum papers and was made in a similar way to the platinum process, the kallitype was especially popular among American amateurs.[15] Another advantage was the wide range of image tones possible: black, blue-black, yellow-ocher and maroon.[16] However, it had a deserved reputation for impermanence, especially because early accounts made poor processing recommendations.[17] These prints are quite vulnerable to fading, and while later articles describe improved fixing procedures,[18] kallitypes today are typically in poor condition with fading overall and the slightly greenish-yellow highlights often seen in deteriorated and poorly processed silver images.

Pigment Processes

A desire for a more permanent photographic image prompted the development of two pigment processes, gum bichromate and carbon. Most pigments are quite lightfast and do not exhibit a tendency to fade. Since there are a wide range of pigments, both of these processes can have virtually any color. In 1852, Henry Fox Talbot discovered that water-soluble colloids, such as gelatin and gum arabic, when in contact with dichromates (then known as bichromates), could be hardened by the action of light. The gum and carbon processes use paper coated with gum arabic and gelatin that have been mixed with dichromates and pigment. Upon exposure to light, image areas are hardened and unexposed areas are not, remaining soluble in water. The unhardened,

non-image areas are then washed away with water. The two processes differ in that the gum process takes place directly on the support of the photograph, while the carbon process requires a transfer step. The negative is contact printed to the light-sensitive material on tissue paper and then the pigment layer is transferred from its original tissue support to another sheet of paper. While this is a more complicated procedure, it typically retains midtone and highlight detail better than the direct process.[19] *Direct pigment print* (commonly known as gum) and *transfer pigment print* (commonly known as carbon) are more exact ways of describing these processes.[20]

Patented by Louis Poitevin in 1855, the gum process was not popular due to its lack of detail and shorter tonal scale compared with the then popular albumen print. Victor Artigue introduced a variant of the gum process in 1889 that revived interest in the process patented by Poitevin. In 1897, Alfred Maskell and Robert Demachy published *The Photo-Aquatint, or the Gum-Bichromate Process*.[21] Arthur von Hügl made a significant innovation in 1898 by devising a means of using multiple printings of gum prints to increase highlights and midtones, the tonal range and contrast. This was also used in combination with platinum prints to increase dark areas.[22] Since the gum print is developed directly on the paper support, local control of the image formation is possible by using brushes during processing.

In 1864, Joseph E. Swan invented the carbon process (also known at the time as the carbon transfer or carbon tissue process). The hardened gelatin was transferred onto the final, gelatin-coated paper support. While adding a step, the carbon transfer process portrayed highlights and midtones better than the direct gum process. In 1868, the Autotype Printing and Publishing Company was founded in London to sell carbon and gum printing materials to individuals and photographic suppliers.[23]

Silver Processes

In 1839, both Louis Daguerre and Henry Fox Talbot announced the invention of photography. Although their processes were quite different from one another, each used the light sensitivity of silver salts to capture the action of light, which remains a fundamental component of photographs made today. In 1840, Talbot expanded on his findings and described the negative/positive system still used today. While Daguerre's system, the daguerreotype, used silver-coated copper plates as the support, Talbot's positive prints were made on paper with no binder (such as albumen or gelatin) using the printing-out technique described earlier. Today these photographs are known as salted paper prints. During the 1890s, there was a revival of the salted paper print, commonly known then as the plain paper or plain silver process.[24] These terms distinguished this silver process from the more common gelatin silver printing-out and developing-out papers.

Gelatin silver printing-out papers became commonly used during the 1880s and gradually began to replace the albumen silver and collodion silver processes popular during the 1860s and 1870s. As the name indicates, these photographs have a gelatin binder and the image is made by printing out. Variations in image color (ranging from a dark, reddish brown to warm, dark brown to a dark purple-black) depend upon the materials in the paper and differences in processing chemistry and procedure.

Gelatin silver developing-out papers became available in 1873, although they were not popular until the late 1880s and early 1890s. The image of these photographs was produced by a very brief exposure to light and then development in a chemical bath, hence the name "developing out." This change in working method took some time to be widely adopted because of the need for a relatively strong, predictable light source. Gaslight papers were one type of developing-out paper using silver chloride salts and could be exposed by the light source of the age, the gaslight. Another type of developing-out paper, the bromide paper, used the faster and more light-sensitive silver bromide salt. These papers are the precursors to today's black-and-white photographs.

Photomechanical Processes

As part of a patent in 1855 for the direct carbon process, Louis Poitevin described the collotype process. Rather than using paper as the support

for transfer of the image, the collotype uses a lithographic stone made light sensitive with dichromated colloid. Hardened areas that received light through the negative absorb lithographic ink while unhardened areas repel it. Improvements in the process by the Bavarian Joseph Albert allowed for the use of glass or copper engraving plates. By 1873, the process was being used for reproducing images in books. It was a less expensive and somewhat easier process than photogravure. It is readily identifiable at 30x magnification by the worm-like reticulation in image areas.

Mounts

The mounts used in the Frances Benjamin Johnston Collection are described in the catalogue entries in the following manner: by type, thickness, texture and color. When more than one mount has been used, the number of intermediate mounts has been listed along with their color. "Board" describes mounts that are rigid and quite thick, and has also been used to describe the thickness of these mounts. Typically, boards are comprised of three layers: a thick core with thin paper on either side. "Paper" is used to describe mounts that are thinner and less rigid. They usually have only one layer. The terms for thickness and texture have been adapted from those used in *The Print Council of America Paper Sample Book.*[25] "Moderately thick" describes a paper similar to that used for a business card. "Thick" describes a paper approximately twice as thick. Mount texture, which is quite varied in the collection, is described by five terms: "very smooth," "smooth," "slightly textured," "moderately textured," and "rough mount color"; there are over thirty colors used to describe mount color. The term "Rembrandt" has been used for mounts that have a gradual darkening across the diagonal. This type of mount was especially popular in 1898 and 1899 and was sold by Willis and Clements as the "Rembrandt Mount" (fig. 3). Other modifications to mounts included embossing, faux plate marks and printed surrounds.

Conservation

Included in the large amount of material in the Frances Benjamin Johnston Collection are the majority of the photographs, Johnston amassed

FIG. 3. Advertisement for the "Rembrandt Mount," in *American Amateur Photographer*, 1899.

while preparing the presentation at the Third International Photographic Congress. These photographs were surveyed in 1999 in order to determine their conservation and preservation needs. The survey found that their condition varied, with some photographs in excellent condition and others requiring significant treatment. The bulk of the treatments were for surface dirt and physical damage to the mounts. In general, the photographs themselves were in good condition.

It is clear that the photographs received a fair amount of wear and tear from handling and poor storage. In a letter she sent in May 1900 to the women photographers whose work she wished to include, Johnston wrote: "In regard to examples of your work, I should like a few prints,—not more than ten—of what you consider your highest and best product, showing as much diversity as possible, and perhaps, covering different perspectives of your progress. These prints should be lightly and compactly mounted, but unframed, and should reach me not later than the 25th of June."[26] As this letter reveals, Johnston was very interested in making transportation of these photographs as compact and light as possible. Over time these photographs went to France, to Russia, back to France and to the United States, where they traveled throughout the country and were used to make reproductions. Johnston appears to have

stored the collection in large manila paper mailing envelopes. Several of these envelopes with writing in Johnston's hand are still with the collection. Soft from wear, they are in a similar condition to many of the mounts.

At the Library of Congress, items were placed in a variety of more protective housings. All items were housed in archival-quality boxes. Items were placed in folders and many were placed in handling mats with off-white back boards and window mats. Much of the matting was done during the 1960s according to the style of the time. Openings in the window mats were cut only as large as the photographs; the window mat covered the entire mount. This approach was in keeping with the Modernist mode of presentation that prevailed during most of the twentieth century— simple, unobtrusive mats that did not compete with the photograph.[27] With the mounts completely covered by the window mat, damage to them was not seen and thus not a high priority for treatment. In the past ten to fifteen years, more attention has been paid to the importance of the mounts and their key role in the visual presentation of these works. This has resulted in reassessment of the treatment and rehousing needs of the collection and focused more attention on the needs of the mounts. For example, in preparing mats for the exhibition in 2001, colored mat boards (now of archival quality) were selected to be sympathetic in color with the mounts. Window mat openings have been cut to show virtually the entire mount.

The treatment of *Portrait* by Mary Bartlett is a good example of this changing attitude. The previous window mat obscured the entire Rembrandt mount including Bartlett's inscription and signature. Treatment included reducing pencil marks, reducing the disfiguring surface dirt on the surface of the mount and removal of small amounts of adhesive along the edges of the photograph. The photograph itself needed no treatment (figs. 4–7). The treatment of *A Portrait* by Eva Walborn was not dissimilar and included reduction of surface dirt and pencil marks. In this case, the edges of the photograph were abraded and there were slight image losses. After consolidation, the edges were inpainted to compensate for the losses (figs. 8–9).

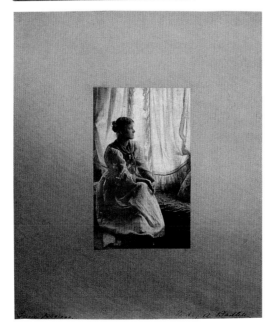

Other treatments performed as part of this project included hinge removal, reduction of accretions, stains and adhesive, mending and reinforcement of tears and creases, inserting mount losses with mat board to appropriate thickness and toned inserts with watercolors and pastels and gouache, and readhering intermediate mounts to subsequent mounts.

Exhibition

It is ironic that light, the very thing needed to create and view photographs, can also cause their deterioration. Image materials, binders and supports for photographs can all be damaged by light. It is for this reason that low light levels between 5 and 10 foot-candles (50 to 100 lux) have been used for the exhibition in 2001. Fading and staining of photographs can occur quite quickly, sometimes in a period of time as short as a few weeks[28] or during a traveling exhibition.[29] Fading of image materials is the most common type of light induced damage. Dyes, such as those used to color papers, can also be very sensitive to light. Light also causes the degradation of cellulose and other organic materials, particularly when a paper contains lignin, and this can result in yellowish staining.

Conservation of a photograph involves many factors: knowledge of the materials used in the photograph and how they age, an understanding of the artistic and historical context of the photograph and the techniques by which it was made, the need to plan a course of treatment that is appropriate for the photograph and its related components, such as mounts, and the ability to conduct successfully delicate procedures that may carry some risk to the appearance or stability of the object.[30] This project has been an opportunity to learn more about the materials, techniques and concerns of photography a century ago. These women photographers have left us with a photographic legacy that serves as a touchstone for an era that we are only beginning to fully appreciate.

FIG. 8. Eva G. Walborn. *A Portrait*, ca. 1900 (cat. 176). Before treatment.

FIG. 9. Eva G. Walborn. *A Portrait*, ca. 1900 (cat. 176). After treatment.

NOTES

1. Frances Benjamin Johnston, "What a Woman Can Do with a Camera," *The Ladies' Home Journal*, 14:10 (1897), pp. 6–7.

2. John Towler, *The Silver Sunbeam* (Hastings-on-Hudson, N.Y.: Morgan & Morgan, 1864; reprinted 1969).

3. Reese V. Jenkins, *Images and Enterprise: Technology and the American Photographic Industry* (Baltimore: The Johns Hopkins University Press, 1975).

4. P. H. Emerson, "Our English Letter," *American Amateur Photographer* 1:11 (November 1889).

5. Albert Myra, "Amateur Photography through Women's Eyes," *The Photo-American*, 5:3 (January 1894), p. 134.

6. Anonymous, "Mounting," *American Amateur Photographer*, 7:3 (March 1897), pp. 138–40.

7. Anonymous, "Mountant," *American Amateur Photographer*, 7:2–3 (February–March, 1895), pp. 94–137.

8. Martin L. Bertram, "Trimming and Framing," *American Amateur Photographer*, 9:3 (March 1897), pp. 102–3.

9. Verna Curtis, "F. Holland Day: The Poetry of Photography," *History of Photography*, 18:4 (winter 1994), p. 311.

10. A. Horsely Hinton, "Influences," *Camera Notes*, 5 (October 1901), p. 86, and William Innes Homer, *Alfred Stieglitz and the Photo-Secession* (Boston: New York Graphic Society, 1983), p. 39.

11. Constance McCabe, with Lisha Glinsman, "Understanding Alfred Stieglitz' Platinum and Palladium Prints: Examination by X-ray Fluorescence Spectrometry," in *Studies in the History of Art*, 53, *Conservation Research* (Washington, D.C.: National Gallery of Art, 1995).

12. Mike Ware, *Cyanotype: the History, Science and Art of Photographic Printing in Prussian Blue* (London and Bradford: Science Museum and National Museum of Photography, Film, and Television, 1999).

13. Giuseppe Pizzighelli and Baron Arthur von Hügl, "The Platinotype" (1883). Reprinted in Peter Bunnell, *Nonsilver Printing Methods* (New York: Arno Press, 1973).

14. Anonymous, "A New Iron Printing Process," *American Amateur Photographer*, 2:5 (May 1890), pp. 190–92.

15. William Crawford, *The Keepers of Light: A History and Working Guide to Early Photographic Processes* (Dobbs Ferry, N.Y.: Morgan & Morgan, 1979), p. 177.

16. Anonymous, "The Improved Kallitype Process," *American Amateur Photographer*, 5:7 (July 1895), pp. 311–13.

17. Anonymous, "A Novel Printing Process," *American Amateur Photographer*, 2:5 (May 1890), p. 190.

18. G. W. Frederick, "Kallitype as a Printing Method," *American Amateur Photographer*, 10:9 (September 1898), pp. 391–92.

19. Crawford, p. 69.

20. Nora Kennedy, "The Reticulation of Gelatine: Observation on the Direct Carbon Process," in *Care of Photographic, Moving Image, and Sound Collections*, Conference Postprints (Leigh Lodge, England: Institute for Paper Conservation, 1998), p. 102.

21. Alfred Maskell and Robert Demachy, *The Photo-Aquatint, or the Gum-Bichromate Process* (1897). Reprinted in Bunnell, *Nonsilver Printing Methods.*

22. Crawford, p. 88.

23. Crawford, p. 72.

24. James Ross, "Printing on Plain Paper," *American Amateur Photographer*, 11:7 (July 1899), pp. 305–6. Also see inscription "Plain Silver" on Bartlett, no. E00-108.

25. Elizabeth Lunning and Roy Perkinson, *The Print Council of America Paper Sample Book: A Practical Guide to the Description of Paper* (The Print Council of America, 1996).

26. Frances Benjamin Johnston, letter sent to American women photographers, May 1900. Frances Benjamin Johnston Papers, Library of Congress, Manuscripts Division, Container 26.

27. Laura Downey and Therese Mulligan, "A Voice for the Prints," in *The Photographs of Alfred Stieglitz: Georgia O'Keeffe's Enduring Legacy* (Rochester, N.Y.: George Eastman House, 2000), p. 12.

28. Nancy Reinhold, "The Exhibition of an Early Photogenic Drawing by Henry Fox Talbot," in *Topics in Photographic Conservation*, 5 (Washington, D.C.: Photographic Materials Group, American Institute for Conservation, 1993), p. 91.

29. Doug Severson, "The Effects of Exhibition on Photographs," in *Topics in Photographic Conservation*, 1 (Washington, D.C.: Photographic Materials Group, American Institute for Conservation, 1986), p. 40.

30. Jose Orraca, "Developing Treatment Criteria in the Treatment of Photographs," in *Topics in Photographic Conservation*, 4 (Washington, D.C.: Photographic Materials Group, American Institute for Conservation, 1991), p. 154.

WOMEN PHOTOGRAPHERS IN THE
FRANCES BENJAMIN JOHNSTON COLLECTION

These biographies are for the women photographers represented in Frances Benjamin Johnston's collection, whether or not they were included in the Universal Exposition of 1900 in Paris. In the words of Zanesville photographer Katharine S. Stanbery, in her handbook for amateur photographers in the December 1908 *Photo Miniature*, what I have written here does not touch "one-twentieth–one-hundredth–of the ground photographic." The complete picture of the lives of many of these women remains only partly developed. This information, which has been collated from a variety of published and unpublished materials, as well as from original research, is presented with the hope it may provide a basis for future study. Birth dates were primarily obtained from Federal population census schedules at The National Archives and Records Administration in Washington, D.C. Dates of death were gleaned from obituaries and city directories. In cases where no death date was found, the last date of activity reflected in the city directory has been indicated. Frances Benjamin Johnston's mother affixed labels to the works assembled for the 1900–1901 exhibitions. In the following entries, they are indicated as "FBJ label" along with the numbers she assigned. They correspond to the list of exhibitors in her *Wanamaker Diary* (see introduction) which also reveals the number of works included by each artist. The asterisk refers to the works included in the present exhibition and reproduced in the plates.

FRANCES STEBBINS ALLEN AND MARY ELECTA ALLEN

FRANCES STEBBINS ALLEN
(1854, Deerfield, Mass. – February 14, 1941, Deerfield, Mass.)

MARY ELECTA ALLEN
(1858, Deerfield, Mass. – February 18, 1941, Deerfield, Mass.)

Active in Deerfield, Mass.

The Allen sisters were prolific professional and artistic photographers whose portraits, genre and scenic views were published widely in books and magazines. By 1884 the Allens had discovered photography. In 1891, they contributed photographs to Charles F. Warner's picture book *Picturesque Franklin* and by the 1890s they were entering competitions. The sisters used a view camera to create images that focus on home, hearth and children, using soft filtered light to create a mood of nostalgia that reflected the aesthetic concerns of the Arts and Crafts movement and the Colonial Revival style.

Daughters of Josiah and Mary Stebbins, both descendants of the town's oldest families, the Allens grew up on a prosperous family farm in the Wapping section of Deerfield. They attended Deerfield Academy, a college preparatory school with a strong commitment to the arts and, between 1874 and 1876, the State Normal School in Westfield, Massachusetts. Both became teachers, yet suffered from a progressive hearing loss, which eventually forced them to leave the teaching profession.

When their father died in 1895, the sisters and their mother moved the farm to a house in the village bequeathed to them by an aunt. At the turn of the century, Deerfield was experiencing a cultural renaissance due to the Colonial Revival and Arts and Crafts movements. Involved in efforts to preserve local history, the Allens photographed the Pocumtuck Valley Memorial Association's museum collection in Memorial Hall. Their photographs also helped to satisfy a growing demand for photographic souvenirs of historic Deerfield and views of New England life. In 1896, the sisters began exhibiting their work both locally and in major salons. Their work appeared at the Washington Salon and Art Photographic Exhibition in 1896 and two of their prints, *Sybill* and *Spring*, were purchased by the National Museum for the Division of Photographs, the first public amateur art photography collection in the country.

The sisters' relationship with Frances Benjamin Johnston was both personal and professional. She visited them for extended periods, occasionally bringing equipment and materials purchased in New York for their use. In June 1900, Mary responded to Johnston's request for a biographical note: "You know already all there is to know. We have no 'methods'… we have had no training, either technical or artistic… and we have no theories." Although photography was a means of income for the Allen sisters, Mary described how they had to combine their photographic endeavors with family obligations: "We take what work comes to hand and it fits itself as it can into the intervals of other duties for it still has to take a secondary place." In Johnston's 1900 exhibition, they were among the older women included and, unlike others, were not sympathetic to the Pictorialist movement. Johnston featured the Allen sisters in one of seven articles profiling "The Foremost Women Photographers of America," in *Ladies' Home Journal* in 1901–2.

After their mother died in 1901, the sisters opened a formal studio, converting an upstairs bedroom into a darkroom and a downstairs parlor into a salesroom. In 1904, they began publishing catalogues of their photographic subjects, which included landscape, figure, country life and costumes, children, and historic Deerfield, and advertised themselves as portrait photographers. The sisters contributed equally to most of the work, but Mary was responsible for the portrait photography and the business affairs. They continued to exhibit locally, publishing their last catalogue in 1920. In the 1920s, Frances's vision began to deteriorate (she was nearly blind by the time she died on February 14, 1941), but Mary carried on the business into the early 1930s. Mary died just four days after her elder sister and they share a single grave marker in Deerfield's Laurel Hill Cemetery.

Frances S. Allen. *Mary Electa Allen*, 1895–1900. Deerfield, Mass., Memorial Hall Museum, 96.14.1116.

Mary E. Allen (attributed). *Frances Stebbins Allen*, ca. 1905. Deerfield, Mass., Memorial Hall Museum, 96.14.255.1.

Exhibitions

Washington Salon and Art Photographic Exhibition, Assembly Hall, Washington, D.C., May 1896

Forty-second annual exhibition, Royal Photographic Society, London, September 1897

American Institute of the City of New York, Photographic Section, National Academy of Design, New York, September 1898

Congrès International de Photographie, Universal Exposition, Paris, July 1900

Third Philadelphia Photographic Salon, Pennsylvania Academy of the Fine Arts, Philadelphia, October 1900

"Les Artistes Américaines," Photo-Club de Paris, Paris, January 1901

Springfield Arts and Crafts Exhibition, Springfield, Mass., 1902

"The Work of Women Photographers of America," The Camera Club of Hartford, Hartford, Conn., April 1906

Exhibition of the Society of Arts and Crafts, Copley Hall, Boston, February 1907

Canadian Pictorialist exhibition, Art Association of Montreal, December 1907

Fifth annual exhibition of photographs, Worcester Art Museum, Worcester, Mass., October 1908

Arts and Crafts Seventh Annual Exhibition, The Art Institute of Chicago, Chicago, December 1908

"Exhibition of the Photographs of Frances and Mary Allen," Charles E. Cobb Gallery, Boston, April 1913

FRANCES ALLEN

Third Chicago Photographic Salon, Art Institute of Chicago, Chicago, January 1902

First American Photographic Salon, New York, December 1904

1. *Calls in Cranford*, ca. 1900
Platinum, 230 x 127 mm.
Mount: Thick black paper with
intermediate black mount,
310 x 221 mm.
LC-USZC2-5914

2. *How D'y Do?*, ca. 1900
Platinum, 206 x 147 mm.
Mount: Thick black paper,
295 x 223 mm.
LC-USZC2-5915

3.* *A 'Crack' with the Blacksmith*,
ca. 1900
Platinum, 209 x 159 mm.
Mount: Gray board, 379 x 306 mm.
Verso: In pencil: "A 'Crack' with
the Blacksmith"; in ink: "Illustration";
stamped: "F.S. & M.E. Allen/Deerfield,
Mass."; FBJ label: 3.
LC-USZC2-5916

4.* *A Holbein Woman*, ca. 1890–92
Platinum, 235 x 187 mm.
In pencil, retraced in ink, l.r. : "Allen"
Mount: Gray board, 379 x 350 mm.
Verso: In pencil: "A Holbein Woman";
in ink: "Rights reserved by Harper
& Bros."; stamped: "F.S. & M.E.
Allen/Deerfield, Mass."; FBJ label: 4.
LC-USZC2-5917

5. *At the Spinet*, ca. 1900
Platinum, 164 x 119 mm.
In pencil, l.r.: "Allen"
Mount: Cream colored board with
printed khaki surround, 356 x 171 mm.
Verso: In pencil: "At the Spinet./
Illustration for old costumes/
Agnes Whiting"; stamped: "F.S. & M.E.
Allen/Deerfield, Mass."
LC-USZC2-5918

6.* *Good Morning!*, ca. 1900
Platinum, 199 x 156 mm.
In pencil, l.r.: "Allen"
Mount: Smooth, gray board,
279 x 226 mm.
Verso: In pencil: "Good Morning!";
stamped: "F.S. & M.E. Allen/Deerfield,
Mass."
LC-USZC2-5919

7. *In May*, ca. 1900
Platinum, 257 x 305 mm.
In ink, l.r.: "Allen"
Mount: Thick dark gray mat,
154 x 208 mm.
Verso: In pencil: "In May"; stamped:
"F.S. & M.E. Allen/Deerfield, Mass."
LC-USZC2-5920

8. *Miss Fidelia with her Lover's Profile*,
1900
Platinum, 206 x 156 mm.
In ink, l.r.: "Allen"
Mount: Thick dark gray mat,
314 x 268 mm.
Verso: In pencil: "Allen"; in ink:
"Miss Fidelia with her lover's profile./
Illustration."; stamped: "F.S. & M.E.
Allen/Deerfield, Mass."
LC-USZC2-5921

9. *Old Burying Ground*, ca. 1892
Platinum, 129 x 102 mm.
Verso: In pencil: "Old Burying
Ground./35/N.E. Magazine"; stamped:
"F.S. & M.E. Allen/Deerfield, Mass."
LC-USZC2-5922

10.* *Old Deerfield*, ca. 1900
21 cyanotypes, 126 x 194 mm.
Album with cream cover bound with
yellow silk cord. Title written by hand
in pencil and painted over in gold,
140 x 240 mm. [Each photograph is
accompanied by an inscription.]
LC-USZC2-6133

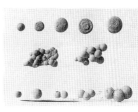

11 and 12. [Specimen illustrations
for a monograph on clay stones
by J. M. Arms Sheldon], ca. 1900
Two platinum prints mounted on single
board, 89 x 123 mm.
In ink, l.r. of bottom photograph: "Allen"
Mount: Thick cream mount,
254 x 203 mm.
Verso: Stamped: "F.S. & M.E.
Allen/Deerfield, Mass."
LC-USZC2-5923 (top) and
LC-USZC2-6130 (bottom)

13. *A New England Sibyl*, before 1890
Gelatin silver, developed out,
221 x 181 mm.
Mount: Pale gray paper, 249 x 213 mm.
[Aunt Judith Allen (1811–1890)]
LC-USZC2-5924

14. Top: *For Alice Morse Earle's*
"Home Life in Colonial Days"
Bottom: *For Article by M. Y.*
Wynne in "The House Beautiful."
Colonial Glassware. Specimen Illustration,
ca. 1898. Two platinum prints mounted
on single board, 100 x 176 mm.
In ink, l.l.: "Allen"
Mount: Gray board, 278 x 227 mm.
Verso: Stamped: "F.S. & M.E.
Allen/Deerfield, Mass."
LC-USZC2-6129 and LC-USZC2-5925

15. *Portrait of the Artist's Mother*,
ca. 1890–95
Platinum, 114 x 159 mm.
In pencil, l.r.: "Allen"
Mount: Thick brown mat,
195 x 239 mm.
Verso: In pencil: "Portrait of the Artist's
Mother"; stamped: "F.S. & M.E.
Allen/Deerfield, Mass."; FBJ label: 1.
LC-USZC2-6011

16. *A 'Crack' with the Blacksmith*,
ca. 1900
Platinum, 200 x 151 mm.
Mount: Thick black mat,
278 x 214 mm.
LC-USZC2-6013

17. *Bread & Milk*, 1894
Carbon, 156 x 110 mm.
Mount: Medium-weight light
gray paper, 209 x 170 mm.
LC-USZC2-6014

18. *A Holbein Woman*, ca. 1890–92
Gelatin silver, developed out,
192 x 142 mm.
Mount: Thick black paper with light
gray intermediate mount,
305 x 208 mm.
LC-USZC2-6015

19. *A Holbein Woman*, ca. 1890–92
Albumen silver, 119 x 96 mm.
Mount: Light gray board,
279 x 229 mm.
LC-USZC2-6016

20. *Willows*, ca. 1900
Platinum, 201 x 149 mm.
In pencil, l.r.: "Allen"
Mount: Thick Rembrandt mount,
304 x 252 mm.
Verso: In pencil: "Willows"; stamped:
"F.S. & M.E. Allen/Deerfield, Mass."
LC-USZC2-6017

21. *The Difficult Step*, ca. 1900
Platinum, 190 x 114 mm.
In pencil, l.r.: "Allen"
Mount: Thick dark gray paper,
364 x 257 mm.
Verso: In pencil: "The Difficult
Step/19/75"; in ink: "Sold to Curtis
Pub. Co."; stamped: "F.S. & M.E.
Allen/Deerfield, Mass."; FBJ label: 2.
LC-USZC2-6018

22. [Portrait of a woman with braids
in front of a paisley backdrop], ca. 1900
Platinum, 254 x 203 mm.
In pencil, l.r.: "Allen"
Mount: Rough, cream board with
printed khaki surround, 117 x 94 mm.
LC-USZC2-6124

23. *Our Margaret*, ca. 1897
Carbon, 156 x 113 mm.
In pencil, l.r.: "Allen"
Mount: Smooth, gray board,
273 x 196 mm.
Verso: In pencil: "Our Margaret"
LC-USZC2-6125

ALICE AUSTIN

(September 1862, Maine – February 3, 1933, Boston)
Active in Boston, Mass.
Studio: Boylston Street, Boston (1900–22; 1926–32)

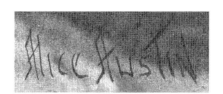

Alice Austin studied sculpture, watercolor and drawing at the Boston Normal Art School and the School of the Museum of Fine Arts, Boston. She then taught drawing in the western United States for six years and traveled abroad before returning to the East to teach drawing in public schools in Brooklyn for five years. While living in Brooklyn, she continued her art studies at the Pratt Institute, where she learned the Dow method of composition. She originally explored photography in "a purely amateurish way," but later studied with Gertrude Käsebier, to whom she gave credit for opening her eyes "to the possibilities of art in photography."

The inventive compositions and lighting techniques of her photographs were widely acclaimed when exhibited locally and abroad. The images, usually scenes of youngsters in upper class settings playing or reading together, expressed turn-of-the-century ideals of childhood. In 1900, Austin's work was included in both F. Holland Day's exhibition "The New School of American Photography" and Johnston's exhibition in Paris. In the biographical sketch sent to Johnston, Austin expressed her desire to represent the personality of her sitter while producing a photograph which "may lay some Claim to Art." The same year, she opened a portrait studio in Boston that remained in operation until 1933, with the exception of 1923–25, during which time she was listed as "artist" rather than "photographer" in the Boston city directories.

Austin was listed as one of twenty successful professional women photographers in an article by Richard Hines, Jr., in *Photo-Era* magazine (September 1906). A member of the Society of Arts and Crafts, Boston, from 1900 until 1927, she served as on officer in the society's department of photographs.

Affiliations
Society of Arts and Crafts, Boston

Exhibitions
Second Philadelphia Photographic Salon, Pennsylvania Academy of the Fine Arts, Philadelphia, October 1899

"Exhibition of the Massachusetts Pictures Shown at the Three Photographic Salons of 1899: London, Philadelphia, and New York," Boston Camera Club, Boston, February 1900

Chicago Photographic Salon of 1900, Art Institute of Chicago, Chicago, April 1900

Congrès International de Photographie, Universal Exposition, Paris, July 1900

"New School of American Photography," Royal Photographic Society, London, October 1900

"Les Artistes Américaines," Photo-Club de Paris, Paris, January 1901

"New School of American Photography," Photo-Club de Paris, Paris, February 1901

Tenth annual exhibition, Society of Arts and Crafts, Copley Hall, Boston, February 1907

Tricentennial exhibition of the Society of Arts and Crafts, Copley Hall, Boston, March 1927

24. [Portrait of a girl with a necklace clasping a shawl], ca. 1900
Platinum, 156 x 109 mm.
In ink on photo, l.r.: "Alice Austin"
Verso: In pencil: "Alice Austin"
LC-USZC2-5926

25.* [Man holding an infant], ca. 1900
Platinum, 153 x 110 mm.
In ink on photo, l.r.: "Alice Austin"
Mount: Dark brown paper with light gray intermediate mount, 210 x 163 mm.
NMAH-C-77.92x

26. *Fairy Tales*, ca. 1900
Platinum, 162 x 111 mm.
In ink on photo, c.: "Alice Austin"
Mount: Green with five intermediate mounts in light brown, green, light brown, dark brown and green, 380 x 295 mm.
Verso: FBJ label: 11.
NMAH-C-77.92.1

27. [Young woman seated by a window], ca. 1900
Platinum, 163 x 113 mm.
In ink on photo, l.l.: "Alice Austin"
Mount: Thick light gray paper with intermediate mounts, 359 x 260 mm.
Verso: FBJ label: 10.
NMAH-C-77.92.2

28.* [Young girl reading], ca. 1900
Platinum, 152 x 108 mm.
In ink on photo, l.l.: "Alice Austin"
Mount: Thick light gray paper with
dark and light gray intermediate
mounts, 363 x 255 mm.
Verso: FBJ label: 8.
NMAH-C-77.92.3

29. [Portrait of a woman], ca. 1900
Platinum, 154 x 69 mm.
In ink on photo, l.l.: "Alice Austin"
Mount: Dark gray thin mat,
342 x 239 mm.
Verso: FBJ label: 6.
NMAH-C-77.92.4

30. [Costumed child], ca. 1900
Platinum, 100 x 65 mm.
Mount: Dark gray paper with dark
brown and dark gray intermediate
mounts, 360 x 250 mm.
Verso: FBJ label: 7.; in pencil on label:
"Alice Austin/Boston, Mass."
NMAH-C-77.92.5

31.* [Portrait of a bearded man], ca. 1900
Platinotype, 167 x 90 mm.
In ink on photo, l.l.: "Alice Austin"
Mount: Olive green paper with beige,
dark green, and gray intermediate
mounts, 358 x 250 mm.
Verso: FBJ label: 5.
NMAH-C-77.92.6

MARY A. BARTLETT (MRS. N. GRAY BARTLETT)

(1847, Ohio – ?)

Active in Chicago, Ill.

Mary A. Bartlett,
in *American Amateur Photographer* (Nov. 1891), p. 416.

In 1894, Mary A. Bartlett was "the leading lady amateur of Chicago" according to Frank W. Crane. Active in photography from about 1887, Bartlett was married to a well-known chemist who assisted her in mastering new techniques: cold-water platinum prints using delicate Japanese and plate papers which she sensitized herself, matte-surface silver paper and unusual gold-toned prints.

It was during summers spent on Lake Geneva, Wisconsin, that Bartlett would pose her friends and children as models to create idealized outdoor images of women and children for books and magazines. The winter months were spent printing in Chicago, where she was an active member of the Chicago Lantern Slide Club and the Photographers Society of Chicago. Bartlett also served as vice president of the Chicago Camera Club in 1890.

Although wary of competition as a motivation for producing art, Bartlett participated with great success in salons and exhibitions. At an open exhibition in Chicago in 1889, she received the society medal and a special prize for the best printing in platinum. Two years later she won a grand diploma in photography at the Vienna Salon and in 1893 she served as chair on the committee of the woman's department of photography at the 1893 World's Columbian Exposition in Chicago. Her book, *Mother Goose of '93: Photographic Illustrations by Mrs. N. Gray Bartlett*, appeared to great acclaim at the World's Columbian Exposition and was published in a popular edition later that year. At the Washington Salon of 1896, the United States National Museum (now Smithsonian Institution) purchased two works by Bartlett—*A Reverie* and *Landscape*—for the first public collection of amateur art photography in the country

Affiliations
Chicago Lantern Slide Club, Chicago

Photographers Society of Chicago, Chicago

Exhibitions
First annual exhibition, Art Institute of Chicago, Chicago, May 1889

Internationale Ausstellung für Künstlerischer Photographien, Vienna, 1891

"George Timmins Collection," Syracuse, N.Y., May 1896

Washington Salon and Art Photographic Exhibition, Washington, D.C., May 1896

Congrès International de Photographie, Universal Exposition, Paris, July 1900

"Les Artistes Américaines," Photo-Club de Paris, Paris, January 1901

32.* [Woman seated with crossed legs in front of sheer curtains], ca. 1900
Gum bichromate, 154 x 97 mm.
In ink, l.l.: "Mary A. Bartlett"; l.r.: "Gum process"
Mount: Thick Rembrandt mount, 304 x 254 mm.
Verso: In pencil: "Mrs. Bartlett/Chicago/Ill."; FBJ label: 16.
LC-USZC2-5927

33.* [Young woman seated by a window with flowers in her lap], ca 1900
Kallitype, 171 x 125 mm.
In ink, l.l.: "Mary A. Bartlett"; l.r.: "….type"
Mount: Thick plum colored paper with torn edges and an ivory intermediate mount, 289 x 232 mm.
LC-USZC2-5928

34.* [Woman on path in the woods], ca. 1900
Gum bichromate, 192 x 155 mm.
In ink, l.r.: "Mary A. Bartlett"; l.l.: "Gum process"
Mount: Thick olive green paper, 285 x 223 mm.
Verso: FBJ label: 15.; in pencil on label: "Miss Prall?"
LC-USZC2-5929

35. [A riverbed in the woods], ca. 1900
Salted paper, 150 x 200 mm.
In ink, l.r.: "Mary A. Bartlett"; l.l.: "Plain Silver"
Mount: Textured, cream stock mount, 258 x 305 mm.
Verso: In pencil: "Mrs. N. G. Bartlett"
LC-USZC2-6020

36. [Women in the woods], ca 1900
Platinum, 182 x 145 mm.
In ink, l.r.: "Mary A. Bartlett"; l.l.: "Plain silver"
Mount: Olive paper with torn edges, 310 x 250 mm.
NMAH-C-77.92.7

37. [Plants], ca 1900
Platinum, 147 x 198 mm.
In ink, l.r.: "Mary A Bartlett"; l.l.: "Plain silver"
Mount: Olive green paper with torn edges, 225 x 280 mm.
NMAH-C-77.92.8

38. *"I'll tell you a story about Jack-a-Nory…"* In *Mother Goose of '93*, before 1893
Platinum, 130 x 178 mm.
In ink on mount, l.r.: "Mary A. Bartlett"; l.l.: "Plain silver"
Mount: Olive green paper with torn edges, 190 x 260 mm.
Verso: FBJ label: 14.
NMAH-C-77.92.9

ZAIDA BEN-YUSUF

(?, Great Britain – ?)

Active in New York City
Studio: 578 Fifth Avenue (1900–5)

F. Holland Day. *Zaida Ben-Yusuf.*
New York, The Metropolitan Museum of Art,
Alfred Stieglitz Collection, 1933. (33.43.367)
Photograph © 2001 The Metropolitan Museum of Art.

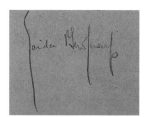

Born in England, Zaida Ben-Yusuf moved to America with her family in the early 1890s where she worked as a milliner. Around 1895 she took up photography with a borrowed hand camera and on a visit to Paris shortly thereafter showed her prints to George Davison (1856–1930), British Pictorialist and Linked Ring co-founder. He "at once advised [her] to go ahead and make more," as he found her fledgling efforts to be representative of "the spirit of the new school of photography." Upon her return to America in 1897, Ben-Yusuf opened a professional portrait studio on Fifth Avenue in New York. Word spread quickly about her work and by October of that year, Stieglitz requested her prints for *Camera Notes*. In 1898, she exhibited jointly with Johnston at the Camera Club of New York. William M. Murray was critical of the "eccentric pose" of some portraits in the exhibition and likened the works to "the cacophony of a great orchestra tuning up for a nervous conductor." However, he admired her daring, stating: "it does not content her to stick to any beaten path or to pay attention to warnings against danger placed along the highway of photography."

In 1899, Sadakichi Hartmann published an in depth essay titled, "Zaida Ben-Yusuf: A Purist." He wrote that Ben-Yusuf's "artist revolt" against the "mechanical precision" of less imaginative portraitists made it "doubtful if there is in the entire United States a more interesting exponent of portrait photography." However, he also criticized her Bohemian airs and accused her of wanting to become the "Mrs. Cameron of America." Ben-Yusuf wrote her autobiographical note to Johnston in the third person, stating that "she is the only photographer in New York who conducts her business without the traditional showcase at the door." Proud of the intimate scale of her studio, one which was "ordinarily used by a painter and contain[ed] no vestage [*sic*] of the customary painted background scenery or iron head rests, etc.," she did all of her own printing and developing, and preferred to work with an assistant. Johnston held her in high regard and asked her for advice in soliciting work for her presentation in Paris, for which Ben-Yusuf recommended the Misses Selby. In her 1901 profile of Ben-Yusuf, Johnston described her work as "daring and original … vivid and striking in treatment … always characteristic, not only of her sitters', but also of her own intense personality."

Magazine work and photojournalism were another strong interest throughout Ben-Yusuf's career. Her first commission was from from *Century* magazine, for celebrity and society portraiture. After 1903, Ben-Yusuf traveled to Europe, and also to Japan several times, sending back articles and photographs which were published in *Architectural Record* and *Century*. Back in America in 1905, Ben-Yusuf published seventeen of her portraits of artists in the magazine *American Art News*. In 1906, she served on the National Preliminary Jury for the Second American Photographic Salon in Chicago, but the next year she ceased participating in exhibitions and dropped out of public view. A mention in *Wilson's Photographic Magazine* (October 1912) notes that Ben-Yusuf "has given up the vanities of the photographic world for an unrestrained life in the South Sea Islands." Her name reappeared in the New York City directories listed with the occupation of photographer for the years 1916 and 1922–23. By 1928, Ben-Yusuf had become the Fashion Editor for the Bulletin of the Retail Millinery Association of America.

Affiliations

Photo-Secession, New York
Salon Club of America

Juror

Second American Photographic Salon, Chicago, 1906

Exhibitions

Photographic Salon, The Linked Ring, Dudley Gallery, London, September 1896

Fifth Annual Exhibition of the Photographic Salon, The Linked Ring, Dudley Gallery, London, October 1897

Photographic Salon, The Linked Ring, Dudley Gallery, London, September 1898

Eastman Photographic Exhibition, National Academy of Design, New York, January 1898

"Zaida Ben-Yusuf," Camera Club of New York, New York, November 1898

Photographic Salon, The Linked Ring, Dudley Gallery, London, September 1899

Second Philadelphia Photographic Salon, Pennsylvania Academy of the Fine Arts, Philadelphia, October 1899

Photographic Salon, American Institute, New York, December 1899

Congrès International de Photographie, Universal Exposition, Paris, July 1900

New School of American Photography, Royal Photographic Society, London, October 1900

Exhibit of Photographs by the Newark Camera Club, Newark, Ohio, November 1900

Glasgow International Exhibition, Glasgow 1901

"Les Artistes Américaines," Photo-Club de Paris, Paris, January 1901

"New School of American Photography," Photo-Club de Paris, Paris, February 1901

The Fourth Philadelphia Photographic Salon, Pennsylvania Academy of the Fine Arts, Philadelphia, November 1901

Tenth Annual Exhibition of the Photographic Salon, The Linked Ring, Dudley Gallery, London, September 1902

Third Annual Exhibition of Photographs, Worcester Art Museum, Worcester, Mass., October 1906

39. *Elsie Leslie*, ca. 1900
Platinum, 244 x 143 mm.
In ink, l.l. (inked out): "Elsie Leslie";
l.r.: "by Miss Ben-Yusuf"
Mount: Cream mat, 253 x 149 mm.
LC-USZC2-5930

40.* *Mr. W. D. Howells*, ca. 1900
Platinum, 125 x 153 mm.
In ink, l.r.: "Zaida BenYusuf"; l.l.: "Mr.
W. D. Howells"
Mount: Thick dark gray paper with
black intermediate mount,
322 x 283 mm.
Verso: FBJ label: 17.
LC-USZC2-5931

41.* *Portrait of Elbert Hubbard*, ca. 1900
Platinum, 234 x 155 mm.
In pencil, l.r.: "Zaida BenYusuf"; in ink
on mount, l.l.: "Frances B.
Johnston,/with all kind wishes/from her
friend/Elbert Hubbard"
Mount: Thick, smooth tan paper with a
dark green intermediate mount,
360 x 275 mm.
Verso: In red ink: "Miss Ben Yusuf/578
Fifth Avenue/New York"
LC-USZC2-5932

42.* *Portrait of Miss K.*, ca. 1900
Gum bichromate, 168 x 135 mm.
In ink l.l.: "Portrait of Miss K."; lower
edge: "A portrait of Miss Florence Kahn
by Miss Ben-Yusuf reproduced Photo.
Times Oct. 1900 frontispiece"
Mount: Thick dark green paper with
light brown intermediate mount,
353 x 135 mm.
Verso: FBJ label: 19.
LC-USZC2-5933

43.* *The Odor of Pomegranates*, ca. 1900
Platinum, 236 x 129 mm.
In pencil, l.l.: "Zaida BenYusuf"; in ink:
"..e Odor of Pomegranates"
Mount: Thick dark green paper with
light brown and ocher intermediate
mounts, 382 x 267 mm.
Verso: In ink: "The Odor of Pomegran-
ates/Miss Ben-Yusuf/578 Fifth
Avenue/New York"; FBJ label: 21.
LC-USZC2-5934

44.* *Portrait of Miss Ben-Yusuf*
[self-portrait], ca. 1900
Platinotype (?), 219 x 94 mm.
In pencil, l.r.: "ZBY"; in ink, l.l.:
"Portrait of Miss Ben-Yusuf"
Mount: Thick dark gray paper,
357 x 254 mm.
Verso: FBJ label: 18.; in pencil on label:
"Miss Ben Yusuf"
NMAH-C-77.92.10

45.* *Portrait of Miss S.*, ca. 1900
Platinum, 214 x 110 mm.
In pencil: "Zaida BenYusuf"; in ink, l.l.:
"Portrait of Miss S."
Mount: Dark gray paper with magenta
intermediate mount, 385 x 273 mm.
Verso: In red ink: "Miss Ben-Yusuf/578
Fifth Avenue/
New York The frame maker is requested
not to change the proportions of the
mat./ It should be left exactly the same
as now is/ZBY"; FBJ label: 20.
NMAH-C-77.92.11

Elizabeth Brownell,
in *Ladies' Home Journal* (Jan. 1902), p. 1.

Exhibitions

Third Philadelphia Photographic Salon,
Pennsylvania Academy of the Fine Arts,
Philadelphia, October 1900

Chicago Photographic Salon of 1900,
Art Institute of Chicago, Chicago, April 1900

Second Chicago Photographic Salon, Chicago,
October 1901

ELIZABETH BROWNELL

(? – ?)

Active in Chicago, Ill.
Studio: 69 Dearborn Street, Room 54, Chicago (Brownell, Page & Co., 1900–1; Brownell, 1902)

Elizabeth Brownell worked principally in the field of photographically illustrated books. At a young age, she married "a man of ample means" with whom she had a daughter, but they subsequently divorced and she returned to the use of her maiden name, Brownell. After a trip abroad, and a rumored "affair of the heart," Brownell returned to Chicago where she rented a room in a house on Maxwell Street, in one of Chicago's poorest neighborhoods. To support herself she began to work for a photographer on Blue Island Avenue, developing photographic plates and films taken by amateurs. She had a close relationship with her cousin, Chicago Pictorialist and Photo-Secessionist William B. Dyer (1860–1931), and worked as his assistant in his studio at 69 Dearborn Street.

She was also a longtime friend of the writer, Clara E. Laughlin (1873–1941), author of a well-known series of travel books. Laughlin wrote the introduction to *Dream Children* (1901), a book of selected poems and essays illustrated with Brownell's photographs of mothers and children. Laughlin's autobiography, *Traveling Through Life*, reveals what little is known about Brownell's life. According to her accounts, Brownell often spent days closely observing people—sitting in train stations, or in the reading room of the Public Library, where she was absorbed by books on philosophy and religion. Nights were spent in her studio developing and printing. Brownell carefully instructed her models for pose and expression, often sketching them for composition before making the portrait. According to Johnston's article in 1902, Brownell was a photographer who worked among poor children, filling her photographs with the "poetic pathos... of humble lives."

"[W]ell grounded in the principles of art," Brownell soon began taking portraits. In 1900, when Dyer relocated his business to 203 Michigan Avenue, Laughlin, with the help of two generous friends, set Brownell up in a large studio in room 54 at 69 Dearborn that attracted various celebrity sitters and became moderately successful. Brownell was in business with another photographer for two years in this studio, listed in the Chicago city directories as Brownell, Page & Co., until 1902, when her name appeared by itself at this address for one additional year.

46. [Elderly woman in a rocking chair peeling apple with young girl standing in front of her], ca. 1900
Platinum, 156 x 134 mm.
Mount: Thick black paper with black intermediate mount, 221 x 185 mm.
LC-USZC2-5937

47. *"We're going to have warm potatoes!,"* ca. 1900
An illustration for "The Candles" in *Dream Children*
Platinum, 210 x 112 mm.
Mount: Thick black paper with black intermediate mount, 310 x 203 mm.
LC-USZC2-5938

48. *"A-listnin' to the witch-tales 'at Annie tells about,"* ca. 1900
An illustration for "Little Orphant [*sic*] Annie" in *Dream Children*
Platinum, 286 x 254 mm.
Mount: Thick black mount, 212 x 130 mm.
Verso: In pencil: "In 'Dream Children'/Copyrighted/Farnsworth"
LC-USZC2-5939

49. Elizabeth Brownell (?)
[Young boy holding a smaller child], ca. 1900
Platinum, 143 x 71 mm.
Mount: Pale blue paper, 147 x 75 mm.
Verso: In ink: "?Käsebier"
LC-USZC2-6021

50. *"Spirit of Tiny Tim! Thy childish essence was from God,"* ca. 1900
An illustration for "From 'A Christmas Carol'" in *Dream Children*
Platinum, 188 x 82 mm.
Mount: Thick black paper with black intermediate mount, 279 x 154 mm.
LC-USZC2-6022

51. [Young woman at her first Communion with an attendant], ca. 1900
Platinum, 189 x 128 mm.
Mount: Thick black paper, 260 x 172 mm.
LC-USZC2-6023

52. [Young boy wearing close fitting cap looking down], ca. 1900
Gum bichromate (?), 205 x 164 mm.
Mount: Thick brown paper with a light brown intermediate mount, 319 x 246 mm.
LC-USZC2-6095

ROSE CLARK AND ELIZABETH FLINT WADE

Active in Buffalo, N.Y.

HARRIET CANDACE "ROSE" CLARK
(1852, La Porte, Ind. – November 28, 1942, Buffalo)

Rose Clark was known as the leading portrait painter of Buffalo. She had extensive art training and for a time taught art at St. Margaret's School in Buffalo. She was a member of the New York Water-Color Club and the Women's Art Club, New York. She exhibited at the Art Club of Philadelphia, the Buffalo Fine Arts Academy (1888), the National Academy of Design (1889, 1890, 1895, 1897), and in the Trans-Mississippi Exposition, Omaha, Nebraska (1898).

Beginning in 1890, she became active as a photographer and worked independently until 1898, when she and Elizabeth Flint Wade began their twelve-year collaboration. Clark received support in her photographic endeavors from Alfred Stieglitz, with whom she corresponded from 1900 to 1902. In a letter dated October 30, 1900, Clark wrote to Stieglitz: "Thank you very much for all your encouragement. I go down into the depths—with all my work—and come up again, and go on trying." Stieglitz cited her, along with Gertrude Käsebier, Eva Watson-Schütze and Mary Devens, as one of ten prominent American Pictorial photographers in his article for *Century Magazine* (1902), "Modern Pictorial Photography." Stieglitz's admired her collaborative work with Wade and acquired three of their photographs for his collection. In addition, Clark participated in the 1902 Photo-Secession Exhibition in Pittsburgh, for which she received praise from Sadakichi Hartmann (also known as Sidney Allen): "The most successful portrait work (next to Steichen's, of course) is furnished by Rose Clark."

After about 1910, Clark returned to painting as her principle medium. In 1920, she moved to New York City and sold portraits in oil for sums ranging from $500 to $2,000. She returned to Buffalo in 1926.

Exhibitions

Loan exhibition, Camera Club of New York, New York, December 1899

Exhibit of photographs by the Newark Camera Club, Newark, Ohio, November 1900

International exhibition of Pictorial photography, Buffalo, November 1910

"An Exhibition of Pictorial Photography," Syracuse, N.Y., December 1915

ELIZABETH FLINT WADE
(? – 1915, Norwalk, Conn.)

In addition to collaborating with Clark, Elizabeth Flint Wade had an established career as a writer, publishing poetry and short stories in *Atlantic Monthly*, *Youth's Companion*, *Collier's Weekly*, *Short Stories*, *Black Cat*, *Everybody's Magazine*, *Herald* and *New York World*, among others. Wade married Frank A. Wade, and had one daughter, Blanche Elizabeth, and two sons, Herman and Frank.

Wade also published articles on photographic subjects in *Photographic Times Bulletin*, *St. Nicholas*, *Photo-American*, *American Amateur Photographer* (where Stieglitz was an editor), *Harper's* and *Photo-Era*. For *Harper's*, Wade was editor for six years of the "Round Table Camera Club." Between 1901 and 1912, she also wrote "The Round Robin Guild," a monthly column in *Photo-Era* which was known for its humor, anecdotes and advice, and became an associate editor of this publication in 1909. In her column, she encouraged women to take up the new craft and she discussed photography's possibilities as a source of income for the serious amateur and opportunities for women in scientific and industrial photography.

In her 1894 article for *The Photo American*, "Amateur Photography through Women's Eyes," Wade wrote, "I believe there is no other vocation open to women in which so much pleasure and profit is combined with so little drudgery."

Juror
Eighth Annual Buffalo Camera Club Exhibition, Buffalo, 1910

CLARK & WADE

Clark & Wade won wide recognition for their photographs, exhibiting widely and winning a gold medal at the Turin exposition in Italy in 1902. They were cited as successful professional photographers by Richard Hines in his article on women and photography in *Photo-Era* in 1906.

Critics often cast Wade in the behind-the-scenes role of darkroom technician in their partnership, working as the printer and managing the business. This misconception may have arisen from the fact that Wade never exhibited her own work, while Clark had several solo exhibitions. Wade described their collaboration in a letter to Johnston in 1900, "Both Miss Clark and myself have used cameras for perhaps ten years or more but it is only two years ago that we took up portrait work as a busines [*sic*]. We have regular days for sittings which are always by appointment and the work of posting, lighting, etc is attended to as carefully as though the sitter was to be painted instead of simply photographed." Their collaboration ended around 1910.

Exhibitions

Chicago Photographic Salon of 1900,
Art Institute of Chicago, Chicago, April 1900

Third Annual Salon and Exhibition,
Carnegie Art Galleries, Pittsburgh, May 1900

Congrès International de Photographie,
Universal Exposition, Paris, July 1900

"Rose Clark and Elizabeth Flint Wade," Camera Club of New York, New York, October 1900

Third Philadelphia Photographic Salon,
Pennsylvania Academy of the Fine Arts,
Philadelphia, October 1900

Pan-American Exposition, Buffalo, March 1901

Glasgow International Exhibition, Glasgow, 1901

"Les Artistes Américaines," Photo-Club de Paris, Paris, January 1901

Esposizione Internationale di Fotografie
Artistica, American Section, Turin, 1902

Leeds-Yorkshire Union of Artists Exhibition,
Leeds, England, 1902

"American Pictorial Photography,"
National Arts Club, New York, March 1902

Photographers Association of New England,
Sixth Convention Exhibition, Boston, August 1902

Fifteenth Annual Exhibition of Picture, City Art Gallery, Leeds, England, October 1902

Photo-Club de Paris, Paris, 1904

Louisiana Purchase Exposition, St. Louis, 1904

"A Collection of American Pictorial Photographs,"
Corcoran Art Galleries, Washington, D.C.,
January 1904

"A Collection of American Pictorial Photographs,"
Carnegie Art Galleries, Pittsburgh, February
1904

Siebente Austellung, Wiener Photo Club,
Vienna, April 1905

53.* *Annetje*, 1898
Platinum, 204 x 128 mm.
In red ink on photo: "R.C./E.F.W."
Mount: Thick pale orange paper, 381 x 299 mm.
LC-USZC2-5942

ANNIE NELSON CROWELL (MRS. A. NELSON CROWELL)

(1862, San Francisco – 1949, Santa Cruz, Cal.)

Active in San Francisco, Cal.

Annie Nelson Crowell was an amateur and professional photographer who specialized in studies of children and still lifes. The daughter of Henry Criticher, a founder of the San Francisco Stock Exchange, she married Charles H. Crowell, with whom she had two children, Carlena and Robinson. In 1884, however, she was listed as a widow in the city directory.

At the First San Francisco Photographic Salon, Crowell exhibited nine photographs and won second prize in the still-life section for *Trillium*. A review of the Second San Francisco Photographic Salon mentioned Crowell's well-lighted study of a Chinese child, *Ah Sue*. Crowell was also known as an accomplished watercolorist and was a member of the Sketch Club, the first women's art club in California, exhibiting her floral still lifes and nature studies throughout the 1890s. At some point after the death of her husband, Crowell moved to an island off the Mediterranean coast of Spain, returning to the United States in 1941.

Affiliations

California Camera Club

Exhibitions

Congrès International de Photographie, Universal Exposition, Paris, July 1900

"Les Artistes Américaines," Photo-Club de Paris, Paris, January 1901

First San Francisco Photographic Salon, San Francisco, January 1901

Second San Francisco Photographic Salon, San Francisco, January 1902

ANNA DESMOND

(1873, California – ?)

Active in Los Angeles, Cal.
Studio: 937 South Hill Street, Los Angeles (1903–9; residence 1892–1904)

Anna Desmond was active in Los Angeles as both a photographer and gallery owner from 1902 to 1909. The unmarried daughter of Irish immigrants Daniel and Ellen Desmond, she initially established her business, Anna Desmond & Company, in the home that she shared with her extended family. For several years the business appeared in the city directory, which indicates that she worked with photographer Theodore Heinig and Nora L. Desmond, a relative and former schoolteacher. Desmond exhibited a number of portraits, mostly of children, in the First Los Angeles Photographic Salon in 1902 and one photograph, *Florence*, was selected for a portfolio of "A Few of the Most Interesting Pictures in the Los Angeles Exhibition" published in *Camera Craft* (1902).

Five portraits of photographer Alvin Langdon Coburn (1882–1966) by Anna Desmond are conserved at the George Eastman House, Rochester, New York.

Affiliations

Los Angeles Camera Club

Exhibitions

First Los Angeles Photographic Salon, Los Angeles, May 1902

54. *Florence*, ca. 1902
Platinum, 153 x 101 mm.
In pencil, l.r.: "Anna Desmond & Co./LA"
Mount: Dark gray mat with light gray intermediate mount, 374 x 253 mm.
LC-USZC2-5945

MARY DEVENS

(1857 – March 13, 1920)

Active in Cambridge, Mass.

Mary Devens, the daughter of Arthur Lithgow Devens and Agnes Howard White Devens, lived with her family in Cambridge, Massachusetts, and spent summers in North Haven, Maine. An amateur photographer with a strong interest in mastering printing techniques that could be manipulated, Devens experimented with both the ozotype and the combination of gum bichromate and platinum printing among others. She presented a lecture on the gum bichromate process at the Old Cambridge Photographic Club in November 1896, after first seeing it in Europe the summer of that year.

She developed a warm relationship with her mentor F. Holland Day, who undeniably influenced her career through encouragement and advocacy of her work, personally submitting five of her prints to the London Salon of 1898 and repeatedly prodding Stieglitz to meet with Devens. Day also showcased Devens's work in his seminal lecture, "Photography as a Fine Art," delivered at the Harvard Camera Club in 1900 and included several of her prints in his 1900–1 exhibition, the "New School of American Photography." In a review of the latter exhibition, A. L. Coburn praised Devens's photographs: "The quality of Miss Devens' 'gum' work is so far above criticism, that for strength and vigor in treatment M. Demachy himself would find it difficult to excel these three prints."

Johnston wished to include Devens's work in her Paris exhibition, but as the latter was traveling abroad throughout most of 1900 and 1901, the letter did not reach her in time. While in Paris, Devens joined Day and Edward Steichen for dinner one evening at Demachy's house, and later attended a party at Steichen's home with fellow Boston photographers and future members of the Linked Ring, Elise Pumpelly Cabot and Margaret Russell. Demachy felt compelled to add some of her photographs to Johnston's exhibition of American women photographers upon its return to Paris for exhibition at the Photo-Club de Paris (1901).

In 1902, Devens was elected to both Stieglitz's Photo-Secession and the prestigious Linked Ring in London and was recognized by Stieglitz in "Modern Pictorial Photography" in *Century Magazine* as one of ten prominent American Pictorial photographers. In 1904, Devens made a rare reference to her failing eyesight when she wrote to Stieglitz asking him to send her any of her prints that he might have, as she needed them for "exhibition almost immediately." After 1904, she only showed work in a handful of exhibitions, and seems to have ceased photographic activity completely after 1905. A memorial retrospective of her photographic work was mounted by the Society of Arts and Crafts, Boston, in January 1921.

Exhibitions

Sixth Annual Exhibition of the Photographic Salon, The Linked Ring, Dudley Gallery, London, September 1898

First Philadelphia Photographic Salon, Pennsylvania Academy of the Fine Arts, Philadelphia, October 1898

Boston Camera Club, Boston, February 1899

Second Annual Exhibition, Society of Arts and Crafts, Boston, April 1899

Ausstellung für künstlerische Photographie, Berlin, February 1899

Old Cambridge Photographic Club, Cambridge, Mass., 1899

Seventh Annual Exhibition of the Photographic Salon, The Linked Ring, Dudley Gallery, London, September 1899

Second Philadelphia Photographic Salon, Pennsylvania Academy of the Fine Arts, Philadelphia, October 1899

Newark Camera Club, Newark, Ohio, November 1899

Loan exhibition, Camera Club of New York, New York, December 1899

Old Cambridge Photographic Club, Cambridge, Mass., 1900

Congrès International de Photographie, Universal Exposition, Paris, July 1900

"New School of American Photography," Royal Photographic Society, London, October 1900

Third Philadelphia Photographic Salon, Pennsylvania Academy of the Fine Arts, Philadelphia, October 1900

Glasgow International Exhibition, Glasgow, 1901

"Les Artistes Américaines," Photo-Club de Paris, Paris, January 1901

"New School of American Photography," Photo-Club de Paris, Paris, February 1901

Second Chicago Photographic Salon, Art Institute of Chicago, Chicago, October 1901

Old Cambridge Photographic Club, Cambridge, May 1902

Second San Francisco Photographic Salon, San Francisco, January 1902

"American Pictorial Photography," National Arts Club, New York, March 1902

Tenth Annual Exhibition of the Photographic Salon, The Linked Ring, Dudley Gallery, London, September 1902

Fifteenth Annual Exhibition of Pictures, Leeds, England, October 1902

"Portraits by a Few Leaders," F. Holland Day Studio, Boston, December 1902

Rochester Camera Club, Rochester, New York, March 1903

First Exhibition, Noble Mechanics Institute, Rochester, N.Y., 1903

Eleventh Annual Exhibition of the Photographic Salon, The Linked Ring, Dudley Gallery, London, September 1903

Old Cambridge Photographic Club, Cambridge, Mass., 1904

City of Bradford Exhibition, Bradford, England, 1904

"Mary Devens," Harcourt Building, Boston, 1904

"American Pictorial Photographs," Corcoran Art Galleries, Washington, D.C., January 1904

"American Pictorial Photographs," Carnegie Art Galleries, Pittsburgh, February 1904

Lewis and Clark Exposition/Alfred Stieglitz, Portland, Oreg. June 1905

Member's work, Photo-Secession, New York, November 1905

Society of Arts and Crafts (posthumous retrospective), Boston, January 1921

SARAH JANE EDDY

(May 1851, Boston – March 29, 1945, Portsmouth, R.I.)

Active in Providence, R.I., and Bristol Ferry, R.I.

Sarah Jane Eddy took up photography in the late 1880s in the belief that it was "only one of the many modes of expression for artistic feeling and that its possibilities in that direction are very great." A student of both the Pennsylvania Academy of the Fine Arts and the Art Students League in New York, Eddy was a member of the National Sculpture Society and exhibited a portrait bust of Samuel S. Fleisher at the Pennsylvania Academy of the Fine Arts, Philadelphia, in 1914. She was adept in the platinotype process and printed her own photographs of genre scenes, portraits, animals and flowers.

In 1892, Eddy won a gold medal for her exhibit at the Eighteenth Triennial Exhibition of the Massachusetts Charitable Mechanics Association. At the Washington Salon of 1896, her photograph *Saint Francis* was given special mention by the jury and purchased by the committee for the United States National Museum (now Smithsonian Institution) as part of the first public amateur art photography collection. A review of the Third Chicago Salon noted that Eddy "handled [her] subject with such rare skill that the picture seemed like a delicate wash drawing, with that lack of suppression of detail that one finds which can be secured with the brush, but with the camera seems impossible."

Eddy had a lifelong commitment to humane causes. She was the founder of the Rhode Island Humane Education Society and, at the time of her death, director of both the American Humane Education Society and the Massachusetts Society for the Prevention of Cruelty to Animals. In her correspondence with the Abolitionist Frederick Douglass (1818–1895), a family friend, she discussed her interest in humane education. She also attended a meeting of the Association for the Advancement of Women. Eddy used photography in connection with her philanthropic causes, illustrating books on the humane treatment of animals and distributing her photographs among hospitals and charitable institutions.

When Johnston asked Eddy for biographical information, Eddy was reluctant, requesting that Johnston reveal simply that she was a member of the Art Students League of New York because "to be known means more care & more demands upon me & I have too many already."

Sarah Jane Eddy,
in Sarah J. Eddy, *Songs of Happy Life for Schools*
(Silver, Burdett and Co., 1901), front.

Affiliations

Postal Photographic Club

Boston Camera Club, Boston

Providence Camera Club, Providence, R.I.

Exhibitions

Sixth Annual Providence Camera Club, Providence, R.I., May 1890

Fifth Annual Joint Exhibition of the Photographic Society of Philadelphia, Boston Camera Club, Boston, May 1892

Thirty-Seventh Annual Exhibition, Royal Photographic Society, London, September 1892

Eighteenth Triennial Exhibition, Massachusetts Charitable Mechanics Association, Boston, October 1892

Boston Camera Club, joint exhibition, Boston, May 1893

Sixth Annual Exhibition of the Boston Camera Club, Boston, January 1894

First Amateur Exhibition of the Hartford Camera Club, Hartford, Conn., March 1894

23rd Regiment Fair, Regiment Armory Building, Brooklyn, November 1894

Seventh Annual Competitive Exhibition, Boston Camera Club, Boston, April 1895

Eighth Annual Competitive Exhibition, Boston Camera Club, Boston, April 1896

"George Timmins Collection," Syracuse, New York, May 1896

Washington Salon and Art Photographic Exhibition, Washington, D.C., May 1896

Tenth Annual Composition Exhibition, Boston Camera Club, Boston, 1898

Postal Photographic Club of the Capital Camera Club, Washington, DC., May 1898

American Institute of the City of New York, Photographic Section, New York, September 1898

Philadelphia Photographic Salon, Pennsylvania Academy of the Fine Arts, Philadelphia, October, 1898

Postal Photographic Club, Camera Club of New York, New York, January 1899

Second Annual International Salon and Exhibition, Carnegie Art Galleries, Pittsburgh, February 1899

Twelfth Annual Club Exhibition, Boston Camera Club, Boston, April 1900

Third Annual Salon, Carnegie Art Galleries, Pittsburgh, May 1900

Congrès International de Photographie, Universal Exposition, Paris, July 1900

"New School of American Photography," Royal Photographic Society, London, October 1900

Boston Camera Club, Camera Club of New York, New York, December 1900

"Les Artistes Américaines," Photo-Club de Paris, Paris, January 1901

"New School of American Photography," Photo-Club de Paris, Paris, February 1901

Thirteenth Annual Exhibition by Members of the Boston Camera Club, Boston, May 1901

Third Chicago Photographic Salon, Art Institute of Chicago, Chicago, December 1902

The Second Competitive Exhibition of Pictures Between the Old Cambridge Photographic Club and Boston Camera Club, Boston, May 1902

First Minneapolis Photographic Salon, Minneapolis, 1903

First Annual Salon, Fenton & Stair's Art Gallery, Cleveland, March 1903

First Salon (Twelfth Annual Exhibition), Toronto Camera Club, Toronto, April 1903

Fourth Chicago Photographic Salon, Art Institute of Chicago, Chicago, December 1903

Fifteen Annual Exhibition of the Boston Camera Club, Boston, May 1904

Annual Members Exhibition, Boston Camera Club, Boston, March 1906

"Exhibition of Photographs: The Work of Women Photographers," Camera Club of Hartford, Hartford, Conn., April 1906

Nineteenth Annual Exhibition, Boston Camera Club, Boston, March 1909

Annual Exhibition, Boston Camera Club, Boston, May 1910

Twenty-First Annual Exhibition, Boston Camera Club, Boston, April 1911

Members One-Print Exhibition, Boston Camera Club, Boston, November 1911

55. *A Welcome Interruption*, ca. 1896
(copyright January 10, 1896)
Platinum, 202 x 153 mm.
Typed on paper pasted at bottom of photo: "'A Welcome Interruption.' Copyright, 1896, by Sarah J. Eddy."; copyright stamp in purple ink, l.r.: 3570 (inside stamp)
Mount: Thick cream mat, 355 x 280 mm.
LC-USZC2-5946

56.* *The Old Mill*, ca. 1900
Platinum, 140 x 202 mm.
In pencil, l.r.: "Sarah J. Eddy"; l.l.: "The Old Mill"
Mount: Dark gray board, 280 x 355 mm.
LC-USZC2-5947

57. *Sitting in the Sun*, ca. 1900
Platinum, 115 x 160 mm.
In pencil, l.r.: "Sarah J. Eddy"; l.l.: "Sitting in the Sun"
Mount: Cream stock mount with olive surround, 250 x 298 mm.
Verso: In pencil: "Sarah J. Eddy/Providence R.I."
LC-USZC2-6030

58.* *Mother and Child*, ca. 1900
Platinum, 185 x 141 mm.
In pencil, l.r.: "Sarah J. Eddy"; l.l.: "Mother and Child"
Mount: Gray board with charcoal intermediate mount, 218 x 171 mm.
Verso: FBJ label: 36.
LC-USZC2-6105

59. *Peace*, ca. 1900
Platinum, 154 x 206 mm.
Mount: Rembrandt mount, 274 x 301 mm.
Verso: In pencil: "Miss Sarah J. Eddy B.C.C./Platinotype"
LC-USZC2-6123

60.* *Contentment*, ca. 1900
Platinum, 202 x 152 mm.
In pencil, l.r.: "Sarah J. Eddy"
Mount: Gray board, 339 x 273 mm.
LC-USZC2-6126

61.* *The Fisherman's Home*, ca. 1893
(copyright deposit July 8, 1893)
Platinum, 152 x 202 mm.
LC-USZC2-6128

62.* *A Welcome Interruption*, ca. 1896
(date of copyright)
Platinum, 203 x 152 mm.
In pencil across bottom: "A Welcome
Interruption/Copyrighted Sarah J. Eddy"
Mount: Dark gray board, 337 x 273 mm.
NMAH-C-7792.12

63. *Sunset, Narragansett Bay*, ca. 1900
Platinum, 148 x 200 mm.
In pencil, l.r.: "Sarah J. Eddy"; l.l.:
"Sunset, Narragansett Bay"
Mount: Dark gray board, 278 x 355 mm.
NMAH-C-77.92.13

64. *Among the Blow-Away Flowers*,
ca. 1900
Platinum, oval: 185 x 140 mm.
Mount: Mat with oval cut
in beveled edge, 295 x 238 mm.
Verso: In pencil: "Among the Blow-away
flowers/Sarah J. Eddy"; FBJ label: 34.
NMAH-C-77.92.14

65. *The Gladness of the Spring*, ca. 1900
Platinum, oval: 180 x 133 mm.
In pencil, l.r.: "Sarah J. Eddy"; l.l.:
"The Gladness of Spring"
Mount: Brown flecked paper with oval
cut, tan oval underneath, 326 x 255 mm.
NMAH-C-77.92.15

66. *Spring Blossoms*, ca. 1900
Platinum, 201 x 150 mm.
In pencil, l.r.: "Sarah J. Eddy"; l.l.:
"Spring Blossoms"
Mount: Dark gray paper, 355 x 280 mm.
NMAH-C-77.92.16

67. *A Pleasant Reflection*, ca. 1900
Platinum, rectangle with rounded upper
edge: 137 x 95 mm.
In pencil, l.r.: "Copyright Sarah J.
Eddy"; l.l.: "A Pleasant Reflection."
Overmount: Gray mat with sage green
silver flecked paper underneath,
340 x 280 mm.
NMAH-C-77.92.17

68. *The Bride*, ca. 1900
Platinum, 201 x 152 mm.
In pencil, l.r.: "Sarah J. Eddy"; l.l.:
"The Bride"
Mount: Pale gray mat, 355 x 280 mm.
NMAH-C-77.92.18

69. *The Last Load*, ca. 1900
Platinum, 150 x 200 mm.
In pencil, l.r.: "Sarah J. Eddy" and
"The Last Load"
Mount: Thick dark gray paper,
280 x 355 mm.
Verso: FBJ label: 35
NMAH-C-77.92.19

70.* *The Spirit of a Flower*, ca. 1900
Platinum, 200 x 152 mm.
In pencil, l.r.: "Sarah J. Eddy"; l.l.:
"The Spirit of a Flower."
Mount: Cream mat with beveled outer
edge with embossed center rectangle
and printed khaki surround,
348 x 300 mm.
NMAH-C-77.92.20

71. *The Spirit of a Flower*, ca. 1900
Platinum, 200 x 152 mm.
In pencil, l.r.: "Sarah J. Eddy"; l.l.:
"The Spirit of a Flower."
Mount: Cream mat with beveled outer
edge with embossed center rectangle
and printed khaki surround,
348 x 300 mm.
NMAH-C-3267

FANNIE L. ELTON (MRS. ELTON SAUNDERS)

(September 1859, Ohio – 1912?)

Active in Cleveland, Ohio
Studio: 127 Euclid Avenue, Cleveland
         The Arcade Building, Euclid Avenue, Cleveland (with Brigden & Geiser)
         166 Euclid Avenue, Cleveland (1895–1907; The Elton Studio, 1901)
         [166 renumbered 734 in 1905]
         10402 Euclid Avenue, Cleveland (The Elton Studio, 1907–12)

72. [Oval portrait of woman with a flower in her hair and a corsage], ca. 1900
Platinum, oval: 126 x 88 mm.
In pencil, l.r.: "Miss Elton/Cleveland/Ohio."
Mount: Black board, 252 x 202 mm.
Verso: FBJ label: 31.; in pencil on label: "Miss Elton"
LC-USZC2-5948

73. [Portrait of man seated with arms crossed in a pinstripe suit], ca. 1900
Platinum, 147 x 108 mm.
In pencil, l.r.: "Miss Elton/Cleveland/Ohio"
Mount: Dark gray board, 305 x 254 mm.
LC-USZC2-5949

Fannie Elton "stepped over into Photography from the kindred art of water color and crayon drawing" in the late 1880s. Of English parentage, Elton was confident that photography was a profession particularly suited to women and opened a professional studio on Euclid Avenue in 1892. In a letter to Johnston, she reveals her desire to surpass the portraits taken by "Men, with a woeful lack of ability and artistic sense ... chiefly of the 'look-pleasant-please' 'rather-go-to-the-Dentist' class."

From 1894 to 1895, Elton worked with photographers Harriet M. Brigden and Franz E. Geisler in the Arcade Building on Euclid Avenue. Professional women photographers were rare in Cleveland, Brigden & Geiser was the only photography firm of fifty-four listed in the 1894–95 city directory to display women's names in its listing. In 1895, Elton opened her own studio at 166 Euclid Avenue and the following year she was one of just two women photographers listed in the business section of the city directory. To help her manage professional demands, Elton employed her boarder, Elsie Upton, as her assistant in 1900. In a letter to Johnston that year, Elton described her ascent to "one of the prettiest studios in the city and a very select trade." Following her marriage to photographer William W. Saunders around 1901, she renamed her studio The Elton Studio, where they worked together until 1911.

Exhibitions
Congrès International de Photographie, Universal Exposition, Paris, July 1900
"Les Artistes Américaines," Photo-Club de Paris, Paris, January 1901

EMMA JUSTINE FARNSWORTH

(1860, Albany, N.Y. – 1952, Albany, N.Y.)
Active in Albany, N.Y.

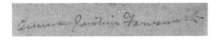

Emma Justine Farnsworth, in *Ladies' Home Journal* (Aug. 1901), p. 1.

The daughter of a successful lumber merchant, Emma Justine Farnsworth lived in Albany all of her life. She was active as a photographer from about 1886 to 1912, specializing in allegorical and narrative studies often created for book illustration. Her photographs were admired for the elegant posing of her models—often friends—and her skillful use of lighting and arrangement of drapery.

In 1892, *In Arcadia* was published, a book of classical verse illustrated by six photographic figure studies. In 1893, Farnsworth illustrated another book, exhibited at the World's Columbian Exposition in Chicago and was the only woman medallist at the joint exhibition in Philadelphia, prompting Alfred Stieglitz to call her the finest lady amateur in the country. At the Washington Salon of 1896, some of her work was purchased by the United States National Museum (now Smithsonian Institution), which established the first public collection of amateur art photography in the country. William Murray spoke highly of her skill when reviewing the fifty works exhibited by Farnsworth at the Camera Club of New York in 1897: "It is impossible not to be struck by the remarkable versatility displayed by this young artist-photographer in the treatment of such a wide range of subjects as this collection embraces. She is gifted certainly with a wonderful power of imagination."

In a letter sent to Johnston in 1900 accompanying prints, Farnsworth made reference to some art training but described herself as "simply an amateur." Due to a "lack of nervous strength" and family obligations she had not been producing new work and submitted work that was less recent than she would have liked. However, in the same letter she estimated that she had won more than twenty-five medals in the United States, Canada, England, France, Germany, Italy and India. She refused to allow images to be reproduced in order to protect their artistic value and revealed the seriousness with which she approached photography: "I know of nothing that requires more energy & patience than to try to realize ones ideas in an artistic attempt with a camera—or 'To catch the spirit of the light./the soul that lurks in shade' with a machine."

Exhibitions

Second Joint Exhibition, Pennsylvania Academy of the Fine Arts, Philadelphia, 1888

Sixth Annual Joint Exhibition, Pennsylvania Academy of the Fine Arts, Philadelphia, April 1893

World's Columbian Exposition, Chicago, 1893

Thirty-Eighth Annual Exhibition of the Royal Photographic Society, London, September 1893

Photographic Salon, The Linked Ring, Dudley Gallery, London, October 1893

Première Exposition d'Art Photographique, Photo-Club de Paris, Paris, January 1894

First Amateur Exhibition, Hartford Camera Club, Hartford, Conn., March 1894

Thirty-Ninth Annual Exhibition of the Royal Photographic Society, London, September 1894

Photographic Salon, The Linked Ring, Dudley Gallery, London, October 1894

Internationalen Ausstellung für Amateur Photographie, Berlin, 1896

"George Timmins Collection," Syracuse, N.Y., May 1896

Washington Salon and Art Photographic Exhibition, Washington, D.C., May 1896

International Exhibition of Pictorial Photography, Laing Art Gallery, Newcastle-upon-Tyne, 1906

Salon de Photographie, Photo-Club de Paris, Paris, May 1897

"Emma Justine Farnsworth," Camera Club of New York, New York, November 1897

First Annual International Salon Exhibition, Carnegie Art Galleries, Pittsburgh, January 1898

American Institute of the City of New York, National Academy of Design, New York, September 1898

Ninth Annual Exhibition, Toronto Camera Club, Toronto, December 1899

Congrès International de Photographie, Universal Exposition, Paris, July 1900

"Les Artistes Américaines," Photo-Club de Paris, Paris, January 1901

Eighth Annual Exhibition of Amateur Photographers, *Youth's Companion* Competition, 1903

The Kodak Exhibition, Kodak Galleries, London, September 1906

The Kodak Exhibition, Eastman Kodak Company, New York, 1912

Annual Exhibition, Portland Society of Art, Portland, Maine, March 1912

74.* [Field with cornstalks twisted into bunches and pumpkins], ca. 1900
Platinum, 169 x 116 mm.
Mount: Gray paper, 237 x 207 mm.
LC-USZC2-5950

75.* *At Dusk*, 1893
Platinum, 102 x 165 mm.
In pencil, l.l.: "E.J.F."
Mount: Dark gray board, 280 x 357 mm.
Verso: In ink: "At Dusk/Copyright 1893 E.J.F."
LC-USZC2-5951

76.* *Diana*, 1898
Platinum, 218 x 163 mm.
In pencil on photo, l.l.: "E.J.F."
Mount: Cream mat with glue remaining from overmatting now removed, 304 x 253 mm.
Verso: In ink: "Diana./Diana/Emma Justine Farnsworth/26 Elk St./Albany NY/USA/ Copyright 1898 To be returned"; FBJ label: 39.
LC-USZC2-5952

77. *To A Greek Girl*, 1873
An illustration of an Austin Dobson poem of the same title published in *In Arcadia*
Carbon, 183 x 130 mm.
Mount: Matted behind tan board with inner beveled edge, 292 x 237 mm.
Verso: Partial inscription in ink "'To a Greek Girl'... you do: where 'er you/gladness on"; in pencil: "Copyrighted 1893"
LC-USZC2-5953

78. *To A Greek Girl*, 1873
An illustration of an Austin Dobson poem of the same title published in *In Arcadia*
Platinum, 195 x 123 mm.
Verso: In pencil: "E.J. Farnsworth"
LC-USZC2-5954

79.* *To A Greek Girl*, 1873
An illustration of an Austin Dobson poem of the same title published in *In Arcadia*
Carbon, 180 x 134 mm.
Mount: Light gray mat glue remains from orange overmat, 263 x 221 mm.
Verso: In pencil: "Carbon/To a Greek Girl"; in ink: "Copyright 1875 E.H. Allen"; FBJ label: 42.
LC-USZC2-5955

80. *At Dusk*, 1894
Platinum, 130 x 184 mm.
In ink, c.: "At Dusk/by/E. J. Farnsworth, Albany, N.Y./Copyright stamp March 30, 1894/17652, Z, 2"
Mount: Light gray board, 210 x 269 mm.
LC-USZC2-6031

81. *At Dusk*, 1894
Platinum, 110 x 161 mm.
LC-USZC2-6032

82. *Diana*, 1898
Platinum, 194 x 137 mm.
LC-USZC2-6033

83. *Diana*, 1898
Platinum, 201 x 138 mm.
Verso: In pencil: "E. J. Farnsworth"
LC-USZC2-6034

84. *Cupid*, ca. 1900
Platinum combination, 159 x 104 mm.
Monogram scratched into negative,
l.r.: "EF"
LC-USZC2-6035

85.* *To A Greek Girl*, ca. 1900
Waxed platinum, 187 x 132 mm.
In red pencil on photo, l.l.:
"Emma J. Farnsworth"
Mount: Matted behind an elaborate gold
mat with beveled edge, 360 x 310 mm.
In black on mat: "To a Greek Girl"/
"Where e'er you go: Where e'er you
pass;/There comes a gladness on the grass."
NMAH-C-77.92.21

86.* *When Spring Comes Laughing
by Vale and Hill*, ca. 1900
Platinum, 229 x 163 mm.
Mount: Dark green mat with two lines
in heavy pencil framing photo,
355 x 280 mm.
Verso: In ink: "'When Spring Comes
Laughing/By Vale and Hill' an illustra-
tion/Austin Dolson [*sic*]/Paris Salon"; in
pencil: "Miss Farnsworth/Albany/'When
Spring Comes Laughing/By Vale &
hill.'/Austin Dolson[*sic*]/Copyrighted"
NMAH-C-77.92.22

87. *In the West Wind Blowing*, ca. 1894
Platinum, 157 x 113 mm.
Overmount: Beige flecked mat,
310 x 267 mm.
Verso: In ink: "Copyrighted 1894
EJF/Negative Broken"; in pencil:
"No. 7/Emma Justine Farnsworth/26
Elk Street./Albany N.Y./ U.S.A./ In the
West Wind Blowing/ Diploma/
On no account to be sold/ 17"
NMAH-C-77.92.23

88.* *The Faggot Gatherers*, ca. 1900
Barytaless gelatin silver print (?),
113 x 162 mm.
Mount: Light gray mat, 260 x 315 mm.
Verso: In pencil: "No. 2/Emma Justine
Farnsworth/26 Elk Street./Albany,
N.Y./U.S.A./Fagot [*sic*] Gatherers/prize
picture/17"
NMAH-C-77.92.24

EMMA L. FITZ

(October 17, 1858, Chelsea, Mass. – June 5, 1926, Marblehead, Mass.)
Active in Boston, Mass.

Emma Fitz was the daughter of the Honorable Eustace C. Fitz (mayor of Chelsea, Massachussetts, during the Civil War) and Sarah J. Blanchard Fitz. In 1875, she was a member of the first class at Wellesley College, where she was enrolled through 1880, though she did not graduate. Fitz was a founder of the Boston Wellesley College Club and remained an active member of this and other college associations throughout her life, including the Wellesley College Art Museum Advisory Committee.

Fitz, who had some training in drawing and painting, took up photography as a "recreation and a pleasure" around 1887, creating images of rural and genre scenes. One of the first American women photographers recognized internationally, Fitz won medals at the annual exhibitions of the Royal Photographic Society, London, in 1894 and 1899. Two of her photographs included in the Washington Salon of 1896 were purchased by the United States National Museum (now Smithsonian Institution), for the establishment of the first public amateur art photography collection in America. In 1899, she won first prize at the annual exhibit of the Boston Camera Club for her photograph *Morning Service,* which was published as the frontispiece of the May issue of *Photo-Era* that year along with the statement that Fitz had "establishe[d] her position among the most enviable in the American ranks."

In 1900, Johnston's letter of invitation to participate in the Paris exhibition did not reach Fitz in time because she was traveling in Europe. In her reply to Johnston, she regretted not being able to participate. Surprisingly, despite years of international recognition for her work she considered it "scarcely worthy of mention." In an article by Hines, she was quoted as saying: "I have great faith in the possibilities of photography as an art, and there is a great field open for women who will go seriously to work."

89.* *The Village Politician*, ca. 1900
Platinum, 187 x 150 mm.
Mount: Cream mat, 250 x 203 mm.
Verso: In pencil: "The Village Politician/by Miss Emma Fitz/253 Commonwealth Ave/Boston"
NMAH-C-77.92.25

FLORIDE GREEN (also referred to erroneously as "Florine" or humorously as "Chloride" Green)

(1863, Eutaw, Ala. – October 24, 1936, San Francisco)

Active in San Francisco, Cal., and New York City
Studio: 41 Union Square, West, New York (1897–98)
20 W. 33rd Street, New York (1898–1901)
1722 Pacific Avenue, San Francisco (1904)
2845b Fillmore, San Francisco (1907)

Floride Green,
in *American Amateur Photographer* (June 1899).

Floride Green was the daughter of Duff C. Green, Jr., and Rebecca Pickens Green, both from prominent Southern families. After losing everything in the Civil War, the Greens fled West like other Southern refugees, settling in Stockton, California. In 1872, they moved to San Francisco, where Floride attended the Valencia Street School and later graduated from the high school at St. Helena. After several years of teaching in San Francisco, Floride Green began her bi-coastal photographic career.

In 1890, she took her first photographs—studies of "Negro life" and landscapes—while visiting her former home in Alabama. The critical acclaim that these works received when exhibited in Europe prompted Green to move to New York in 1897 to become a professional photographer. As a society photographer, she specialized in portraits at the sitter's home. Green received her first commission for an "at home" portrait after a society woman with a restless child saw four of her photographs in the window of an art store. Word of her skill soon spread and her business expanded until it occupied the entire top floor of the building at 20 W. 33rd Street. Her portraits were also exhibited publicly: five in Johnston's exhibitions (1900–1) and seven in the First San Francisco Photographic Salon (1901).

From 1904 to 1906, Green traveled through Europe, Africa and Egypt with lifelong friend, the famous San Franciscan Lillie Hitchcock Coit (1843–1949). She returned to San Francisco to care for her sick mother. An active member of the California Historical Society, Green continued to work as a photographer until around 1907, when she went into real estate. Later she worked in insurance brokerage.

Estelle Huntington Huggins

(February 1870, Ohio – ?)
Active in London, Ohio, and New York City
Studio: London, Ohio (1896–99)
        57 East 59th Street, New York (and residence 1901–18)

90. [Young fair haired girl seated with hands in her lap], ca. 1900
Platinum, 80 x 55 mm.
In pencil on front: "Huggins/57 E 39th St./N.Y."
Bifold business card of thick cream paper, 173 x 128 mm.
LC-USZC2-5961

Estelle Huntington Huggins was a portrait photographer who operated studios in both London, Ohio, and New York City. She worked with her sister at the studio in London from 1896 to 1899. In an advertising pamphlet which lists both studios, Huggins detailed her abilities in the platinotype process and touted eight years' experience. She also referred to her classical art training at the Art Students League in New York by listing her distinguished teachers: muralist Kenyon Cox (1856–1919), landscape artist John Henry Twachtman (1853–1902), and portraitists Douglas Volk (1856–1935) and James Carroll Beckwith (1852–1917).

In addition to her photographic portraits, Huggins may have worked professionally in other media, as she is listed variously in the New York city directories as "artist" and "photographer."

Gertrude Stanton Käsebier

(1852, Des Moines – 1934, New York City)
Active in Brooklyn, N.Y., and New York City
Studio: 273 Fifth Avenue, New York

Baron A. DeMeyer, *Gertrude Stanton Käsebier*. Washington, D.C., Library of Congress, Frances Benjamin Johnston Collection, LC-USZC2-5943

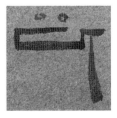

Gertrude Käsebier was born in Des Moines, Iowa, but in 1860 the family moved to Eureka Gulch, Colorado, where her father ran a lumber mill and mineral refinery. After the sudden death of her father John W. Stanton in 1864, the family moved to Brooklyn where her mother, Muncy Boone Stanton, opened a boarding house to support the family. A few years later, Käsebier attended the Moravian Seminary for Women in Bethlehem, Pennsylvania, before returning to Brooklyn in 1874 to marry German immigrant and successful shellac importer, Eduard Käsebier. The Käsebiers stayed in Brooklyn for ten years before moving to a farmhouse in New Durham, New Jersey, and had three children, Frederick William, Gertrude Elizabeth and Hermine Mathilde. In the late 1880s, Käsebier began photographing her family, and in 1889, despite the objections of her husband, she moved the family back to Brooklyn and enrolled at the Pratt Institute of Art and Design. Here she studied drawing, painting and design, but maintained an interest in photography. In 1892, Käsebier won first prize in a photography competition sponsored by *The Monthly Illustrator* magazine, but her teachers disapproved so vehemently that she gave away the prize money in shame. Käsebier spent 1894 in France, where she painted with Frank DuMond, photographed the local peasants and experimented with portrait photography.

Upon her return from Europe, Käsebier became a professional photographer, in part because of her husband's declining health. She had already apprenticed with a chemist in Germany to master the technical side of photography, and in 1896 began to work with Samuel H. Lifshey, a portrait photographer in Brooklyn, to learn the business of running a studio and to further her knowledge of techniques. Over the following two years, she would be honored by a solo exhibition of one hundred and fifty of her works at both the Boston Camera Club and the Pratt Institute. In 1897–98, Käsebier opened her first studio in Manhattan. Her husband disapproved, fearing that the business might reflect poorly on his ability to support the family. Favoring simplicity and individuality over elaborate backdrops, props and artificial looking poses, Käsebier quickly carved out her own niche in portrait photography. She did not advertise per se, but instead generated publicity through her celebrity portraits and story illustrations for magazines such as *Ladies' Home Journal*, *The World's Work* and *Everybody's Magazine*.

In July 1899, Stieglitz published five of Käsebier's photographs in *Camera Notes*, declaring her "beyond dispute, the leading artistic portrait photographer of the day." In 1900, Käsebier and British Pictorialist Carine Cadby became the first women to be elected to the Linked Ring. Invited by Johnston that year to submit photographs for her presentation in Paris, Käsebier wrote that she simply did not have time to make prints. However, after several pleas, Johnston convinced Käsebier to send a group of prints. Johnston profiled Käsebier in her series for the *Ladies' Home Journal* (May 1901), writing that Käsebier had "probably done more than any other American woman to lift Pictorial photography to the high plane of a fine art." In 1902, Käsebier became a founding member of the Photo-Secession and was honored in the first issue of *Camera Work* (1903) by the reproduction of six of her photographs.

During the summer of 1905, Käsebier and Johnston—who had opened a portrait studio in New York that year—traveled to Venice together, where they visited photographer Baron Adolf DeMeyer. Käsebier then traveled alone to Paris, where she was introduced to the reclusive Auguste Rodin, who allowed her to photograph him. Käsebier joined Johnston at the end of the summer and visited French Pictorialist Robert Demachy in Normandy. Käsebier's relationship with Stieglitz had begun to sour in 1905 and in 1907 tensions peaked when Käsebier joined the Professional Photographers of New York, an organization that Stieglitz regarded as too commercial, Stieglitz published a parody of Käsebier by Caffin in the October 1907 issue of *Camera Work* and five years later Käsebier was the first member to resign from an unraveling Photo-Secession.

Following her husband's death in 1909, Käsebier began to teach composition to women photographers through the Women's Federation of the Photographers' Association of America. In 1910, she opened a summer studio in Newport, Rhode Island, and exhibited twenty-two prints in the grand finale exhibition of the Photo-Secession, at the Albright-Knox Gallery in Buffalo. She continued to make painterly, hand-manipulated prints and found an ally in White. She occasionally taught classes at the Clarence White School. In 1916, Käsebier became honorary vice-president of the Pictorial Photographers of America, an organization founded by White that year.

In 1924, Käsebier's daughter Hermine Turner joined her in her portrait business. In 1929, the Brooklyn Institute of Arts (now the Brooklyn Museum) mounted a retrospective exhibition of Käsebier's work.

Affiliations

The Linked Ring, London

The Photo-Secession, New York

Pictorial Photographers of America, Boston

Juror

Second Philadelphia Photographic Salon, Philadelphia, 1899

Third Philadelphia Photographic Salon, Philadelphia, 1900

Brooklyn Camera Club, Brooklyn, 1904

International Salon of the Pictorial Photographers of America, New York, 1923

Exhibitions

"Gertrude Käsebier," Boston Camera Club, Boston, 1896

"Gertrude Käsebier," Pratt Institute, New York, February 1897

First Philadelphia Photographic Salon, Pennsylvania Academy of the Fine Arts, Philadelphia, October 1898

Ausstellung für künstlerische Photographie, Berlin, February 1899

"Collection of Prints by Mrs. Gertrude Käsebier and Mr. William J. Cassard," Camera Club of New York, New York, February 1899

Seventh Annual Exhibition of the Photographic Salon, The Linked Ring, Dudley Gallery, London, September 1899

Second Philadelphia Photographic Salon, Pennsylvania Academy of the Fine Arts, Philadelphia, October 1899

Exhibit of Photographs by the Newark Camera Club, Newark, Ohio, November 1899

"Gertrude Käsebier," Minneapolis Camera Club, Minneapolis, December 1899

Exhibit of Photographs by the Newark Camera Club, Newark, Ohio, November 1900

Chicago Photographic Salon of 1900, Art Institute of Chicago, Chicago, April 1900

Members' Third Annual Exhibition of Prints, Camera Club of New York, New York, May 1900

Congrès International de Photographie, Universal Exposition, Paris, July 1900

"New School of American Photography," Royal Photographic Society, London, October 1900

Third Philadelphia Photographic Salon, Pennsylvania Academy of the Fine Arts, Philadelphia, October 1900

Fifth Salon and Exhibition of Amateur Photography, Case Library, Cleveland, November 1900

"Les Artistes Américaines," Photo-Club de Paris, Paris, January 1901

"New School of American Photography," Photo-Club de Paris, February 1901

Glasgow International Art Exhibition, Glasgow, 1901

Twenty-First Annual Photographers Association of America Convention Exhibition, Detroit, January 1901

Ninth Annual Exhibition of the Photographic Salon, The Linked Ring, Dudley Gallery, London, October 1901

"American Pictorial Photography," National Arts Club, New York, March 1902

Neunte Internationale Ausstellung von Kunst-Photographien, Kunsthalle, Hamburg, 1902

Fifteenth Annual Exhibition of Pictures, City Art Gallery, Leeds, England, 1902

Photographers Association of New England, Sixth Convention Exhibition, Boston, August 1902

"Portraits by a Few Leaders in the Newer Photographic Methods," F. Holland Day Studio, Boston, December 1902

Esposizione Internazionale di Fotografie Artistica, American Section, Turin, 1902

Tenth Annual Exhibition of the Photographic Salon, The Linked Ring, Dudley Gallery, London, September 1902

Fifteenth Annual Exhibition of Pictures, City Art Gallery, Leeds, England, October 1902

Eleventh Annual Exhibition, Toronto Camera Club, Toronto, December 1902

First Annual Salon, Fenton & Stair's Art Gallery, Cleveland, March 1903

Fourth Denver Photographic Salon, Colorado Camera Club, Denver, March 1903

First Exhibition, Noble Mechanics Institute, Rochester, N.Y., March 1903

Erste Internationale Ausstellung für künstlerische Bildnis-Photographie, Wiesbaden, April 1903

Eleventh Annual Exhibition of the Photographic Salon, The Linked Ring, Dudley Gallery, London, September 1903

First Exhibition, Rochester Camera Club, Rochester, N.Y., 1903

First Minneapolis Photographic Salon, Minneapolis, 1903

"A Collection of Pictorial Photographs," Photo-Secession, Corcoran Art Galleries, Washington, D.C., January 1904

"A Collection of Pictorial Photographs," Photo-Secession, Carnegie Art Galleries, Pittsburgh, February 1904

City of Bradford Exhibition, Bradford, England, 1904

Wiener Photo Club, Vienna, April 1904

Members' Exhibition, Camera Club of New York, New York, April 1904

Photographische Ausstellung im Park der grossen Kunstausstellung, Dresden, May 1904

Twelfth Annual Exhibition of the Photographic Salon, The Linked Ring, Dudley Gallery, London, September 1904

Internationale Ausstellung ausgewählter künstlerischer Photographien, Vienna, February 1905

Third Salon of the Toronto Camera Club, Toronto, April 1905

Wiener Photo Club, Vienna, April 1905

Lewis and Clark Exposition, Portland, Oregon, June 1905

Members' Exhibition, Camera Club of New York, New York, November 1905

Second Annual Exhibition of Photographs, Worcester Art Museum, Worcester, Mass., November 1905

Members' Work, Gallery of the Photo-Secession, New York, February 1906

Exhibition of Photographs, Photo-Secession, Pennsylvania Academy of the Fine Arts, Philadelphia, April 1906

International Exhibition of Pictorial Photography, Laing Art Gallery, Newcastle-upon-Tyne, 1906

Canadian Pictorialist Exhibition, Art Association of Montreal, Montreal, November 1907

Members' Exhibition, Camera Club of New York, New York, 1908

International Exhibition of Pictorial Photography, National Arts Club, New York, February 1909

Twenty-Ninth Annual Photographers Association of America Convention Exhibition, Rochester, N.Y., July 1909

International Exhibition of Pictorial Photography, Albright Art Gallery, Buffalo, November 1910

Modern Photography, Public Library, Newark, N.J., April 1911

Portland, Maine Society of Art, Photographic Section, Portland, Maine, March 1912

Thirty-Second Annual Photographers Association of America Convention, Philadelphia, July 1912

"An Exhibition Illustrating the Progress of the Art of Photography," Montross Art Galleries, New York, October 1912

"An International Exhibition of Pictorial Photography," New York, January 1914

Second Annual Pittsburgh Salon of National Art, Pittsburgh, March 1915

"American Pictorial Photography," Syracuse, N.Y., May 1915

"An Exhibition of Pictorial Photography," The Print Gallery, New York, December 1915

First Annual Arts and Crafts Salon, Los Angeles, February 1916

Twenty-Sixth Annual Exhibition, Department of Photography of the Brooklyn Institute of Arts and Sciences, Brooklyn, April 1916

International Salon of the Pictorial Photographers of America, New York, May 1923

"Exhibition of Photographs by Gertrude Käsebier," Brooklyn Institute of Arts and Sciences, Brooklyn, 1929

American Retrospective, Julien Levy Gallery, New York, November 1933

91. [Three young girls reading a book], ca. 1900
Platinum, 201 x 155 mm.
Monogram in ink, l.r.
Mount: Thick dark gray mat with black and sage green intermediate mounts, 365 x 322 mm.
LC-USZC2-5962

92. *The Manger*, ca. 1900
Platinum, 207 x 145 mm.
Mount: Gray paper. Two sets of holes far right indicate that it was possibly bound, vertical line in white gouache at far right, 281 x 195 mm.
LC-USZC2-5963

93. *Venice*, 1905
Platinum, 265 x 130 mm.
In pencil: "To Miss F. B. Johnston/Venice Aug. 1905"
Mount: Brown paper with torn edges with cream and black intermediate mounts
Verso: Monogram stamped on back of mount partially cut off.
LC-USZC2-5964

94.* *Blessed Art Thou Among Women*, 1899
Photogravure, 236 x 141 mm.
Mount: Thick gray mat with ivory intermediate mount, 382 x 271 mm.
LC-USZC2-6115

95.* *The Manger*, 1899
Photogravure, 208 x 145 mm.
Mount: Thick dark gray mat, 382 x 271 mm.
LC-USZC2-6116

EDITH C. HAGGIN LOUNSBERY (MRS. RICHARD P. LOUNSBERY)

(July 1858, California – ?)
Active in New York City

Edith Haggin Lounsbery.
Goodrich-Blanding Family Photographs, ca. 1874-1920.
Courtesy of the Bancroft Library,
University of California, Berkeley, 1979.082.

The daughter of James B. Haggin, of the prominent Wall Street brokerage Haggin & Lounsbery, Edith Haggin married her father's business partner, Richard P. Lounsbery, in 1878. The couple had three children, Ben Ali, Richard, and Edith. An amateur photographer, Lounsbery was described in *Photogram* as a leading figure in New York society "who finds time amongst her other engagements for a great deal of very beautiful photographic work."

In 1893, she organized a slide presentation at the Camera Club of New York in aid of the St. Andrew's Convalescent Hospital in New York, thus using amateur photography to benefit a charitable cause. Although she remained an amateur photographer, Lounsbery was interested in being recognized for her photography and agreed to let Johnston reproduce any of her works, provided they were properly credited to her.

Lounsbery specialized in "at home" portraits, taken either in her own home or in the homes of her sitters using side lighting. The effects of this simple technique won much praise—one reviewer characterized her work as "graceful and natural," while Margaret Bisland, in her article on women photographers, challenged professional portraitists to achieve the excellence of Lounsbery's work.

Affiliations
Camera Club of New York, New York

Exhibitions
First Exhibition, Camera Club of New York,
New York, April 1890

Second Annual Exhibition, Camera Club
of New York, New York, March 1891

Third Annual Exhibition, Camera Club
of New York, New York, March 1892

Annual Exhibition, Camera Club of New York,
New York, March 1893

Members' Exhibition, Camera Club
of New York, New York, April 1894

Exhibition of Photographs by Members
of the Camera Club of New York and the Boston
Camera Club, Boston, December 1900

Congrès International de Photographie,
Universal Exposition, Paris, July 1900

"Les Artistes Américaines," Photo-Club de Paris,
Paris, January 1901

96.* *Portrait of John Lane, Publisher,*
ca. 1900
Salt print (?) or warm tone platinum,
130 x 102 mm.
In pencil, l.r.: "Edith H. Lounsbery"
Mount: Embossed cream mat with
cream intermediate mount,
253 x 202 mm.
Verso: In pencil: "Portrait of John
Lane/publisher _(English)/Property
of E. Lounsbery/12 East 35th St/N.Y.";
FBJ label: 59.
NMAH-C-77.92.61

97.* *Portrait Study,* ca. 1900
Salt print (?) or platinum, 197 x 146 mm.
In pencil on mount: "Edith H.
Lounsbery"
Mount: Cream colored stock mat,
305 x 255 mm.
Verso: In pencil: "Portrait study./Property
of Mrs. R. P. Lounsbery/12 East 35th
St./New York City"; FBJ label: 60.
NMAH C-77.92.62

98. *Portrait of Hubert Vos, Dutch Painter,*
ca. 1900
Platinum, 103 x 76 mm.
In pencil, l.r.: "Edith H. Lounsbery"
Mount: Thin cream mat with cream
intermediate mount, 254 x 203 mm.
Verso: In pencil: "Portrait of Hubert
Vos (Dutch Painter)/Property of E. H.
Lounsbery/ 12 East 35th St/New York";
FBJ label: 57.
NMAH-C-77.92.62A

99. *Portrait of Hubert Vos, Dutch Painter,*
ca. 1900
Platinum, 144 x 74 mm.
In pencil, l.r.: "Edith H. Lounsbery"
Mount: Cream paper; 261 x 197 mm.
Verso: In pencil: "Portrait of Hubert
Vos/Dutch Painter/12 E. 35/N.Y."; FBJ
label: 58.
NMAH-C-77.92.62B

EMILY G. MEW

(May 1863 – ?)

Active in Washington, D.C.

Eager to enter the field of photography, Emily Mew wrote to Frances Benjamin Johnston in November 1894, humbly asking if she might be taken on as a pupil. Though Johnston's response is not known, Mew did later receive technical assistance from Johnston's former teacher Thomas W. Smillie of the Smithsonian Institution and became active professionally around 1898.

When contacted by Johnston for inclusion in her exhibition of American women photographers, Mew considered her work inferior to that of other women and was fearful that it would not "compare favorably." Overcoming her apprehension, Mew sent some prints and for her biography simply stated that she had "no artistic training." In the May 1901 review of the Photo-Club de Paris exhibition in *Le Monde moderne,* Constant Puyo made particular mention of Mew's "very beautiful portrait of a man."

Exhibitions

Congrès International de Photographie, Universal Exposition, Paris, July 1900

"Les Artistes Américaines," Photo-Club de Paris, Paris, January 1901

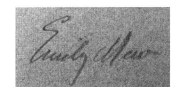

100. *Portrait of E. C. Messer*, ca. 1900
Platinum, 199 x 137 mm.
In pencil, l.l.: "Emily Mew"
Mount: Rembrandt mount,
304 x 253 mm.
Verso: In ink: "Emily Mew/Washington D.C."; FBJ label: 63.
LC-USZC2-5965

101.* [Girl in period dress with headband], ca. 1900
Platinum, 212 x 165 mm.
In pencil, l.l.: "Emily Mew"
Mount: Rembrandt mat,
305 x 253 mm.
Verso: In ink: "Emily Mew/Washington D.C."; FBJ label: 62.
LC-USZC2-5966

102. [Young girl in profile], ca. 1900
Platinum, 158 x 102 mm.
In pencil, l.l.: "Emily Mew"
Mount: Rembrandt mat,
350 x 251 mm.
Verso: In ink: "Emily Mew/Washington D.C."
LC-USZC2-5967

103.* *Prince Pierre Troubetskoy, Painter*, ca. 1900
Platinum, 181 x 153 mm.
In pencil, l.l.: "Emily Mew"
Mount: Rembrandt mat,
350 x 251 mm.
Verso: In ink: "Emily Mew/Washington D.C."; in pencil: "Prince Pierre Troubet-skoy"; FBJ label: 61.
LC-USZC2-5968

104. *Max Wegl*, ca. 1900
Platinum, 120 x 98 mm.
In pencil, l.r.: "Emily Mew/Max Wegl"
Mount: Gray mat, 170 x 125 mm.
LC-USZC2-6107

105. [Woman wearing a bonnet], ca. 1900
Platinum, 140 x 84 mm.
Mount: Rembrandt mat, 300 x 254 mm.
Verso: In pencil: "Hollinger/NY"
LC-USZC2-6108

Mary F. Carpenter Paschall. August 29, 1896. Doylestown, Penn., Mercer Museum, Bucks County Historical Society.

MARY FRANCES CARPENTER PASCHALL (MRS. ALFRED PASCHALL)

(April 1854, Boston – ?)

Active in Doylestown, Pa.

In 1879, Bostonian Mary F. Carpenter married Alfred Paschall, with whom she had one son, Irvin Francis, and moved to Doylestown, Pennsylvania. She took up photography as a "pastime" while recovering from a "severe illness" in 1893. In a letter responding to Johnston's invitation to send work for exhibition, she described her first photographic experience: "One day my husband brought me home a 4 x 5 Hawkeye with developing and printing outfit. We immediately loaded it for action, posed our small son with his bicycle... That evening a closet served as darkroom, the plate was developed and before noon the next day a print made and mounted all according to the little handbook which came with the camera."

"Intensely interested at once," Paschall continued to work in photography "as time, strength, and money (all of this limited) would permit." She reported that she had no training, either technical or artistic and no permanent darkroom—using the bathroom or the kitchen at night.

From 1898 to 1900, Mary Paschall made a collection of photographs of "old buildings, utensils, and processes of the past" for the Bucks County Historical Society, which her husband helped to found. The Mercer Museum of the Bucks County Historical Society still holds many of these photographs. She also treated other subjects—floral images, landscapes and genre scenes—also took photographs to illustrate her husband's newspaper, the *Bucks County Intelligencer*. Preferring sharply focused images to the work of the Pictorialists, Paschall wrote to Johnston: "I am very old fashioned in my ideas as I cannot get used to the modern way of little or no focus." Paschall stayed active in photography after her husband died in 1912.

Affiliations

Lenape Valley Photographic Club, Pa.

Exhibitions

Congrès International de Photographie, Universal Exposition, Paris, July 1900

"Les Artistes Américaines," Photo-Club de Paris, Paris, January 1901

106.* *An Old Porch*, ca. 1900
Platinum, 115 x 159 mm.
Mount: Dark gray board, 253 x 304 mm.
Verso: In pencil, u.r.: "M. F. C. Pascall"; u.l.: "An Old Porch"; FBJ label: 73.
LC-USZC2-5970

107. *Hawthornes*, ca. 1900
Platinum, 115 x 156 mm.
Mount: Gray board, 254 x 340 mm.
Verso: In pencil, u.r.: "M. F. C. Pascall"; u.l.: "Hawthornes"
LC-USZC2-5971

108.* *Milkweed*, ca. 1900
Platinum, 162 x 114 mm.
Mount: Gray board, 304 x 253 mm.
Verso: In pencil, u.r.: "M. F. C. Paschall";
u.l.: "Mrs. Alfred/Paschall/Doylestown P.A."; FBJ label: 72.
LC-USZC2-5972

109.* *Picking Geese*, ca. 1900
Platinum, 114 x 165 mm.
Mount: Gray board, 252 x 303 mm.
FBJ label: 74.
LC-USZC2-5973

110. *Poke Berry*, ca. 1900
Platinum, 115 x 165 mm.
Mount: Thin black mat, 253 x 305 mm.
Verso: In pencil, u.l.: "Poke Berry"; u.r.: "M. F. C. Paschall"
NMAH-C-77.92.26

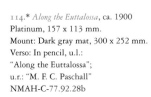

111. *Thomas Tucker*, ca. 1900
Platinum, 95 x 120 mm.
Mount: Gray board, 176 x 227 mm.
Verso: In pencil, u.l.: "Thomas Tucker"; u.r." M. F. C. Paschall"
NMAH-C-77.92.27

112. *A Few Chestnuts*, ca. 1900
Platinum, 106 x 150 mm.
Mount: Gray board, 252 x 302 mm.
Verso: In pencil, u.l.: "A Few Chestnuts"; u.r. "M. F. C. Paschall"
NMAH-C-77.92.28

113.* *An April Snow*, ca. 1900
Platinum, 113 x 164 mm.
Mount: Thin black mat, 254 x 305 mm.
Verso: In pencil, u.l.: "An April Snow"; u.r.: "M. F. C. Paschall"
NMAH-C-77.92.28a

114.* *Along the Euttalossa*, ca. 1900
Platinum, 157 x 113 mm.
Mount: Dark gray mat, 300 x 252 mm.
Verso: In pencil, u.l.: "Along the Euttalossa"; u.r.: "M. F. C. Paschall"
NMAH-C-77.92.28b

ANNE K. PILSBURY

(1875, Maine – ?)

Active in Boston, Mass.
Studio: 248 Boylston Street, Boston (1899–1903)

Although she was an active professional photographer, Anne K. Pilsbury also participated in amateur art circles and was a member of the Society of Arts and Crafts, Boston, from 1901 to 1904. From 1899 to 1903, she operated a portrait studio at 248 Boylston Street in Boston. Pilsbury exhibited photographs at many prestigious salons and exhibitions, including the Second Philadelphia Photographic Salon in 1899 and F. Holland Day's "New School of American Photography," and received praise from critics at home and abroad. In 1904, Pilsbury moved to Washington, D.C., after which time there are no further records of her photographic activity.

Affiliations
Society of Arts and Crafts, Boston

Exhibitions
First Annual Exhibition, Society of Arts and Crafts, Boston, April 1899

Third Philadelphia Photographic Salon, Pennsylvania Academy of the Fine Arts, Philadelphia, October 1900

Eighth Annual Exhibition of the Photographic Salon, The Linked Ring, Dudley Gallery, London, September 1900

"New School of American Photography," Royal Photographic Society, London, October 1900

Third Annual Salon and Exhibition, Carnegie Art Galleries, Pittsburgh, May 1900

Congrès International de Photographie, Universal Exposition, Paris, July 1900

"Les Artistes Américaines," Photo-Club de Paris, Paris, January 1901

Ninth Annual Exhibition of the Photographic Salon, The Linked Ring, Dudley Gallery, London, September 1901

Fourth Philadelphia Photographic Salon, Pennsylvania Academy of the Fine Arts, Philadelphia, October 1901

Tenth Annual Exhibition of the Photographic Salon, The Linked Ring, Dudley Gallery, London, September 1902

First American Photographic Salon at New York, Clausen Galleries, New York, April 1904

115.* [Bearded man in spectacles reading a newspaper], ca. 1900
Platinum, 153 x 119 mm.
Mount: Dark brown with charcoal and black intermediate mounts, 279 x 201 mm.
Verso: FBJ label: 64.
LC-USZC2-5974

116.* [Portrait of a boy in a round hat], ca. 1900
Platinum, 164 x 115 mm.
In pencil on photo, l.l.: "A.P./"
Mount: Thick dark gray mat with black intermediate mount, 278 x 203 mm.
Verso: FBJ label: 70.
LC-USZC2-5975

117. [Young girl in white dress, seated and holding teacup and saucer], ca. 1900
Platinum, 170 x 120 mm.
In pencil, l.l.: "A.P./"
Mount: Thick dark gray mat with black intermediate mount, 280 x 120 mm.
Verso: FBJ label: 69.
LC-USZC2-5976

118. [Young girl in a white off-the-shoulder dress with a ribbon in her hair], ca. 1900
Platinum, 170 x 120 mm.
In pencil on photo, l.l.: "Anne Pilsbury/"
Mount: Thick gray mat with black surround, 273 x 206 mm.
Verso: FBJ label: 71.
LC-USZC2-6036

F. C. Clark. *Virginia M. Prall,*
in *The Delineator* (Oct. 1901), p. 78.

VIRGINIA M. PRALL

(May 1866, Tennessee – 1945?)

Active in Washington, D.C.

Virginia M. Prall had less than two years experience when she was contacted by Johnston for her Parisian exhibition, yet she had already been commended for her portrayals of religious subjects and genre studies. A letter responding to Johnston in 1900 reveals an enthusiasm for her newfound love of photography:: "My very first photographic experience was only one year and eight months ago, when in a spirit of fun and on a wager that I would have no success, I undertook to take a group of family portraits in the house, with a borrowed Kodak, being entirely unfamiliar with any-thing in connection with it. I succeeded fairly well and won the wager."

Though Prall's art training only included a few drawing lessons as a girl, her technical training came from what experience taught her "from day to day." Soon after beginning, she purchased a professional 8 x 10 camera and a Voigtlander Euryscope. She took great care with her photographs and "never let a print be made from my negatives by any one but [herself]" and did her own retouching. For her costume pieces, Prall often used her sister, niece, and other family members for models.

By 1900, she had exhibited in a total of ten salons and that year would be honored with a solo exhibition at the New York Camera Club in 1899, and would be included in both Johnston's exhibition of American women photographers and F. Holland Day's "New School of American Photography." Sadakichi Hartmann was critical of her work, particularly the religious images, describing it as "undeveloped" despite her "decided talent." However, another critic praised her religious images which he found "for composition and effects of light and shade as well as in point of imaginative beauty, [were] entitled to high artistic rank."

Affiliations

Capital Camera Club, Washington, D.C.

New York Camera Club

Exhibitions

Second Annual International Salon and Exhibition, Carnegie Art Galleries, Pittsburgh, February 1899

Eighth Annual Exhibition, Capital Camera Club, Washington, D.C., May 1899

Second Philadelphia Photographic Salon, Pennsylvania Academy of the Fine Arts, Philadelphia, October 1899

Photographic Salon, American Institute, New York, December 1899

Congrès International de Photographie, Exposition Universelle, Paris, July 1900

"New School of American Photography," Royal Photographic Society, London, October 1900

Chicago Photographic Salon of 1900, Art Institute of Chicago, Chicago, April 1900

Third Annual Salon and Exhibition, Carnegie Art Galleries, Pittsburgh, May 1900

"New School of American Photography," Royal Photographic Society, London, October 1900

"Virginia M. Prall," Camera Club of New York, New York, November 1900

"Les Artistes Américaines," Photo-Club de Paris, Paris, January 1901

"New School of American Photography," Photo-Club de Paris, Paris, February 1901

Second Chicago Photographic Salon, Art Institute of Chicago, Chicago, October 1901

Fourth Philadelphia Photographic Salon, The Pennsylvania Academy of the Fine Arts, Philadelphia, November 1901

Third Chicago Photographic Salon, Art Institute of Chicago, Chicago, December 1902

Thirteenth Annual Exhibition of the Capital Camera Club, Washington, D.C., May 1904

Second American Salon, Metropolitan Camera Club of New York, New York, December 1905

Second American Photographic Salon, Art Institute of Chicago, Chicago, March 1906

"Exhibition of Photographs—The Work of Women Photographers of Camera Club of Hartford," Hartford, Conn., April 1906

Thirty-Second Annual Photographers Association of America, Philadelphia, July 1912

119.* [Portrait of a woman in a floral dress adorned with diamond brooches and bows], ca. 1900
Platinum, 213 x 164 mm.
Mount: Thick Rembrandt mount, 427 x 351 mm.
LC-USZC2-5977

120.* [Two girls wearing white dresses and dark stockings reading a book], ca. 1900
Platinum, 235 x 143 mm.
Mount: Thick black paper with black intermediate mount, 325 x 213 mm.
Verso: In pencil: "Miss Prall"
LC-USZC2-5978

121.* *From Old Virginia*, ca. 1900
Platinum, 241 x 191 mm.
Mount: Black board, 375 x 275 mm.
Verso: In pencil partially cut off:
"…irginia Prall"; FBJ label: 81._
LC-USZC2-5979

122. [Woman descending the stairs
with her white dog], ca. 1900
Platinum, 207 x 104 mm.
In pencil, l.r.: "…ss Pra…"
Mount: Green paper, 222 x 131 mm.
Verso: FBJ label: 76.
LC-USZC2-5980

123. [Seated woman petting her white
dog], ca. 1900
Platinum, 199 x 149 mm.
Mount: Thick black with black inter-
mediate mount, 284 x 230 mm.
Verso: In pencil: "Miss Prall"
LC-USZC2-6112

ADDIE KILBURN ROBINSON

(October 1860, New Hampshire – January 29, 1935, Belmont, Mass.)

Active in Boston, Mass.
Studio: 729 Boylston Street, Boston (1900)
        727 Boylston Street, Boston (1901)

E. F. Hall. *Addie Kilburn Robinson*,
in *Photo-Era* (Aug. 1899), p. 388.

Although her father was a photographer and surrounded himself with artist friends, professional photographer Addie Kilburn Robinson was allowed no formal art training. By her own account, her initial
training was simply an "unconscious adoption of methods" witnessed in her father's studio.

In 1897, after her sons (Edward K. and Frank O.) had grown up, and with her husband's "cordial
co-operation," Robinson spent seven weeks in the studio of Pictorialist E. F. Hall (1857–1910), in Buffalo. She received both technical and business training and benefited from Hall's "unsparing criticism."
The death of her husband, Benjamin Frank Robinson, the following year altered her plans for a "gradual
entrance into the actual business world of picture taking" and compelled her to open a professional portrait studio, in Melrose, Massachusetts. She soon outgrew the space and in the spring of 1899 opened a
larger studio on Boylston Street in Boston. By virtue of the "very efficient assistance" Robinson
employed, she was free to attend to her favorite aspect of photography: "operating."

Less than a year after she opened her studio, a profile was published in *Photo-Era* heralding Robinson's successful portraits of young women and children. The "artistic and lifelike results" of her portraits
were quickly recognized, as was her process for making portrait photographic miniatures on porcelain.
She disavowed "theatrical methods," preferring methods of the "greatest simplicity" to obtain a simple,
graceful pose of the head.

Robinson was a member of the Corliss Art and Camera Club in Newburyport, Massachusetts. A
review of the Corliss's 1900 annual exhibition praises the overall improvement in the quality of work
presented, yet mentions that no group of photographs equaled Robinson's "London Heads" series exhibited the previous year.

In addition to sending examples of her own work to Johnston, Robinson sent three 8 x 10 portraits
made by her assistant, Fr[?]y Gercher. These photographs, which bear the inscription "From the Studio
of Addie Kilburn Robinson" on the back, were not included in the Paris exhibition.

Exhibitions
Corliss Art and Camera Club, Newburyport,
Mass., 1899

Corliss Art and Camera Club, Newburyport,
Mass., 1900

Congrès International de Photographie,
Universal Exposition, Paris, July 1900

"Les Artistes Américaines," Photo-Club de Paris,
Paris, January 1901

124. *Geraldine Farrar*, 1897
Platinum, 166 x 119 mm.
Mount: Thick white mat,
353 x 278 mm.
Verso: In pencil: "Geraldine Farrar
189?"; FBJ label: 85.; blank label.
LC-USZC2-6039

125.* *Geraldine Farrar*, 1898
Platinum, 164 x 116 mm.
In ink on photo: "Copyrighted/1898
By/Addie K. Robinson."
Mount: Thick cream paper,
354 x 279 mm.
Verso: FBJ label: 84.
LC-USZC2-6040

126. [Portrait of little girl in frilly hat],
ca. 1900
Platinum, 160 x 110 mm.
Mount: Thick white mat,
350 x 280 mm.
Verso: In pencil: "Photographed by
Addie Kilburn Robinson/Boston, Mass.
U.S.A."
LC-USZC2-6041

127. [Little girl with fair, wavy hair],
ca. 1900
Platinum, 160 x 110 mm.
Mount: Thick white mat,
350 x 280 mm.
Verso: In pencil: "Photographed
by/Addie Kilburn Robinson/Boston,
Mass. U.S.A."
LC-USZC2-6042

128. F. Gercher (?)
[Portrait of woman wearing pearls and
an off-the-shoulder dress], ca. 1900
Platinum, 240 x 180 mm.
Mount: Embossed thick white paper
with cream intermediate mount,
440 x 380 mm.
Verso: In pencil: "From the studio
of/Addie Kilburn Robinson/Boston,
Mass. U.S.A."
LC-USZC2-6043

129. F. Gercher (?)
[Portrait of man with gray mustache
and beard, hair parted down the middle],
ca. 1900
Platinum, 240 x 180 mm.
Mount: Embossed thick white paper
with cream intermediate mount,
440 x 380 mm.
Verso: In pencil: "From the studio
of/Addie Kilburn Robinson/Boston,
Mass. U.S.A."
LC-USZC2-6044

130. F. Gercher (?)
*Vladimir Vasilevich Stasov, Art & Music
Historian*, ca. 1900
Platinum, 240 x 180 mm.
Mount: Embossed thick white paper
with cream intermediate mount,
440 x 380 mm.
Verso: In pencil: "From the studio
of/Addie Kilburn Robinson/Boston,
Mass. U.S.A."
LC-USZC2-6132

Mary Townsend Sharples Schäffer, in Mary T. S. Schäffer, *Old Indian Trails of the Canadian Rockies* (New York: G. P. Putnam's sons, 1912).

Exhibitions

Congrès International de Photographie, Universal Exposition, Paris, July 1900

"Les Artistes Américaines," Photo-Club de Paris, Paris, January 1901

Exhibition of Prints by Members of the Photographic Society of Philadelphia, Camera Club of New York, New York, April 1901

Canadian Exhibit, Congress of Alpinism, Monaco, 1920

MARY TOWNSEND SHARPLES SCHÄFFER

(1861, West Chester, Pa. – 1939, ?)

Active in Philadelphia, Pa.

Born to moderately wealthy Quaker parents in West Chester, Pennsylvania, Mary Townsend Sharples Schäffer is best known for her exploration of the Canadian Rockies. In a lengthy letter to Johnston, Schäffer tells the story of how she "turned from the brush to the camera" during a period when she tended to a member of her household confined with a long illness: "An idea suddenly developed... To photograph some of the invalid's beautiful flowers appealed to my long training with the brush. I knew no more about lenses, stops, shutters, plates, or any other part of the instrument, than what I had heard from daily conversation."

The letter also reveals Schäffer's awareness of the evolving styles of photography. She described the pictures enclosed for exhibition as made "with the old fashioned idea that a good photo was to be as near an absolute presentation of the object as possible, clear & clean & sharp & all study of light & shade was but to enhance this condition." She and her husband, Dr. Charles Schäffer, pursued a mutual interest in botany and the natural sciences. Photography was crucial to their botanical work—"the camera help[ed] materially to classify" and allowed them to bring "much valuable material" from their summer explorations of the Canadian Rockies.

By 1900, Schäffer's interest in photography seemed to have grown beyond the purely documentary, as she expressed the desire to "learn new tricks in developing, printing, etc." She also addressed the debate raging in photographic circles with regard to her own work: "As my work lies in realism rather than idealism, it seems scarce fair to call them pictures but records of objects & places, two separate schools. Will the modern photographer blend the two, or must one go to the wall & disappear utterly? Let there be a happy tempering of both & then we may have reached art in photography."

After her husband's death in 1903, Schäffer charted new territory in the Rockies. She wrote several articles on the topic for the *Bulletin of the Geographical Society of Philadelphia* and *The Canadian Alpine Journal*. In 1905, she traveled to Asia, making photographic prints and slides of Formosa, Taiwan and Japan. In 1907, using her late husband's data and her own drawings and photographs, she completed *Alpine Flora of the Canadian Rocky Mountains*. In 1913, she settled in Banff and continued to work in the Canadian wilderness. She later married mountain guide William Warren.

131. *Epigaea Refiens—Trailing Arbutus, Botanical Study*, ca. 1900
Platinum, 118 x 150 mm.
In pencil on mount, l.r.: "Mrs. Chas. Schäffer"
Mount: Gray mat with a white intermediate mount, 203 x 254 mm.
NMAH-C-77.92.29

132.* *La France Rose, Sprinkled with Water*, ca. 1900
Platinum, 151 x 105 mm.
In pencil, l.r.: "Mrs. Chas. Schäffer"
Mount: Gray mat, 253 x 203 mm.
Verso: In ink: "La France Rose/Sprinkled with water"
NMAH-C-77.92.30

133.* *Chalk Mushroom from the Selkirk Mountains of Canada*, ca. 1900
Platinum, 114 x 166 mm.
In pencil, l.r.: "Mrs. Chas Schäffer"
Mount: Dark gray mat white intermediate mount, 202 x 253 mm.
Verso: In ink: "Chalk mushroom from the Selkirk Mountains of Canada";
FBJ label: 87.
NMAH-C-77.92.31

134. *La France Rose. Indoor Study*, ca. 1900
Platinum, 169 x 118 mm.
In pencil, l.r.: "Mrs. Chas. Schäffer"
Mount: Dark gray mat, 253 x 203 mm.
Verso: In ink: "La France Rose. Indoor Study."
NMAH-C-77.92.32

135. *Sedum Latifolium*, ca. 1900
Platinum, 110 x 167 mm.
In pencil on mount, l.r.: "Mrs. Chas.
Schäffer"
Mount: Gray mat, 203 x 254 mm.
Verso: In ink: "'Sedum latifolium'/
Taken for botanical study/in the Rocky
Mountains of/Canada"; FBJ label: 88.
NMAH-C-77.92.33

136.* *Mount Sir Ronald*, ca. 1900
Platinum, 162 x 102 mm.
In pencil, l.r.: "Mrs. Chas. Schäffer"
Mount: Dark gray mat, 254 x 202 mm.
Verso: In ink: "Mount Sir Ronald. The
Matterhorn of America, in the Canadian
Rockies. Height 10646 ft Taken from
an elevation of 6000 ft"
NMAH-C-77.92.34

137. *Lake Marion in the Canadian
Rockies*, ca. 1900
Platinum, 167 x 87 mm.
In pencil, l.r.: "Mrs. Chas. Schäffer"
Mount: Dark gray mat with white
intermediate mount, 253 x 204 mm.
Verso: In ink: "Lake Marion in the
Canadian Rockies./5000 ft above the sea."
NMAH-C-77.92.35

138. *Cornus Florida*, ca. 1900
Platinum, 159 x 114 mm.
In pencil, l.r.: "Mrs. Chas. Schäffer"
Mount: Dark gray mat with white
intermediate mount, 253 x 203 mm.
Verso: In ink: "Cornus Florida 'dog-wood
tree.' Botanical study."
NMAH-C-77.92.36

139.* *Easter Morning*, ca. 1900
Platinum, 145 x 102 mm.
In pencil: "Mrs. Chas. Schäffer"
Mount: Dark gray mat, 253 x 203 mm.
Verso: In ink: "Calla lillies. / Easter
Morning."
NMAH-C-77.92.37

SARAH CARLISLE CHOATE SEARS (MRS. J. M. SEARS)

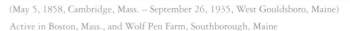

(May 5, 1858, Cambridge, Mass. – September 26, 1935, West Gouldsboro, Maine)

Active in Boston, Mass., and Wolf Pen Farm, Southborough, Maine

Gertrude Käsebier. *Sarah Carlisle Choate Sears*.
(Included in Frances B. Johnston's exhibition
under the title *Le Collier de perles*.)
Private collection.

Sarah Choate Sears, née Sarah Carlisle Choate, was the daughter of Charles Francis and Elizabeth Carlisle Choate and a prominent member of Boston society. In 1877, she married real estate magnate Joshua Montgomery Sears (d. 1905), with whom she had two children: Helen and Joshua Montgomery Sears. While a student at the Cowles Art School and the School of the Museum of Fine Arts, Boston, in the mid-1870s, Sears studied art with Ross Turner, Joseph DeCamp, Dennis Miller Bunker, Edmund C. Tarbell and George De Forest Brush. A member of both the New York and Boston watercolor clubs, and the Society of Arts and Crafts, Boston, she was an accomplished watercolorist who won prizes at the World's Columbian Exposition in Chicago (1893), the Universal Exposition in Paris (1900), the Pan-American Exposition in Buffalo (1901) and the Louisiana Purchase Exposition in St. Louis (1904). Sears also collected paintings by contemporaries John Singer Sargent, Mary Cassatt, John La Farge and Edgar Degas, and later watercolors by John Marin, Alfred Henry Maurer and Charles Demuth.

Sears entered the field of photography "only for an amusement" in the 1890s, yet soon began to participate in salons. She joined the Boston Camera Club in 1892, where she was honored with a solo exhibition in 1899. A review in *Photo-Era* likened her photographs to "filmy wash drawings laid in as with a thought, and so delicate as to be destroyed by too rude a breath." In 1900, she was represented in both Johnston's Paris exhibition and Day's exhibition "New School of American Photography." Both included prints of the *Portrait of Mrs. J. W. H.*, which A. L. Coburn noted was "one of the most dignified pieces of composition exhibited, [carrying] with it a conviction regarding its qualities of portraiture seldom surpassed."

An avid supporter of the cause of art photography, Sears developed strong ties with both its leaders, F. Holland Day and Alfred Stieglitz. She encouraged Day to start a national association of Pictorial photographers and secured a permanent exhibition space at the Museum of Fine Arts for a Boston photography salon. This complicated her relationship with Stieglitz, who saw this as a threat to New York's status as the center of art photography. Nonetheless, Sears was elected a fellow of the Photo-Secession in 1903, to which she made several generous financial contributions. In 1904, Sears was elected to the Linked Ring. After her husband's death in 1905, she spent much of the next two years traveling throughout Europe and spent time in Paris with Mary Cassatt and Gertrude Stein. Two of Sears' portraits, *Mary* and *Miss Julia Ward Howe,* appeared in *Camera Work* in April 1907, but shortly thereafter Sears shifted her attention primarily to working in watercolor and collecting art.

Exhibitions

Fifth Annual Joint Exhibition, Boston Camera Club, Boston, May 1892

Tenth Annual Composition Exhibition, Boston Camera Club, Boston, 1898

Ausstellung für künstlerische Photographie, Berlin, February 1899

"Portrait Photographs by Mrs. J. Montgomery Sears," Boston Camera Club, Boston, February 1899

First Annual Exhibition, Society of Arts and Crafts, Boston, April 1899

Second Philadelphia Photographic Salon, Pennsylvania Academy of the Fine Arts, Philadelphia, October 1899

Photographic Salon, American Institute, New York, December 1899

"Exhibition of the Massachusetts Pictures Shown at the Three Photographic Salons of 1899: London, Philadelphia, and New York," Boston Camera Club, Boston, February 1900

Twelfth Annual Club Exhibition, Boston Camera Club, Boston, April 1900

Congrès International de Photographie, Universal Exposition, Paris, July 1900

"New School of American Photography," Royal Photographic Society, London, October 1900

Boston Camera Club at the Camera Club of New York, New York, December 1900

Glasgow International Exhibition, Glasgow, 1901

"Les Artistes Américaines," Photo-Club de Paris, Paris, January 1901

"New School of American Photography," Photo-Club de Paris, February 1901

Second Chicago Photographic Salon, Art Institute of Chicago, Chicago, October 1901

Tenth Annual Photographic Exhibition of the Photographic Salon, The Linked Ring, Dudley Gallery, London, September 1902

Second San Francisco Photographic Salon, San Francisco, January 1902

Eleventh Annual Photographic Exhibition of the Photographic Salon, The Linked Ring, Dudley Gallery, London, September 1903

City of Bradford Exhibition, Bradford, England, 1904

"A Collection of American Pictorial Photographers," Corcoran Art Galleries, Washington, D.C., January 1904

"A Collection of American Pictorial Photographers," Carnegie Art Galleries, Pittsburgh, February 1904

Affiliations

Boston Camera Club, Boston

Society of Arts and Crafts, Boston

Juror

Seventh Annual Exhibition, Old Cambridge Photographic Club, Cambridge, Mass., March 1900

Wiener Photo Club, Vienna, April 1904

Twelfth Annual Photographic Exhibition of the Photographic Salon, The Linked Ring, Dudley Gallery, London, September 1904

Internationale Ausstellung ausgewählter künstlerischer Photographien, Vienna, February 1905

Wiener Photo Club, Vienna, April 1905

Lewis and Clark Exposition, Portland, Oregon, June 1905

Second Annual Exhibition of Photographs, Worcester Art Museum, Worcester, Mass., November 1905

Members' Work, Gallery of the Photo-Secession, New York, November 1905

"An Exhibition of Photographs Arranged by the Photo-Secession," Pennsylvania Academy of the Fine Arts, Philadelphia, April 1906

Canadian Pictorialist Exhibition, Montreal, November 1907

International Exhibition of Pictorial Photography, National Arts Club, New York City, February 1909

140. *Julia Ward Howe,*
before February 1899
Platinum, 243 x 190 mm.
Mount: Thick dark gray mat, 382 x 295 mm.
Verso: FBJ label: 95. 98.
LC-USZC2-6046

141. [Woman wearing a veil], ca. 1900
Platinum, 235 x 179 mm.
Mount: Gray paper, 380 x 305 mm.
Verso: FBJ label: 94. 99.; on label: "Mrs. J. S. Sears./12 Arlington St./Boston./Mass."
NMAH-C-77.92.38

142. [Young girl], ca. 1900
Platinum, 229 x 178 mm.
Mount: Gray paper, 380 x 310 mm.
Verso: FBJ label: 96. 97.
NMAH-C-77.92.57

143. [Young girl seated in a carved wooden chair with a young man kneeling near her], ca. 1900
Platinum, 240 x 190 mm.
Mount: Gray paper, 380 x 305 mm.
Verso: In pencil: "Mrs. Sears?"
NMAH-C-77.92.59

144. [Profile portrait of a young man],
ca. 1900
Platinum, 245 x 190 mm.
Mount: Gray paper, 380 x 305 mm.
NMAH-C-77.92.60

145. [Profile portrait of Julia Ward
Howe], before February 1899
Platinum, 240 x 187 mm.
Mount: Gray paper, 383 x 305 mm.
Verso: FBJ label: ~~93~~. 100.; on label:
"Mrs. J. S. Sears./12 Arlington
St./Boston./Mass."
NMAH-C-77.92.60A

THE MISSES SELBY

EMILY SELBY
(April 1868, Great Britain – 1909?, New York)

LILLIAN SELBY
(December 1866, Great Britain – ?, New York)

Active in New York City
Studio: 292 Fifth Avenue, New York (1900–11)
            628 Fifth Avenue, New York (1911–25)
            54 East 57th Street, New York (1933–34)

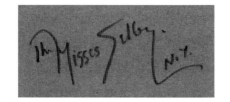

The British-born Selby sisters, Emily and Lillian, were successful portrait photographers, who worked together from about 1895 to 1911, and Lillian Selby continued to work under the business name "The Misses Selby" until 1934. According to Jane C. Gover, Emily and Lillian were seeking an artist's studio in New York when they happened to be offered a photographer's studio with all its equipment. Relying on Emily's business experience and Lillian's degree in science, the sisters established a portrait studio and quickly became well known in Manhattan.

Zaida Ben-Yusuf suggested that Frances Benjamin Johnston contact the Selby sisters for her Paris exhibition. Emily Selby responded to Johnston's invitation on business letterhead, revealing the demands of the Selby studio: "It is impossible for me to say for certain if we could let you have the prints & the little personal sketch by the date you name, as the time is very short & we are constantly busy just now." Selby also felt obliged to explain that she and her sister were English and had only been in the United States "a comparatively short time" and so perhaps should not be included in the exhibition. Ultimately, Johnston must have felt that the Selbys' New York studio work established them as American, as she included four of their photographs in the exhibit. The Selbys were also members of the Photographer's Association of America, with whom they exhibited work in 1901.

As the Misses Selby seldom exhibited their work, reviews are scarce; however, in the special women's issue of the *Bulletin of Photography* of October 18, 1911, critic Professor Miller assessed their photograph, *Some One Coming*. He wrote: "This is an exquisitely beautiful print. The key is very properly kept high ... and the whole thing has been kept pure and delicate as a sympathetic appreciation of the character demands."

146. [Portrait of a young boy standing
in short pants and belted shirt], ca. 1900
Platinum, 156 x 71 mm.
In pencil, l.r.: "The Misses Selby./N.Y."
Mount: White stock mat, 332 x 158 mm.
Verso: In pencil: "May be reproduced."; stamp: "THE
MISSES SELBY,/292 FIFTH Avenue,/BET. 30TH &
31ST Sts,/NEW YORK"; FBJ label: 101.
LC-USZC2-6047

Exhibitions
Congrès International de Photographie,
Universal Exposition, Paris, July 1900
Boston Camera Club at the Camera Club
of New York, New York, December 1900

"Les Artistes Américaines," Photo-Club de Paris,
Paris, January 1901
Twenty-First Annual Photographers Association
of America Convention Exhibition, Detroit,
August 1901

147.* [Portrait of woman in walking dress holding a fur muffler], ca. 1900
Platinum, 243 x 118 mm.
In white, l.r.: "The Misses Selby/N.Y."
Mount: Dark gray mat, 431 x 229 mm.
Verso: FBJ label: 102.
LC-USZC2-6048

148. [Profile portrait of a woman seated in chair, facing left with hands on her knees], ca. 1900
Platinum, 158 x 103 mm.
In pencil, l.l.: "The Misses Selby./N.Y."
Mount: Thick gray mat, 355 x 273 mm.
Verso: FBJ label: 103.
LC-USZC2-6049

149.* [Portrait of a young girl with tousled hair], ca. 1900
Platinum, 206 x 187 mm.
In pencil, l.r.: "The Misses Selby N.Y."
Mount: Thick white paper, 447 x 365 mm.
Verso: Stamp: "The Misses Selby/292 FIFTH Avenue,/BET. 30TH & 31ST STS./NEW YORK"; FBJ label: 104.
LC-USZC2-6050

150.* [Old woman reading a book], ca. 1900
Platinum, 157 x 115 mm.
In pencil, l.r.: "The Misses Selby/N.Y."
Mount: Cream mat, 344 x 261 mm.
Verso: In pencil: "NOT to be reproduced.";
stamp: "THE MISSES SELBY,/292 FIFITH Avenue,/BET. 30TH & 31ST STS./NEW YORK"
LC-USZC2-6121

VIRGINIA GUILD SHARP

(May 25, 1857, Bangor, Maine – July 6, 1946, Nantucket, Mass.)
Active in Roxbury, Nantucket, Mass., and Philadelphia, Penn.

Virginia Sharp moved from Maine to Nantucket, Massachusetts, with her mother and sister. There she met Dr. Benjamin Sharp, a prominent philanthropist from Philadelphia, whom she married in 1881. The Sharps traveled extensively abroad and maintained homes in Philadelphia, Nantucket, and Roxbury, Massachusetts, frequently hosting charitable and cultural events.

Virginia Sharp studied at the Académie Julian in Paris during two winters and with Eastman Johnson at the Museum of Fine Arts in Boston for three years, but as she wrote to Johnston in 1900, "The care of a family of children put a stop to all art." A shortage of free time led Sharp to pick up the camera "to satisfy the longing I had to do something in the art line." She specialized in portrait photography, and often chose children as sitters. Photography was an interest she shared with her husband. Both Sharps exhibited work in the First Chicago Salon (1900), the Third Philadelphia Photographic Salon (1901), and the Members' Exhibition of the Photographic Society of Philadelphia at the Camera Club of New York (1901).

Head of a Young Girl by Virginia Sharp won a blue ribbon at the Chicago Salon of 1900 and was the first photograph purchased by the Art Institute for its permanent collection. Fellow Philadelphian Eva L. Watson, upon hearing the news of the purchase, wrote to Sharp: "This marks an epoch in the history of photography." Chicago photographer William Dyer congratulated Sharp on the purchase, "a veritable triumph for our art."

Virginia Guild Sharp.
Private collection.

Affiliations
Philadelphia Photographic Society, Philadelphia

Exhibitions
First Philadelphia Photographic Salon, Pennsylvania Academy of the Fine Arts, Philadelphia, October 1898

Chicago Photographic Salon of 1900, Art Institute of Chicago, Chicago, April 1900

Congrès International de Photographie, Universal Exposition, Paris, July 1900

Third Philadelphia Photographic Salon, Pennsylvania Academy of the Fine Arts, Philadelphia, October 1900

"Les Artistes Américaines," Photo-Club de Paris, Paris, January 1901

Photographic Society of Philadelphia at the Camera Club of New York, New York City, April 1901

Fourth Philadelphia Photographic Salon, Pennsylvania Academy of the Fine Arts, Philadelphia, November 1901

Third Chicago Photographic Salon, Art Institute of Chicago, Chicago, December 1902

First Minneapolis Photographic Salon, Minneapolis, 1903

ALTA BELLE SNIFF

(November 1874, Ohio – ?)

Active in Columbus, Ohio

Studio: 43 S. High Street, Columbus (1900–4)
      515 East Broad, Columbus (1904–5)
      1208 Harrison Building, Columbus (1905–6)
      49 North High, Columbus (1906–7)
      76 North High, Columbus (1908–9)

Exhibitions

American Institute of the City of New York, Photographic Section, National Academy of Design, September 1898

Congrès International de Photographie, Universal Exposition, Paris, July 1900

"Les Artistes Américaines," Photo-Club de Paris, Paris, January 1901

Alta Belle Sniff owned and operated a prominent portrait studio in Columbus, Ohio, for ten years. She made her first attempts at photography in 1896. She purchased a 4 x 5 outfit and studied photographic chemistry with Dr. L. M. Early. She soon discovered that she could do better with portrait photography than with landscape, thereby finding her future profession. In the summer of 1899, Sniff opened a studio with "no previous experience under a skylight except two weeks with James Inglis at Chicago." One year later, she wrote to Johnston, enthusiastic about her own accomplishments and about the possibilities for women in the photography business: "I consider the field of photography very large and comparatively unworked, as a profession for women." With no formal art training, she attempted to capture "a pleasing likeness, best lines, and some of the personality of the subject," and thought it "better to sacrifice some technical point in order to catch some of the real character."

Johnston noted that Sniff's studio, which employed two women assistants and charged the highest prices in town, was doing "the best work" in Columbus. Sniff was active professionally until at least 1909 or 1910, after which time her occupation changes to "artist" in the Columbus city directory, which also indicates that Sniff lived with her father, Bennett, her sister, Anna, and other family members in Columbus until 1910–11.

151. [Portrait of a bearded man], ca. 1900
Platinum, oval: 87 x 125 mm.
In pencil, l.r.: "Alta Belle Sniff/1900/Columbus Ohio"
Mount: Thin Rembrandt mount, 203 x 252 mm.
NMAH-C-77.92.50

152. [Portrait of a young woman in a white dress], ca. 1900
Platinum, 110 x 168 mm.
In pencil, l.r.: "Alta Belle Sniff/Columbus Ohio"
Mount: Thin Rembrandt mount, 278 x 354 mm.
NMAH-C-77.92.51

153.* [Boy with suspenders], ca. 1900
Toned platinum, 145 x 94 mm.
In pencil, l.r.: "Alta Belle Sniff/Columbus Ohio"
Mount: Thin Rembrandt mount, 253 x 203 mm.
NMAH-C-77.92.52

154. [Portrait of a man with mustache in a tuxedo], ca. 1900
Platinum, oval: 87 x 127 mm.
In pencil, l.r.: "Alta Belle Sniff/1900 Columbus Ohio"
Mount: Thin Rembrandt mount, 204 x 254 mm.
NMAH-C-77.92.53

EMA SPENCER

(1857, Brownsville, Ohio – August 30, 1941, Newark, Ohio)

Active in Newark, Ohio

The daughter of Dr. Benjamin F. and Susan Porter Spencer, Ema Spencer was the eldest of three children. In 1827, the well-known and affluent Spencer family founded the *Newark Advocate*, a newspaper for which Spencer would later become the art and theater critic and write a long-running column titled "Aunt Ca'line of the Meltin' Pot." A lifelong passion for the printed word led her to operate a lending library out of her home with her niece and to serve as a trustee of the New York Public Library. After graduation from Newark High School as valedictorian, she attended Shepardson College for Women in Granville, Ohio, and then worked for a time as a schoolteacher.

As a photographer, Spencer operated a studio out of her family home taking informal portraits of local people in domestic settings. She also frequently posed her nieces and nephews outdoors and created costume pieces. Spencer was a founding member of the Newark Camera Club, which began in February 1898 with a charter membership of fifteen representative amateurs of the city. The first exhibition of the Newark Camera Club was held in her home. In 1898, she wrote an article for *Brush and Pencil* which echoed the club's "universally recognized" principle that "mere mechanical processes are entirely subordinate to the higher qualities essential to an artistic picture."

Spencer strongly encouraged the young club member Clarence H. White (1871–1925) and curated a solo exhibition of his work at the Boston Camera Club in 1899. As White's reputation spread, Spencer publicly credited his connections to F. Holland Day and Gertrude Käsebier with helping the Newark Camera Club become more involved with the established centers of artistic photography in Boston and New York.

Spencer enjoyed great success in her own right, winning a silver medal in Turin in 1902 and bronze medals in Germany in 1903 and 1911. She also became a member of Stieglitz's Photo-Secession in 1907, after sending a letter expressing her sympathies with the movement and containing a humble inquiry about applying for membership. Two years later *Girl with a Parasol* was published in *Camera Work*.

Affiliations

Newark Camera Club, founding member, Newark, Ohio

Photo-Secession, New York

Exhibition Curator

"Exhibition of Photographs by Clarence H. White of Newark, Ohio," Boston Camera Club, Boston, December 1899

Exhibitions

First Exhibition of the Newark Camera Club, Newark, Ohio, 1898

Second Philadelphia Photographic Salon, Pennsylvania Academy of the Fine Arts, Philadelphia, October 1899

Exhibition of Photographs by the Newark Camera Club, Newark, Ohio, November 1899

Chicago Photographic Salon of 1900, Art Institute of Chicago, Chicago, April 1900

Third Philadelphia Photographic Salon, Pennsylvania Academy of the Fine Arts, Philadelphia, October 1900

Exhibit of Photographs by the Newark Camera Club, Newark, Ohio, November 1900

Ninth Annual Exhibition of the Photographic Salon, The Linked Ring, Dudley Gallery, London, September 1901

Newark Camera Club at the Camera Club of New York, New York, December 1901

Neunte Internationale Ausstellung von Kunst-Photographien, Hamburg, 1902

Esposizione Internazionale di Fotografie Artistica, American Section, Turin, Italy, 1902

"American Pictorial Photography," National Arts Club, New York, March 1902

Erste Internationale Ausstellung für künstlerische Bildnis-Photo, Wiesbaden, April 1903

Photographische Ausstellung im Park der grossen Künstausstellung, Dresden, May 1904

Fourteenth Annual Exhibition of the Photographic Salon, The Linked Ring, London, 1906

Sixth Annual Exhibition of Photographs, Worcester Art Museum, Worcester, Mass., October 1909

International Exhibition of Pictorial Photography, Albright Art Gallery, Buffalo, November 1909

"An International Exhibition Illustrating the Progress of the Art of Photography," Montross Art Galleries, New York, October 1912

"Ema Spencer," Brooklyn Institute of Arts and Sciences, Brooklyn, 1914

Royal Photographic Society, London, 1914

155. *A Mute Appeal*, ca. 1900
Platinum, 191 x 124 mm.
Monogram in pencil on photo, l.l.: "ES"
Mount: Dark gray mat, 196 x 128 mm.
Verso: In pencil: "A Mute Appeal/Ema Spencer/Newark.Ohio."
LC-USZC2-5981

156. *Child With Apple*, ca. 1900
Platinum, 114 x 65 mm.
Monogram in pencil on photo, l.l.: "ES"
Mount: Gray mat, 116 x 67 mm.
Verso: In pencil: "Child with Apple/Ema Spencer/Newark, Ohio"
LC-USZC2-5982

157. *Dandelions*, ca. 1900
Platinum, 194 x 118 mm.
Monogram in pencil on photo, l.l.: "ES"
Mount: Thin charcoal mat, 198 x 124 mm.
Verso: In pencil: "Dandelions/Ema Spencer/Newark, Ohio"
LC-USZC2-5983

158. *Melody*, ca. 1900
Platinum, 89 x 110 mm.
Monogram in pencil on photo, l.r.: "ES"
Mount: Charcoal mat light gray
intermediate mount, 100 x 98 mm.
Verso: In pencil: "Melody/Ema
Spencer/Newark, Ohio."
LC-USZC2-5984

159. *Young Bacchus*, ca. 1900
Platinum, 261 x 102 mm.
Monogram in pencil on photo, l.r.: "ES"
Mount: Charcoal mat, 211 x 104 mm.
Verso: In pencil: "Young Bacchus/Ema
Spencer/Newark, Ohio."
LC-USZC2-5985

Mary R. Stanbery. *Katharine Sheward Stanbery*, 1901.
Washington, D.C., Library of Congress,
LC-USZC2-5989

MARY R. STANBERY AND KATHARINE SHEWARD STANBERY

Active in Zanesville, Ohio

MARY R. STANBERY (MRS. GEORGE A. STANBERY)
(February 22, 1842, Ohio – June 9, 1906, Ohio)

KATHARINE SHEWARD STANBERY (MRS. LEVI J. BURGESS)
(March 1870, New York – 1928, ?)

Mary R. and her daughter Katharine Sheward Stanbery took up photography together in 1897, beginning as amateurs but aspiring to "something more pretentious." The only child of Mary and George A. Stanbery, superintendent of the American Encaustic Tiling Company, Katharine lived in her parents' home until her marriage to the artist, Levi J. Burgess, around 1909.

In 1897, after just two months of "Kodak work," Katharine wrote to Johnston, asking her to recommend a photography handbook and an amateur photographic journal. Confessing their desire to advance into portrait work, she was "bold enough" to enclose "a few specimens" of their work, asking for Johnston's opinion as to whether they were "fair enough … to warrant further efforts." While the Stanberys were not members of the Newark Camera Club, they were closely associated with it and were "in sympathy with its aims." The club provided an entrée into the eastern centers of photography, particularly New York, where Katharine Stanbery spent time in Zaida Ben-Yusuf's studio. Katharine corresponded for five years with Alfred Stieglitz and became a member of the Photo-Secession in 1904. Mary Stanbery was also a member of the Photo-Secession by 1904, although the exact date of her election is not known. Although the Stanberys collaborated on many of their portraits, they were better known for the individual works.

Early in her photographic career, Katharine authored a technical article on platinum printing for *The Photo-American*. Later, *The Photo-Miniature* published her unpretentious but detailed handbook for amateur photographers, which was illustrated with her own work and offered advice on all aspects of photography, from the general question of "realism vs. suggestion" to the specifics of accurately measuring one's chemicals.

Following the death of her mother in 1906, Katharine thanked Stieglitz for his condolences: "All words of appreciation of her as a woman or as an artist help to keep her very much alive to me, and that is what I want—always to have her … I have let my pictures go, but I mean to take them up again—as much to carry out her life as to satisfy my own instincts." Katharine Stanbery continued to exhibit for six years after her mother's death.

Affiliations
Photo-Secession, New York

Exhibitions
Chicago Photographic Salon of 1900, Art Institute of Chicago, Chicago, April 1900

Third Philadelphia Photographic Salon, Pennsylvania Academy of the Fine Arts, Philadelphia, October 1900

Exhibit of Photographs by the Newark Camera Club, Newark, Ohio, November 1900

Ninth Annual Exhibition of the Photographic Salon, The Linked Ring, Dudley Gallery, London, September 1901

Fourth Philadelphia Photographic Salon, Pennsylvania Academy of the Fine Arts, Philadelphia, November 1901

Newark Camera Club at the Camera Club of New York, New York, December 1901

Fourth Annual Exhibition, Akron Camera Club, Akron, Ohio, 1902

Fourth Denver Photographic Salon, Colorado Camera Club, Denver, March 1903

Eerste Internationale Salon von Kunstfotografie, `s Gravenhage, Holland, 1904

"A Collection of American Pictorial Photographs," Corcoran Art Galleries, Washington, D.C., January 1904

"A Collection of American Pictorial Photographs," Carnegie Art Galleries, Pittsburgh, February 1904

Second Annual Exhibition of Photographs, Worcester Art Museum, Worcester, Mass., November 1905

Members' Work, Gallery of the Photo-Secession, New York, November 1905

Exhibition of Photographic Art, Cincinnati Museum, Cincinnati, 1906

International Exhibition of Pictorial Photography, Laing Art Gallery, Newcastle-upon-Tyne, 1906

Glasgow International Exhibition, Glasgow, 1901

Esposizione Internationale di Fotografie Artistica, American Section, Turin, Italy, 1902

Tenth Annual Exhibition of the Photographic Salon, The Linked Ring, Dudley Gallery, London, September 1902

Thirteenth Annual Exhibition of the Photographic Salon, The Linked Ring, London, 1905

"An Exhibition of Photographs Arranged by the Photo-Secession," Pennsylvania Academy of Fine Arts, Philadelphia, 1906

L'Effort Vᵉ Salon, Paris, 1905

Fourth American Photographic Salon, Worcester Art Museum, Worcester, Mass., November 1907

Fifth Annual Exhibition of Photographs, Worcester Art Museum, Worcester, Mass., October 1908

International Exhibition of Pictorial Photography, National Arts Club, New York, February 1909

International Exhibition of Pictorial Photography, Albright Art Gallery, Buffalo, November 1910

"An Exhibition Illustrating the Progress of the Art of Photography," Montross Art Galleries, New York, October 1912

"An International Exhibition of Pictorial Photography," Ehrick Art Galleries, New York, January 1914

160. Katharine Sheward Stanbery
At the Dawn, 1900
Platinum, 185 x 233 mm.
Verso: In pencil: "Katharine Sheward Stanbery/At the Dawn"
LC-USZC2-5986

161. Katharine Sheward Stanbery
Clarence White, 1900
Platinum, 185 x 233 mm.
In pencil, l.r.: "Katharine Sheward Stanbery 1900."
Mount: Thick gray paper, 456 x 351 mm.
Verso: Label with notation in ink: "No. 6 Portrait of Clarence H. White./Katharine Stanbery./433 Adair Avenue,/Zanesville, Ohio./not for sale"
LC-USZC2-5987

162. Mary R. Stanbery
Good Model, 1901
Platinum, 146 x 199 mm.
In pencil on photo, l.l.: "Mary R. Stanbery 1901"
Mount: Charcoal colored mat, 255 x 350 mm.
Verso: In pencil: "Good Model"
LC-USZC2-5988

163. Mary R. Stanbery
K. S. Stanbery, 1901
Platinum, 136 x 78 mm.
In pencil on photo, l.l.: "Mary R. Stanbery 1901"
Mount: Thick dark gray paper folded in half, 269 x 210 mm.
Verso: Inside of fold, label with notations in ink: "No. 4/Portrait of K.S.Stanbery/Mary R. Stanbery/433 Adair Avenue/Zanesville Ohio"
LC-USZC2-5989

166. Katharine Sheward Stanbery
Harry Pollock, 1901
Kallitype, 145 x 96 mm.
In pencil on photo, l.r.:
"Katharine Stanbery./1901."
Mount: Thick tan paper, 251 x 154 mm.
Verso: In pencil: "Harry Pollock.
Katharine Sheward Stanbery."
LC-USZC2-6052

164. Katharine Sheward Stanbery
Louise, 1900
Platinum, 150 x 43 mm.
Verso: In pencil: "Mary R. Stanbery
1900."; in ink: "Louise"
LC-USZC2-5990

165. Katharine Sheward Stanbery
The Great Dane, ca. 1900
Platinum, 225 x 120 mm.
In pencil on photo, l.l.:
"Katharine Sheward Stanbery. 1900."
Verso: In pencil: "The Great Dane.
Katharine Stanbery"
LC-USZC2-5991

AMELIA C. VAN BUREN

(? – 1917?)

Active in Detroit, Mich., and Philadelphia, Pa.
Studio: Van Husen Building, 106 Miami Avenue, Detroit (1899–1913, renamed Broadway in 1906)

Van Buren was a painter and portrait photographer, who specialized in figure studies and biblical themes, often using her friends and associates to pose as the Virgin Mary and other biblical characters. Trained as a painter, she was a student and friend of Thomas Eakins at the Pennsylvania Academy of the Fine Arts, where she studied around 1885.

After graduating from the Pennsylvania Academy of the Fine Arts, Van Buren worked in photogravures for a time. She then opened a small studio and gallery in the country, from which she tried to sell her paintings. Finding the aesthetic compromises of this business too much to bear, Van Buren staged her "revolt" against these "cheap commercial" endeavors and determined to use photography "solely as a medium through which to express artistic ideas." She and her former classmate Eva Lawrence Watson (later Eva Watson-Schütze) then opened a studio in Atlantic City, New Jersey, which they shared from 1894 to 1896.

Returning to Detroit in 1898, Van Buren soon opened a professional studio, and continued to exhibit in amateur venues. She wrote to Johnston in 1900 that her "road to photography was like so many other's through painting." She confessed that when she was a student of painting, she expressed so much scorn for photographs "that a friend of mine said she always put hers away when she saw me coming." She shared her aspirations with Johnston: "I hope to make portraits to stand with Sargent and Watts and the other masters." Her studio at 106 Miami Avenue was open from 1899 until 1913. From 1913 until 1917, when she disappeared from the city directory, Van Buren was listed as a photographer at her home address.

Thomas Eakins. *Amelia Van Buren*, ca. 1891.
Philadelphia, Pennsylvania Academy of the Fine Arts,
Charles Bregler's Thomas Eakins Collection,
1985.68.2.702.

Exhibitions

First Philadelphia Photographic Salon,
Pennsylvania Academy of the Fine Arts,
Philadelphia, October 1898

Second Annual International Salon and Exhibition,
Carnegie Art Galleries, Pittsburgh, February 1899

Second Philadelphia Photographic Salon,
Pennsylvania Academy of the Fine Arts,
Philadelphia, October 1899

Exhibition of Photographs by the Newark
Camera Club, Newark, Ohio, November 1899

Photographic Salon, American Institute,
New York, December 1899

Loan exhibition, Camera Club of New York, 1899

Chicago Photographic Salon of 1900,
Art Institute of Chicago, Chicago, April 1900

Congrès International de Photographie,
Universal Exposition, Paris, July 1900

New School of American Photography, Royal
Photographic Society, London, October 1900

Third Philadelphia Photographic Salon,
Pennsylvania Academy of the Fine Arts,
Philadelphia, October 1900

Fifth Salon and Exhibition of Amateur
Photography, Cleveland, November 1900

"Les Artistes Américaines," Photo-Club de Paris,
Paris, January 1901

"New School of American Photography,"
Photo-Club de Paris, February 1901

Third Chicago Photographic Salon, Art Institute
of Chicago, Chicago, December 1902

First Minneapolis Photographic Salon,
Minneapolis, 1903

First Annual Salon, Fenton & Stair's Art Gallery,
Cleveland, March 1903

Fourth Chicago Photographic Salon,
Art Institute of Chicago, Chicago, December 1903

Seventh American Photographic Salon,
John Herron Art Institute, Indianapolis,
November 1910

167. *A Rainy Day*, ca. 1900
Platinum, 119 x 166 mm.
In pencil on photo, l.l.: "A. C. Van
Buren"
Mount: Thick tan paper, 326 x 231 mm.
Verso: In pencil: "Miss Van Buren_
Pluta./Miss Watson's/partner?";
FBJ label: 109.
LC-USZC2-5992

168.* [Profile portrait of woman draped
with a veil], ca. 1900
Platinum, 149 x 111 mm.
In pencil, l.r.: "A. C. Van Buren"
Mount: Black mat, 290 x 230 mm.
Verso: In pencil: "A. C. Van Buren";
FBJ label: 106.; in pencil: "A. C. Van
Buren./Detroit"
LC-USZC2-5993

169. [Profile portrait of woman draped
with a veil], ca. 1900
Platinum, 150 x 100 mm.
In pencil, l.r.: "A. C. Van
Buren/Detroit."
Mount: Rembrandt mount,
301 x 250 mm.
Verso: Torn label from the Philadelphia
Photographic Salon with notation in
pencil: "C. Van Buren"
LC-USZC2-6055

170. [Woman with urn], ca. 1900
Salt print or platinum, 149 x 87 mm.
In pencil on photo, l.l.:
"A. C. Van Buren"
Mount: Gray paper, 370 x 263 mm.
Verso: FBJ label: 105.
NMAH-C-77.92.39

171. [Woman looking at herself in a
mirror held in her lap], ca. 1900
Platinum, 166 x 118 mm.
In pencil on photo, l.l.: "A. C. Van
Buren"
Mount: Brown paper, 352 x 253 mm.
Verso: FBJ label: 108.
NMAH-C-77.92.40

172. *Madonna*, ca. 1900
Platinum, 239 x 162 mm.
In pencil on photo, l.l.:
"Amelia/Van Buren"
Mount: Thin Rembrandt,
354 x 280 mm.
Verso: In pencil: "Miss Van Buren"
NMAH-C-77.92.41

173.* *Madonna*, ca. 1900
Platinum, 214 x 142 mm.
In pencil on photo, l.l.:
"A. C. Van Buren"
Mount: Gray paper, 350 x 252 mm.
NMAH-C-77.92.42

174. [Autumn landscape on a canal
or river lined with trees], ca. 1900
Platinum, 117 x 93 mm.
Mount: 355 x 254 mm.
Verso: FBJ label: 110.
NMAH-C-77.92.54

175. [Alice Austin reading], ca. 1900
Platinum, 163 x 113 mm.
In pencil on photo, l.l.:
"A. C. Van Buren"
Mount: Brown paper, 353 x 253 mm.
NMAH-C-77.92.56

EVA GAMBLE WALBORN

(January 1874, Ohio – ?)

Active in Akron, Ohio

Eva Gamble Walborn, a widow who lived with her father William Gamble, was inspired to enter the field of photography by the work of photographer H. W. Minns of Akron, Ohio. Minns was an active member of the Photographers Association of America and took Walborn on as a student in 1898. In a letter to Johnston, Walborn enclosed a portrait of herself made by Minns and credited him with her progress, particularly because he insisted that she "follow the fruit of [her] own mind and feelings in regard to what constitutes a picture."

Although Walborn's exhibition history is short, her work met with critical success. In his review of the First Chicago Salon (1900), William B. Dyer noted that Walborn contributed pictures "of a high order." The following year, Robert Demachy wrote at length of her work included in Johnston's exhibition at the Photo-Club de Paris: "One searches in vain for what could be added or subtracted to this small portrait, so simple and so complete."

H. W. Minns. *Eva Gamble Walborn.*
Washington, D.C., Library of Congress,
LC-USZ-62-85822

Exhibitions

Second Philadelphia Photographic Salon,
Pennsylvania Academy of the Fine Arts,
Philadelphia, October 1899

Case Library Annual Salon, Cleveland, 1900

Congrès International de Photographie,
Universal Exposition, Paris, July 1900

"Les Artistes Américaines," Photo-Club de Paris,
Paris, January 1901

Chicago Photographic Salon of 1900,
Art Institute of Chicago, Chicago, April 1900

Exhibit of Photographs by the Newark Camera
Club, Newark, Ohio, November 1900

"Exhibit of Pictorial Photography," Newark,
Ohio, 1901

176.* *A Portrait*, ca. 1900
Platinum, 152 x 105 mm.
In pencil, l.r.: "Eva Gamble Walborn.";
c.: "A Portrait"
Mount: Charcoal colored mat,
326 x 257 mm.
Verso: In pencil: "Eva Gamble Walborn";
FBJ label: 129.
LC-USZC2-5994

177.* *Interest*, ca. 1900
Platinum, 169 x 116 mm.
In pencil, l.l.: "Eva Gamble Walborn";
on brown mount, c.: "Interest"
Mount: Thin charcoal mat with brown
and pale green intermediate mounts,
357 x 281 mm.
Verso: In pencil: "Eva Gamble Walborn";
FBJ label: 130.
LC-USZC2-5995

178.* *Sweet Peas*, ca. 1900
Platinum, 229 x 161 mm.
In pencil, l.l.: "Eva Gamble
Walborn"; on cream intermediate
mount: "Sweet Peas"
Mount: Cream mat with cream, pale
yellow and pale pink intermediate
mounts, 431 x 331 mm.
Verso: In pencil: "Sweet Peas.";
FBJ label: 132.
LC-USZC2-5996

179.* *Zylpha*, ca. 1900
Platinum, 161 x 113 mm.
In pencil, l.r.: "Eva Gamble Walborn";
in pencil centered below image: "Zylpha"
Mount: Thick white paper,
356 x 281 mm.
Verso: In pencil: "Eva Gamble Walborn";
FBJ label: 131.
LC-USZC2-5997

Eva Lawrence Watson-Schütze,
in *Ladies' Home Journal* (Oct. 1901), p. 1.

EVA LAWRENCE WATSON (MRS. WATSON-SCHÜTZE)

(1867, Jersey City, N.J. – 1935, ?)

Active in Atlantic City, N.J., Philadelphia, Pa., and Chicago, Ill.
Studio: 1520 Atlantic Avenue, Atlantic City, N.J. (1897)

Eva Watson-Schütze began her artistic career at the age of fifteen, when she entered the Pennsylvania Academy of the Fine Arts and began to study drawing and painting with Thomas Eakins. She gained competency in drawing and modeling during her six years of study, though she "hated the Classics, especially Greek and Latin and the old Flemish Masters." Her first job was making photo-copper reproductions of "Masterpieces of Art" in Philadelphia, an experience which, by her account, she "nearly died of."

From 1894 to 1896, Watson shared a photography studio in Atlantic City, New Jersey, with fellow Eakins student, Amelia Van Buren. She opened her own studio in 1897 in Philadelphia and wrote to Johnston of the growing popularity of the medium among her fellow Philadelphians: "There will be a new era and women will fly to photography." Watson was in sympathy with the aims of the Pictorialists in Philadelphia. Her studio became the "recognized rendezvous" for disenchanted members of the Philadelphia Photographic Society which split bitterly over the issue of Pictorialism.

Watson's solo exhibition at the Camera Club of New York in April of 1900 received wide critical acclaim. Joseph Keiley (1869–1914) reported that the exhibition was "markedly artistic in feeling and purpose, serious and thoughtful in its conception and, as a whole, entirely harmonious and generally pleasing." He noted the mounting of the photographs, commenting that "the unframed pictures were mounted in a way that displayed great taste and a keen understanding and appreciation of tone mass and line values, spacing and artistic proportion." Chicago Pictorialist and Photo-Secessionist William B. Dyer (1860–1931) remarked that Watson's work in this show "demonstrate[d] the forceful elements of an artist's personality … The pictures … tell of a thoughtful mind, a skillful hand, and a keen appreciation. There is not one that is trivial, for Miss Watson does not trifle."

Two months later, Johnston approached Watson about submitting her work for her presentation of American women photographers in Paris. Watson objected at first: "It has been one of my special hobbies— and one I have been very emphatic about, not to have my work represented as 'women's work.' I want [my work] judged by only one standard irrespective of sex." Ultimately, she agreed to participate in the exhibition and twelve photographs—the largest group by a single artist—were shown. In her series "The Foremost Women Photographers in America" (1901), Johnston praised Eva Watson-Schütze as a "true artist—with the true artist's delight in all the beautiful things of life and nature."

Watson-Schütze was elected to the Linked Ring in 1901. Her correspondence with Alfred Stieglitz helped to lay the groundwork for the founding of the Photo-Secession in 1902. Watson-Schütze suggested the formation of an independent group "to make use of the three first salons as the foundation of an American Salon … surely fifty people at least would be ready to join such a society … I feel very strongly that now is the time for action." Drafts for a statement of the aims of the group went back and forth between Watson-Schütze and Stieglitz. In December 1902, Watson-Schütze became one of thirteen members of the founding governing council for the Photo-Secession. Keiley, Stieglitz's right-hand man, described her as "one of the staunchest and sincerest upholders of the pictorial movement in America." In 1902, Watson-Schütze submitted the sole photograph among paintings and sketches at the annual members' exhibition of the Pennsylvania Academy of the Fine Arts, which signaled recognition of Pictorial photography as an art form among the fellows of the Academy.

In 1901, Watson married Professor Martin Schütze, a German–born and –trained lawyer, who had received his Ph.D. in German literature from the University of Pennsylvania in 1899. He took a teaching position that took the couple to Chicago, where Watson-Schütze established a new portrait studio, catering mainly to friends and family of university faculty. However, the move to Chicago made it difficult to keep up her level of involvement with the Photo-Secession, and her relationship with Stieglitz gradually soured. She felt slighted by what she felt was an unglamorous presentation of her work in the January 1905 issue of *Camera Work*. In 1909, she had seven prints in a retrospective of the Photo-Secession, but her name was no longer on the member list.

In 1902 or 1903, Watson-Schütze began to spend summers at Byrdcliffe, an artists' colony in Woodstock, New York. The Schützes later bought land nearby and built Hohenwiesen (High Meadows), where Watson-Schütze would eventually spend between three and six months each year. Her involvement with the Byrdcliffe community led her back to painting, around 1912. Even though she continued to make photographs until the early 1920s, she thought of herself increasingly as a painter, as reflected in her later autobiographical notes. From 1929 until her death, she presided over the University of Chicago's Renaissance Society, a society designed to "stimulate love of the beautiful and to enrich the life of the community through the cultivation of the arts." Watson-Schütze wrote the forward to *Plastic Redirections in 20th Century Painting*, published by the Renaissance Society in 1934.

Affiliations

Photographic Society of Philadelphia, Philadelphia

Linked Ring, London

Photo-Secession, New York

Juror

Chicago Photographic Salon of 1900, Art Institute of Chicago, Chicago, April 1900

Second Philadelphia Photographic Salon, Pennsylvania Academy of the Fine Arts, Philadelphia, October 1899

Third Philadelphia Photographic Salon, Pennsylvania Academy of the Fine Arts, Philadelphia, October 1900

Exhibitions

Philadelphia Photographic Salon, Pennsylvania Academy of the Fine Arts, Philadelphia, October 1898

Second Annual International Salon and Exhibition, Carnegie Art Galleries, Pittsburgh, February 1899

Seventh Annual Photographic Salon, The Linked Ring, Dudley Gallery, London, September 1899

Second Philadelphia Photographic Salon, Philadelphia, October 1899

Exhibition of Photographs by the Newark Camera Club, Newark, Ohio, November 1899

Loan exhibition, Camera Club of New York, December, 1899

Chicago Photographic Salon of 1900, Art Institute of Chicago, Chicago, April 1900

"Eva L. Watson," Camera Club of New York, New York, April 1900

"An Unique Exhibition of Photographs," Boston Art Club, Boston, May 1900

Congrès International de Photographie, Universal Exposition, Paris, July 1900

"New School of American Photography," Royal Photographic Society, London, October 1900

Third Philadelphia Photographic Salon, Philadelphia, October 1900

Fifth Salon and Exhibition of Amateur Photography, Cleveland, Ohio, November 1900

"Exhibit of Photographs by the Newark Camera Club," Newark, Ohio, November 1900

Glasgow International Exhibition, Glasgow, 1901

"Les Artistes Américaines," Photo-Club de Paris, Paris, January 1901

Annual Exhibition of the Work of the Members of the Photographic Society of Philadelphia, Philadelphia, January 1901

"New School of American Photography," Photo-Club de Paris, February 1901

Photographic Society of Philadelphia at the Camera Club of New York, New York City, April 1901

Ninth Annual Exhibition of the Photographic Salon, The Linked Ring, Dudley Gallery, London, October 1901

Second Chicago Photographic Salon, Art Institute of Chicago, Chicago, October 1901

Neunte Internationale Ausstellung von Kunst-Photographien, Hamburg, 1902

Eleventh Annual Exhibition, Toronto Camera Club, Toronto, 1902

Esposizione Internationale di Fotographie Artistica, American Section, Turin, Italy, 1902

"American Pictorial Photography," National Arts Club, New York, March 1902

Tenth Annual Exhibition of the Photographic Salon, The Linked Ring, Dudley Gallery, London, September 1902

Fifteenth Annual Exhibition of Pictures, Leeds, England, October 1902

"Portraits by a Few Leaders in the Newer Photographic Methods," F. Holland Day Studio, Boston, December 1902

Fourth Denver Photographic Salon, Colorado Camera Club, Denver, March 1903

Erste Internationale Ausstellung für künstlerische Bildnis-Photographie, Wiesbaden, April 1903

Eleventh Annual Exhibition of the Photographic Salon, The Linked Ring, Dudley Gallery, London, September 1903

City of Bradford Exhibition, Bradford, England, 1904

"A Collection of American Pictorial Photographs," Corcoran Art Galleries, Washington, D.C., January 1904

"A Collection of American Pictorial Photographs," Carnegie Art Galleries, Pittsburgh, April 1904

Photographische Ausstellung im Park der grossen Kunstausstellung, Dresden, May 1904

Twelfth Annual Exhibition of the Photographic Salon, The Linked Ring, Dudley Gallery, London, September 1904

Internationale Ausstellung ausgewählter künstlerischer Photographien, Vienna, February 1905

Third Salon of the Toronto Camera Club, Toronto, April 1905

Wiener Photo Club, Vienna, April 1905

Second Annual Exhibition of Photographs, Worcester Art Museum, Worcester, Massachusetts, November 1905

Members' Work, Gallery of the Photo-Secession, New York, November 1905

Canadian Pictorialist Exhibition, Montreal, November 1907

International Exhibition of Pictorial Photography, Laing Art Gallery, Newcastle-upon-Tyne, 1906

International Exhibition of Pictorial Photography, National Arts Club, New York, February 1909

"An Exhibition Illustrating the Progress of the Art of Photography," Montross Art Galleries, New York, October 1912

180. [Seated girl reading a book],
ca. 1900
Platinum, 167 x 113 mm.
Monogram in green on photo, l.r.
Mount: Thick tan paper with gray
intermediate mount, 349 x 255 mm.
Verso: FBJ label: 122.
LC-USZC2-5998

181. [Girl sitting with legs folded,
reading a book], ca. 1900
Platinum, 153 x 110 mm.
Monogram in green on photo, u.r.
Mount: Thick tan paper with orange
intermediate mount, 354 x 253 mm.
Verso: FBJ label: 121.
LC-USZC2-5999

182.* [Woman in a kimono standing
looking at a sculpted bust], ca. 1900
Platinum, 164 x 102 mm.
Monogram in black on photo, l.r.
Mount: Thick tan paper,
376 x 278 mm.
LC-USZC2-6000

183.* *The May Apple Leaf*, ca. 1900
Platinum, 172 x 121 mm.
Monogram in black on photo, l.l.
Mount: Thick tan paper,
377 x 286 mm.
LC-USZC2-6001

184. *Dr. Morgan Frederick Mount*, ca. 1900
Platinum, 158 x 113 mm.
Monogram in green on photo, u.r.
Mount: Tan, 160 x 115 mm.
Verso: In pencil: "Mount, Morgan F."
LC-USZC2-6056

185. *Dr. Morgan Frederick Mount*, ca. 1900
Platinum, 161 x 114 mm.
Monogram in green on photo, l.r.
Verso: In pencil: "Mount"
LC-USZC2-6057

186. *Dr. Morgan Frederick Mount*, ca. 1900
Platinum, 158 x 113 mm.
Monogram in green on photo, u.r.
Verso: In pencil: "Mount"
LC-USZC2-6058

187. *Dr. Morgan Frederick Mount*, ca. 1900
Platinum, 164 x 114 mm.
Monogram in green on photo, u.r.
Mount: Thick dark brown paper with
beige intermediate mount,
350 x 253 mm.
Verso: FBJ label: no number
LC-USZC2-6059

188. [Woman standing in a park, trees
in background], ca. 1900
Platinum, 201 x 149 mm.
Monogram in green on photo, l.r.
Mount: Thick dark brown paper,
254 x 191 mm.
LC-USZC2-6060

189. [Profile of young woman wearing
bonnet], ca. 1900
Platinum, 158 x 115 mm.
Monogram in green on photo, l.l.
Mount: Thick gray paper with dark gray
and light gray intermediate mounts,
374 x 279 mm.
Verso: In pencil: "Not for reproduction";
FBJ label: 116.
LC-USZC2-6061

190. [Girl sitting cross legged, book in
her lap, looking at the camera],
ca. 1900
Platinum, 163 x 117 mm.
Monogram in green on photo, l.l.
Mount: Thick brown paper with cream
intermediate mount, 354 x 255 mm.
Verso: FBJ label: 123.
LC-USZC2-6062

191.* [Child standing with piece of
paper looking at a book held by a seated
infant], ca. 1900
Platinum, 157 x 110 mm.
Monogram in green on photo, l.r.
Mount: Thick ocher paper,
355 x 254 mm.
Verso: FBJ label: 120.
LC-USZC2-6063

192. [Portrait of man wearing glasses, seated with elbow resting on right knee], ca. 1900
Platinum, 164 x 117 mm.
Monogram in green on photo, u.r.
Mount: Thick tan paper with brown intermediate mount, 360 x 255 mm.
LC-USZC2-6064

193. [Portrait of a young girl with a scarf tied around her head], ca. 1900
Platinum, 157 x 106 mm.
Monogram in green on photo, l.r.
Mount: Thick dark gray paper with light gray intermediate mount, 384 x 291 mm.
Verso: FBJ label: 118.
LC-USZC2-6065

194. *Child with Oak Branch*, ca. 1900
Platinum, 169 x 118 mm.
Monogram in green on photo half way up right edge
Mount: Thick dark gray paper, 379 x 274 mm.
Verso: FBJ label: 124.
LC-USZC2-6106

195. [Portrait of a woman in kimono], ca. 1900
Platinum, 165 x 115 mm.
Mount: Gray paper, 368 x 270 mm.
Verso: In pencil: "Miss Watson"
NMAH-C-77.92.44

196.* [Woman with cat], ca. 1900
Warm tone platinum (salt?), circle: 92 mm.
Monogram in green on photo, l.l.
Mount: Thick gray paper, 354 x 233 mm.
Verso: In pencil: "Eva Watson/Not to be reproduced"; FBJ label: 115.
NMAH-C-77.92.46

197.* [Portrait of William Rau leaning on sword], ca. 1900
Platinum, 164 x 114 mm.
Monogram in green center of right edge
Mount: Thick dark green paper with light gray intermediate mount, 351 x 274 mm.
Verso: FBJ label: 117.
NMAH-C-77.92.47

198. [Woman in kimono beside sculptured bust], ca. 1900
Platinum, 165 x 107 mm.
Mount: Gray paper, 377 x 290 mm.
NMAH-C-77.92.48

199. *Woman Holding Parrot*, ca. 1900
Platinum, 85 x 108 mm.
Monogram in green ink on photo, l.r.
Mount: Gray paper with orange intermediate mount, 253 x 360 mm.
Verso: FBJ label: 119.
NMAH-C-77.92.49

200.* [Still life with chrysanthemums], ca. 1900
Platinum, 188 x 105 mm.
Mount: Gray paper, 340 x 230 mm.
Verso: FBJ label: 126.
NMAH-C-77.92.63

MATHILDE WEIL

(1872, Philadelphia – 1943?, Philadelphia)

Active in Philadelphia, Pa.
Studio: 604 Baker Building, Philadelphia (1898)
    1520 Chestnut Street, Philadelphia (1898–99)
    1628 Chestnut Street, Philadelphia (1900)
    1716 Chestnut Street, Philadelphia (ca. 1905–8)
    1730 Chestnut Street, Philadelphia (1909–17)

Eva L. Watson-Schütze. *Mathilde Weil*, in *Photo-Era* (Jan. 1901), p. 213.

Upon graduation from Bryn Mawr College, Mathilde Weil moved to New York where she worked in a publishing house for three years reading manuscripts. She spent the winter of 1896–97 in Philadelphia, only to find that she could not obtain the type of library work she desired, so she "bought a small camera and started to work with it." After only six private lessons, and within three months of obtaining her first camera, Weil began to photograph professionally. While learning about photography, she also studied drawing and painting at the Pennsylvania Academy of the Fine Arts, the Decorative Art League and the Museum of Industrial Art.

In 1900, she wrote to Johnston that she had "entered the ranks of wage-earners" in 1898, opening a studio in the heart of Philadelphia's business district where, as she told Hines, she was "charging from the beginning the highest prices … and have always had more work than I could do, refusing many orders." Weil became a specialist in portraits of children "at home" and outdoors, with the belief that she could create more "characteristic likenesses" of her subjects in their personal surroundings. She employed an assistant yet insisted on doing her own developing and retouching, in order to avoid becoming what she called "a department-store photographer."

In a handful of essays for photo journals, Weil wrote about her theories, techniques and equipment. In one article, she addressed the artistic limitations of professional portraiture: "It is unfortunately the case that an artistic picture and a good likeness are by no means always synonymous." Weil struggled with these limitations, complaining in her correspondence with Stieglitz about the lack of freedom in her choice of subjects and methods: "The comparative success I may be said to have attained has been the greatest possible surprise to me. I cannot regard my work very highly, for though I never consciously work to please the public, still I have no time ever for the things I would do specifically to please myself. Everything in my studio with the exception of half a dozen prints has been made in the course of my regular professional work."

From 1897 to 1908, Weil exhibited prolifically with artistic photographic societies. Elected to membership in the Photographic Society of Philadelphia in 1896, she exhibited in the Philadelphia and London salons, and with the Photo-Secession, though she was not a member. Stieglitz published her portrait *Beatrice* in the portfolio *American Pictorial Photography, Series I* (1899) and in *Camera Notes* (1900). In addition to many medals and diplomas, Weil's work received favorable reviews, emphasizing her command of composition and the delicate modeling and harmony of tones achieved through her use of natural light. A review of the Pictorial section of the 1901 exhibition at the Royal Photographic Society reflected on the artistic qualities of Weil's work: "'Mrs. G.' is one of those portraits that are peculiar to modern photography in its highest flights … This style of portraiture is so eminently fitted to photography that when it is adopted as Miss Weil knows so well how, it can hold its own with any portrait method in the various branches of art." Her portrait studio remained in operation until 1917.

Affiliations
Photographic Society of Philadelphia, Philadelphia

Exhibitions
Forty-Second Exhibition of the Royal Photographic Society, London, September 1897

Sixth Annual Photographic Salon, The Linked Ring, Dudley Gallery, London, September 1898

First Annual International Salon Exhibition, Carnegie Art Galleries, Pittsburgh, January 1898

American Institute of the City of New York, Photographic Section, National Academy of Design, New York, September 1898

Forty-Third Exhibition of the Royal Photographic Society, London, September 1898

Philadelphia Photographic Salon, Pennsylvania Academy of the Fine Arts, Philadelphia, October 1898

Eighth Annual Exhibition, Toronto Camera Club, Toronto, December 1898

Second Annual International Salon and Exhibition, Carnegie Art Galleries, Pittsburgh, February 1899

First Annual Exhibition, Society of Arts and Crafts, Boston, April 1899

Seventh Annual Photographic Salon, The Linked Ring, Dudley Gallery, London, September 1899

Forty-Fourth Annual exhibition of the Royal Photographic Society, London, September 1899

Second Philadelphia Photographic Salon, Pennsylvania Academy of the Fine Arts, Philadelphia October, 1899

Third Annual Exhibition, Detroit Camera Club, Detroit, Michigan, November 1899

Exhibition of Photographs by the Newark Camera Club, Newark, Ohio, November 1899

Photographic Salon, American Institute, New York, December 1899

Ninth Annual Exhibition, Toronto Camera Club, Toronto, December 1899

Congrès International de Photographie, Universal Exposition, Paris, July 1900

Chicago Photographic Salon of 1900, Art Institute of Chicago, Chicago, April 1900

Third Annual International Salon Exhibition, Carnegie Art Galleries, Pittsburgh, 1900

Forty-Fifth Annual Exhibition of the Royal Photographic Society, London, October 1900

"New School of American Photography," Royal Photographic Society, London, October 1900

Third Philadelphia Photographic Salon, Pennsylvania Academy of the Fine Arts, Philadelphia, October 1900

Fifth Salon and Exhibition of Amateur Photography, Case Library, Cleveland, Ohio, November 1900

Glasgow International Exhibition, Glasgow, 1901

Annual Exhibition of the work of the Members, Photographic Society of Philadelphia, Philadelphia, January 1901

"Les Artistes Américaines," Photo-Club de Paris, France, January 1901

"New School of American Photography," Photo-Club de Paris, February 1901

Photographic Society of Philadelphia at the Camera Club of New York, New York, April 1901

Forty-Sixth Annual Exhibition of the Royal Photographic Society, London, September 1901

Ninth Annual Exhibition of the Photographic Salon, The Linked Ring, Dudley Gallery, London, October 1901

Neunte Internationale Ausstellung von Kunst-Photographien, Kunsthalle, Hamburg 1902

Esposizione Internazionale di Fotografie Artistica, American Section, Turin, Italy, 1902

"American Pictorial Photography," National Arts Club, New York, March 1902

Photographers Association of New England, Sixth Convention Exhibition, Boston, August 1902

Tenth Annual Exhibition of the Photographic Salon, The Linked Ring, Dudley Gallery, London, September 1902

Erste Internationale Ausstellung für künstlerische Bildnis-Photographie, Wiesbaden, April 1903

Eleventh Annual Exhibition of the Photographic Salon, The Linked Ring, Dudley Gallery, London, September 1903

Forty-Eighth Annual Exhibition of the Royal Photographic Society, London, September 1904

"A Collection of American Pictorial Photographs," Corcoran Art Galleries, Washington, D.C., January 1904

"A Collection of American Pictorial Photographs," Carnegie Art Galleries, Pittsburgh, February 1904

Photographische Ausstellung im Park der grossen Kunstausstellung, Dresden, May 1904

International Exhibition of Pictorial Photography, Laing Art Gallery, Newcastle-upon-Tyne, 1906

201.* *The Embroidery Frame*, ca. 1900
Platinum, 224 x 163 mm.
Monogram in red on photo, u.l.
Mount: Thick dark brown paper with teal intermediate mount,
294 x 230 mm.
LC-USZC2-6002

202.* *Constance*, ca. 1900
[Also published in *Camera Notes* January 1901 as *Beatrice*]
Platinum, 239 x 120 mm.
Monogram in red on photo, l.l.
Mount: Thick gray paper with light brown and cream intermediate mounts, 412 x 242 mm.
Verso: FBJ label: 133.; in ink on label: "Mathilde Weil. On Constance/Mathilde Weil"
LC-USZC2-6003

203.* *Il Penseroso*, ca. 1900
Platinum, 160 x 100 mm.
Monogram in red on photo, l.r.
Mount: Black mat, 357 x 227 mm.
Verso: In ink: "Il Penseroso/Mathilde Weil"
LC-USZC2-6004

204. *Lady With Muff*, ca. 1900
Platinum, 250 x 181 mm.
Monogram in red on photo, l.l.
Mount: Cream paper folded over mat, 432 x 304 mm.
Verso: FBJ label: 139.; label from Third Annual International Salon and Exhibition of the Pittsburgh Amateur Photographer's Society, completed in ink with the following information: "Lady with Muff/(Miss) Mathilde Weil/1628 Chestnut Street/Philadelphia and..."
LC-USZC2-6005

205.* *Song of the Meadow Lark*, ca. 1900
Platinum, 189 x 154 mm.
Monogram in red on photo, l.r.
Mount: Dark gray paper folded over mat with cream and sage intermediate mounts, 359 x 268 mm.
Verso: In ink: "The Song of the Meadowlark/Mathilde Weil"; FBJ label: 135.
LC-USZC2-6006

206. *Constance*, ca. 1900
[Also published in *Camera Notes* January 1901 as *Beatrice*]
Platinum, 237 x 109 mm.
Monogram in red on photo, l.l.
Verso: In pencil: "Reduce to 3 1/2 in #1192/385"
LC-USZC2-6066

207. [Girl in a plaid dress seated with a book in her lap], ca. 1900
Platinum, 307 x 225 mm.
Monogram in red on photo, u.l.
In pencil, l.r.: "Mathilde Weil"
Mount: Thin dark brown mat, 244 x 158 mm.
LC-USZC2-6117

208.* [Old woman in an armchair with an open book in her lap], ca. 1900
Platinum, 210 x 160 mm.
Monogram in red on photo, l.r.
Verso: In pencil: "Reduce to 4 1/2 in #1192"
LC-USZC2-6118

Myra Albert Wiggins.
(Possibly the portrait by Gertrude Käsebier
exhibited by Frances B. Johnston.)
Washington, D.C., Library of Congress,
Frances Benjamin Johnston Collection.

MYRA ALBERT WIGGINS

(1869, Salem, Oregon – 1956, Seattle)

Active in Salem, Ore.

Myra Albert was the daughter of John and Mary Holman Albert, both from pioneer families of the American West. In the spring of 1889, Wiggins made her first picture with a "cheap box" she and her brother had purchased together, but of which she soon became sole owner. That same year, she traveled on horseback into the wilderness around Mount Jefferson in central Oregon, carrying her wooden camera, tripod and thirteen glass plates. She wrote of this adventure into an area where "The foot of woman never trod, nor feet of camera ever prod" in her illustrated essay "Amateur Photography through a Woman's Eyes" for *The Photo American*. The photographs were also published in the *New York Herald*, *Camera Mosaics*, the *Amateur American Photographer* and *Photograms of the Year*.

Educated at both Willamette University in Salem and Mills College in San Fransisco, Wiggins moved east in 1891 to become a student at the Art Students League in New York, where she studied painting under William Merritt Chase, George DeForest Brush, John H. Twachtman and Kenyon Cox until 1894. To have access to a darkroom, she joined the Camera Club of New York. Wiggins (then Albert) returned to Oregon in 1894 and married Frederick Wiggins, a merchant of farm equipment, photographing her own wedding. In 1896, their daughter Mildred was born. Wiggins would pose Mildred and her housekeeper Alma in vintage Dutch garments that she had inherited from her aunt to create Dutch genre scenes inspired by Old Master paintings. She would also transform her home by stretching burlap over the walls of her dining room, laying rough-cut boards on the floor, and pasting strips of black paper on the large window pane, to make it look like several small ones. Evidence of Wiggins's "set design" may be seen in the uncropped print of her famous work, *Hunger ist der Beste Koch* (1898). This photograph was originally used by the Malted Cereal Co. of Burlington, Vermont, as an advertisement without Wiggins' permission, but the company later paid her for the rights of reproduction.

Although she developed her photographs "in a series of bathrooms and cellars," Wiggins won wide recognition and was able to pay for a ticket to Paris in 1900 with the winnings from a Rochester Optical Company competition. She spent much of 1900 traveling overseas and documenting her travels with photographs, drawings and writing. In a letter to Johnston, who presented four of her photographs at the Universal Exposition in Paris, she reported that she had no formal training in photography, and attributed her improvement to the photographic magazines that she read avidly. Her photograph *Head of the Grand Court* earned *Leslie Magazine's* first prize for best photograph of the Exposition. In 1902 Wiggins, whose work had previously been selected by Stieglitz for publication in *Camera Notes*, was elected a member of the Photo-Secession. Her travels continued in 1904 when she journeyed to Jerusalem and through Turkey and Europe, taking snapshots of people's daily lives and historical sites. Some of these pictures are illustrations in her book, *Letters from a Pilgrim*, accompanied by text from letters she had sent home while abroad.

In 1907, her husband's business took them to Toppenish, Washington. The geographical isolation was hard on Wiggins's photographic career, as she explained in a letter to Stieglitz: "Indians and sage brush must here-after be my inspiration, with now and then an irrigation ditch for variety … Yes, I think my work would be better if I could only be with the Eastern workers once in awhile or even see a good exhibition." Wiggins won over fifty prizes in photography exhibitions, yet after about 1913 she gradually returned to painting and writing. As a painter of still lifes, Wiggins received numerous prizes and notices and exhibited her work in Vancouver, Los Angeles, Seattle, Spokane, Chicago, New Orleans, Buffalo, New York, London and Paris.

In 1930, Wiggins and her husband moved to Seattle, where they spent the remainder of their lives. Here she opened a painting studio, became one of six founding members of Women Painters of Washington and chaired the Division of Art in the Washington State Federation of Women's Clubs. Major retrospectives including both painting and photography were held at the Seattle Art Museum and the M. H. de Young Memorial Museum in San Francisco.

Affiliations

Camera Club of New York, New York

Photo-Secession, New York

Exhibitions

First Annual Members' Exhibition,
Society of Amateur Photographers, New York,
March 1893

Eastman Photographic Exhibition, National
Academy of Design, New York, January 1898

American Institute of the City of New York,
Photographic Section, New York, September 1898

Collection of Prints by Members of the Camera
Club of New York, New York, May 1899

Second Philadelphia Photographic Salon,
Pennsylvania Academy of the Fine Arts,
Philadelphia, October 1899

Photographic Salon, American Institute,
New York, December 1899

Congrès International de Photographie,
Universal Exposition, Paris, July 1900

Members' Third Annual Exhibition of Prints,
Camera Club of New York, New York, 1900

Exhibition of Photographs by Members of the
Camera Club of New York at the Boston Camera
Club, Boston, 1900

"Les Artistes Américaines," Photo-Club de Paris,
Paris, January 1901

First San Francisco Photographic Salon,
San Francisco, January 1901

Fourth Members' Exhibition, Camera Club
of New York, New York, May 1901

Second Chicago Photographic Salon,
Art Institute of Chicago, Chicago, October 1901

Fourth Philadelphia Photographic Salon,
Pennsylvania Academy of the Fine Arts,
Philadelphia, November 1901

Second San Francisco Photographic Salon,
San Francisco, January 1902

Los Angeles Photographic Salon, Los Angeles,
May 1902

Competitive Print Exhibition, Camera Club
of New York, New York, May 1902

Members' Exhibition, Camera Club
of New York, New York, May 1902

Tenth Annual Exhibition of the Photograph
Salon, The Linked Ring, Dudley Gallery,
London, September 1902

Forty-Seventh Annual Exhibition of the Royal
Photographic Society, London, September 1902

Third Chicago Photographic Salon, Art Institute
of Chicago, Chicago, December 1902

First Minneapolis Photographic Salon, Minneapolis,
1903

Eleventh Annual Exhibition of the Photographic
Salon, The Linked Ring, Dudley Gallery, London,
September 1903

"A Collection of American Pictorial Photographs,"
Corcoran Art Galleries, Washington, D.C.,
January 1904

"A Collection of American Pictorial Photographs,"
Carnegie Art Galleries, Pittsburgh,
January 1904

Wiener Photo Club, Vienna, 1905

"Exhibition of Photographs: The Work of
Women Photographers of Hartford," Camera
Club of Hartford, Hartford, Conn., April 1906

The Kodak Exhibition, Kodak Galleries,
London, September 1906

Arts & Crafts Exhibition, Idora Park, Oakland,
1908

International Exhibition of Pictorial Photography,
National Arts Club, New York, February 1909

International Exhibition of Pictorial Photography,
Albright Art Gallery, Buffalo, November 1910

The Kodak Exhibition, Eastman Kodak Company,
New York, 1912

Annual Exhibition, Washington Art Association,
Seattle, January 1913

209. [Seated girl with body facing left
looking at the camera], ca. 1900
Platinum, 190 x 149 mm.
Mount: Gray mat, 355 x 279 mm.
Verso: In pencil: "Portrait./Myra A.
Wiggins/Salem/Oregon"
LC-USZC2-6007

210. *Mildred*, ca. 1900
Platinum, 177 x 127 mm.
Mount: Gray mat, 357 x 281 mm.
Verso: In pencil: "Mildred./Myra A.
Wiggins/Salem/Oregon"
LC-USZC2-6008

211.* *Hunger ist der Beste Koch*, 1898
Carbon, 166 x 235 mm.
Monogram in ink on photo, l.l.
Verso: In pencil, retraced in ink:
"'Hunger ist der Beste Koch'/Photo-
graph by./Myra Albert Wiggins
(1898)/Subject.Mildred Wiggins./1899
(Hung) Phila. Salon etc./Prizes London
& Buffalo, N.Y."
LC-USZC2-6009

212. *Mother and Child*, ca. 1900
Platinum, 193 x 152 mm.
Mount: Black mat, 376 x 308 mm.
Verso: In pencil: "Mother and
Child./Myra Albert
Wiggins/Salem/Oregon"
LC-USZC2-6010

213. *The Babe*, ca. 1900
Gelatin silver, developed out,
123 x 158 mm.
Mount: Gray mat with light gray
intermediate mount, 279 x 355 mm.
Verso: In pencil: "The Babe./Myra
Albert Wiggins/Salem/Oregon."
LC-USZC2-6070

214. [Seated woman looking right],
May 1918
Platinum, 250 x 200 mm.
Verso: In pencil: "Willis Clements/
Palladiotype/May 1918"
LC-USZC2-6109

215. [Woman at mantel with mirror],
ca. 1900
Platinum, 243 x 173 mm.
Verso: In pencil: "Myra Albert
Wiggins/Salem. Ore"
LC-USZC2-6110

216. *The Mother*, ca. 1900
Gelatin silver, developed out,
234 x 117 mm.
Mount: Black mat with beveled outer
edge and a gray intermediate mount,
290 x 149 mm.
Verso: In pencil: "The Mother/Myra A.
Wiggins/Salem/Oregon."
LC-USZC2-6111

217.* *Looking Seaward*, 1889
Carbon (?), 92 x 157 mm.
In pencil, l.r.: "_Myra A. Wiggins.-1889_"; c.l.: "_Looking Seaward_"
Mount: Light gray embossed stock mat, 179 x 229 mm.
Verso: In pencil: " Seaward-1889-/Myra A. Wiggins/Salem./Oregon.U.S.A."
LC-USZC2-6120

James Osborne Wright. *Mabel Osgood Wright.*
Washington, D.C., Library of Congress,
Frances Benjamin Johnston Collection.

MABEL OSGOOD WRIGHT (MRS. JAMES OSBORNE WRIGHT)

(1859, New York – 1934, Fairfield, Conn.)
Active in Fairfield, Conn., and New York City

An active photographer, popular author, advocate of the preservation of nature and passionate gardener, Mabel Osgood Wright was raised in New York City and Fairfield, Connecticut, the youngest of three daughters by Ellen and Dr. Samuel Osgood, a Unitarian minister and writer. In 1884, she married James Osborne Wright, an English bookseller with whom she traveled abroad for several years before settling at Mosswood (originally called Waldstein), the summer home built by her father in Fairfield.

Wright began publishing nature essays anonymously in the *Evening Post* and *The New York Times* in the early 1890s. Around this time, she also took up photography after some chemistry lessons from "old Dr. Ehrmann." In an article for *Munsey's Magazine*, Frank W. Crane stated that Wright had diplomas from the Chautauqua School of Photography and Boston in 1892, and that her pictures had hung in the rooms of the Royal Society of Photographers of Great Britain (although no records confirm these statements). In 1900, Wright wrote to Johnston: "I had begged for a Kodack [*sic*] to catch some of the lovely scenes that I was always finding in the course of a life very largely spent out of doors." Her husband gave her a "fine lens and a complete 5 x 5 tripod outfit," in order that she "'take up photography... at the right end.'" Her studio was a "small tower room (lighted by windows on three sides, which are screened by curtains so that many effects of light may be had) for portrait heads and such flowers as it is impossible to take out of doors." Wright printed most of her photographs herself in her "dark House near the garden." She confided to Johnston that she did not work "for pay" but "Con Amore," and that her ambition was not "to become a photo-artist," rather to "take the humble position of one who loves the beautiful [*sic*] so keenly that I must try to make pictures from pure enthusiasm."

Wright illustrated her first book, *The Friendship of Nature* (1894), with her own photographs. After two winters at the American Museum of Natural History's ornithology department, she wrote *Birdcraft* (1895), a handbook on birds which was reprinted nine times. Wright created images to illustrate books by other authors and also used her camera to document historic and natural sites in the Fairfield area.

Interested in protecting birds from being slaughtered for use in fashion, Wright was one of thirteen women who founded the Connecticut Audubon Society in 1898, and was elected its first president. She wrote a steady column on bird observation and preservation for *Bird-Lore,* the Audubon publication, from 1911 until her death. In 1914, through the anonymous sponsorship of Annie Burr Jennings, Wright created the Birdcraft Sanctuary in Fairfield (now the Connecticut Audubon Birdcraft Museum). Wright continued her active involvement both with the Audubon Society and the Birdcraft Sanctuary until her death in 1934.

Exhibitions
Congrès International de Photographie, Universal Exposition, Paris, July 1900

"Les Artistes Américaines," Photo-Club de Paris, Paris, January 1901

218.* *Feeding the Calves*, ca. 1900
Platinum, 183 x 241 mm.
Verso: In pencil: "Mrs. Mabel Osgood Wright"
LC-USZC2-6119

After viewing the selection of photographs by American women photographers assembled by Frances Benjamin Johnston, W. I. Sreznewsky, a Russian attendee to the International Congress of Photography in Paris, requested that the collection be loaned for exhibition in Russia. Johnston honored the request and the photographs were exhibited first in St. Petersburg and then Moscow in the autumn of 1900, before returning to the Photo-Club de Paris in January 1901. Two reviews and one mention of the exhibition from Russian periodicals were found while preparing this exhibition. They reveal a fascination with the works, particularly those in the Pictorial style, virtually unknown in Russia at that time, and comment upon the original mounting techniques.

"American Ladies Collection of Photographic Works," trans. Thomas Hoisington, *Amateur Photographer*, 11 (1900), pp. 401–404.

Organ of the Odessa, Kazan, Crimean, Saratov, Estonian Photography Society, of the Ladies Photography Circle of the R[ussian]. W[omen's]. Ch[aritable]. S[ociety], the Baku Photography Circle, and the Tiflis Society of Amateur Photographers.

Recently W. I. Sreznewsky invited us to view a collection of works by American ladies sent at the latter's request to Russia so that photography groups in St. Petersburg and Moscow could familiarize themselves with this original style of photographic reproduction.

By way of brief explanation as to why the American ladies decided to send their works to us, at the Paris photography congress Miss Benjamin Johnston set up a stall exhibiting the work of 29 of her female compatriots to familiarize the congress with the American style, probably of one of the ladies clubs that does nature photography. After members of the congress had viewed these works, W. I. Sreznewsky, representing the 5th Section of the Imperial Russian Technical Society, asked Miss Johnston to send these works to Russia so that he could display them in IRTS's 5th Section and at the Russian Photographic Society in Moscow. Miss Johnston promised to ask her compatriots and, if they agreed, to send the photos to St. Petersburg. The group's permission was secured and W. I. Sreznewsky now has the collection. We were able to familiarize ourselves with the collection before the photography groups mount it.

There are 142 prints, all of them done on three types of paper, platinum, pigment, and gum arabic, and therefore in various colors, ranging from black to a brown that verges on red. The shapes of the prints are extremely varied. Round, oblong, patterned, or in the style that the Decadents favor, i.e., without background above the head, or for a subject seated in profile the shape fitted to the shoulder, part of which is missing from the print. But yet this is not what makes the work original. That finds its main expression not only in the shots themselves, but also in how the prints are mounted and about which we want to speak here.

Our remark above that these photographs belong to a ladies society or club was based on the fact that, in examining the works, one seems to find answers to posed topics, topics implemented by several authors quite individually, authors who infuse their works with taste and technical skill. One example is "A Mother Holding Her Small Child," a subject used by almost all of the authors. A second subject is the photographic portrait taken in front of window light, not a silhouette but incorporating shade as a factor. These subjects are executed in quite different ways by many of these misses. A third subject consists of a portrait lighted from behind against dark backgrounds so as to provide full detail to the shaded portion of the face. Besides such difficult and complex subjects, in the American ladies' album there are many portraits, genres, i.e., whole scenes done in rooms with the help of daylight or flash. It's not the chance aspect of an on-the-spot photo that one notices in these works but rather carefully constructed scenes with specially prepared lighting. When these scenes are done al fresco by the American ladies, they are weaker than those done inside. In several works it is clear what ideas the author wants to impart to them. This is the case, for example, in the depiction of a woman holding outstretched a string of pearls from a necklace she is wearing. The woman is lost in thought, but about what? The author furnishes the answer in the background: The woman is photographed against a dark background which has been converted to white except for the area around the woman's head. Looking closely at the dark part that remains one can make out the profile of a man's head with a beard, a large head of hair, and part of a torso. But this silhouette is executed subtly; someone unaccustomed to looking at pictures might not even notice it. In a similar vein is the portrait of a woman wearing the white dress of a nun and holding a lily. She is also sunk in thought, expressed in a grayish background by means of a cross the barely perceptible contours of which are colored only a bit stronger than the background. This idea is entirely new and thus attracted our attention.

Moving on to the technical aspect of the works, it's clear that the entire ladies circle has given itself over to a certain type of *flou*. This *flou* is executed to the degree that willy-nilly it becomes a blind alley since with contemporary objects one can achieve not only a lack of sharpness but take only patches from nature and not light ones but half-toned, shadowed ones. In order to convey this more clearly we cite several photos. A portrait of an artist in his studio: The face, torso, palette, and picture are all in halftones, with such lack of sharpness in the contours and gradations of tones that only at a distance can everything we've enumerated be distinguished in the print. And suddenly in this almost dark print there are several light strokes in the hair and on the paints of the palette, and so strong that the entire print seems to be receiving light only here while otherwise wrapped in halftone and shadow.

Similarly, a portrait of an old woman wearing glasses. All gray against a similar background—and also in the very same way several light-colored glints (rendered by retouching the negative) on her gray hair, which lends a special effect to the whole portrait. Another feature of the ladies circle, observable in all their works and executed with greater or lesser skill is the generally grayish tone of the prints where there is a general, artificially created lack of sharpness, half-tinted photos of faces, the direct indication of a trend.

One gets used to anything, and so the first print that fell into our hands we simply didn't like. But when we had viewed several very similar works, we got used to them, and in these allusions to nature we began to find nature, and that's why the remaining prints elicited an entirely different feeling, and it isn't really only a matter of searching in them for the object of the exposure as much as understanding precisely what the author wanted to invest, i.e., understanding the authorial "I," that which compels the viewer to meditate on the thought and aim

of the reproduction. As for the matter of a viewer being influenced by such work, one can judge that by works encountered in this original collection, both ordinary shots of groups and of scenes splendidly executed on platinum paper, shots which however seem for some reason strange, dry, licked clean. Examining anew an indistinct print, it's as if again one passes into an incomplete world, so that one is forced to guess what is missing in the print. Naturally, this is simply a matter of photographic focus, though of what kind it is hard to tell. The only thing that is clear is that in most instances all retouching is done on the exposure itself and not on the positive. This way of doing things is what makes the exposure original. Also, the mounting of the prints is original: Several of them are pasted only at the corners on two or three pieces of colored paper chosen according to the print's tone and comprising as it were a passe-partout or frame. The first piece of paper under the print is cut using a somewhat larger format than the copy and of the same color; the second piece is a liner of another tone, a neutral one corresponding to the "lights" in the sense of their distribution in the print. Finally, there's a third layer that joins the improvised frame with the larger uneven pasteboard and constitutes the general background against which the print itself stands out, in the form of a patch. Non-use of white bristol board is the chief characteristic of the mounting of all these works. Colored paper or heavy-duty bristol board, very distinctive for its unevenness as well as its tone, are like folios from an album. Among these large pieces of paper there are also original ones which begin in one corner with a dark tone and change gradually to a lighter tone in the opposite corner. This in several prints, in particular platinum ones, gives the work a special cachet.

Authors' signatures are done in the conventional manner or the whole surname simply appears on a large bristol board under the print or at the bottom of it. Often

the bristol board is not cut in linear fashion as we are accustomed to, but as if it were roughly torn, and this too gives the mounting an original quality.

So, this roughly speaking is what we took away from looking at this collection, and if, after thinking about all we had seen, we wanted to define what impression the work of the American ladies had made on us, then we would respond as follows: All the work shows a striving, with the help of contemporary photographic apparatus, to change the photograph as much as possible, so that it seems to be not a print from a negative but a sketch done by hand in the form of a study. This gives the work of several members the appearance of being a copy of a very old oil in which over time the dark colors have blended so that they no longer even hint at the detail of the painting; only the light places of the portrait are preserved, and these to the degree that they would be in an old picture. The whole group pursues this objective. It requires not only special technique but also well-known methods that form the object of experience and study in this mode of work.

All the works of the lady photographers exhibit great deliberateness as much in terms of pose and lighting, singling them out and developing them in a completely original manner. Hence the absence of banality in the collection. Finally, all these prints, in spite of their album mountings, are such that the general and the whole result not from the proximity of the eye to the work but the opposite, when all these spots, which at first seem imperceptible, acquire something resembling the form of a model.

Thus, in general concerning these ladies' work, there is much that is original in terms of contemporary techniques and modes. But then the question arises: Is this the work of a school or of something else? We are inclined to think that this is not a school but merely the resolute aim of the entire circle, one which is not easily executed even by one very knowledgeable in photographic modes, and it is namely this that constitutes the originality in the works of the American ladies.

W. I. Sreznewsky, "The Collection of Photographs Taken by American Women Amateur Photographers," trans. Harold M. Leich, *Fotograficheskoe obozrienie*, 1 (1901), pp. 1–5.

This collection was presented at a congress on photography held in Paris, during the exposition. Miss Frances Benjamin Johnston, from Washington, brought it over and showed it at the congress at the request of American women amateur photographers.

At its first viewing, the collection drew the general attention of congress attendees for its artistic treatment, the originality of the majority of images, the wide variety of topics, as well as the faithful transmission of chiaroscuro.

Notwithstanding technological advances that have simplified photographic composition, in Russia we rarely see amateur photographs in which there is any attempt to develop the subject, or provide any artistry or idea to this or that group or individual figure. Meanwhile, photographic composition has arisen in Russia, and the first person who demonstrated this new way in Europe was Karelin, in Nijni Novgorod. For his efforts, he was awarded a major prize at the international photographic exhibition in Edinburgh. His successor was Soloviev. Both these men achieved artistic merit under the most difficult conditions of the older technology (1878–1882). Since that time, with the exception of only a few professional photographers and two or three amateurs, we have not seen attempts to work on this subject or to find a form for this emerging concept. The wide dissemination of snapshot photography has somehow halted the attempts of Russian amateur photographers at artistic composition, and has weakened the desire to use photography as a technological method and as a means of recording the beautiful—not in the random way it appears in nature, but in a form that is arbitrarily directed and generalized by means of taste and the understanding of artistry, and by the subjective temper of personality.

And this is why, at the first brief look at the collection of American photographs, I wanted to acquaint Russian amateurs and lovers of photography with the images made by the young contingent of American women, using new technological means and accepting new ways of printing that allow for the implementation of artistic goals without using the hands.

My request to allow the collection to stay for a while in Russia was graciously fulfilled by Miss Frances Benjamin Johnston, and so we can now examine in detail the collection, note its particulars, and assess its value.

The collection consists of 142 photographs taken by 29 young American ladies. The collection was drawn together to familiarize representatives of various countries at the Paris Exhibition with the nature, direction, and goals of amateur work in far-off America. It is quite probable that it was intended for the Paris Exposition, but did not in fact end up there, either for missing the deadline, or for overall lack of space. And, in fact, this collection of artistic works would most likely not have been noticed at the exhibition, since the building allocated to American photography was even worse than that for Russian photography—cramped and completely dark. In general, the good space at the exposition went only to the French and English photographers; the Germans, not wanting to subject themselves to impossible conditions, used the German palace on the "embankment of nations."

Among the pictures in the collection there are a few that have already been shown at special American exhibits and awarded prizes; however, the majority here are new.

The participants in the collection do not comprise any permanent, organized society. They live in several states and are from a number of cities: nine from New York, five from Boston, one from Chicago, three from Ohio, one from Providence, two from Washington, five from Pennsylvania, etc.

After returning from Europe, the photographs will go back to their authors. Of the 142 pictures, 18 are owned by their authors and are not authorized for publication. Three authors have completely forbidden reproduction of all their works; twenty have granted the freedom both to reproduce and to be published. In all probability, the prohibitions were caused by the desire not to disseminate personal portraits of the relatives and close family members who served as models.

As to the technical aspects, we should note that almost all the photographs have been done on platinum paper, providing half-tones in the deepest shadows. Comparatively few of the photographs have been done in a pigmented fashion, and even fewer on gum or bromide paper. The photographs have been mounted on dark, rough paper, of brown, dark gray, or steely color, or gradually darkening along the diagonal—or else on coarse paper that resembles wrapping paper. The photographs are for the most part glued along the upper edge, sometimes not symmetrically—sometimes in the left corner, sometimes in the center. The sizes in which the photos are cut likewise do not conform to generally accepted ones, and the forms are not fancy. One photograph is in an oval shape, while all the others are cut up in the form of rectangles, with great differences in size and relations of the sides.

Examining the subjects of the photographs, one must note that there are several general motifs in the collection which were likely proposed to the participants as themes or goals, such as: mother and child, or woman with child; a woman's figure in the bright side of a window, the dark side being lit from behind; the female figure in profile; portraits of men; etc. Such motifs have been elaborated on by participants with great variety. Each decision is connected with a certain idea, and therefore monotony in the subjects is avoided. Thus, for example, the first topic, "woman with child," is treated in the following pictures: the Virgin Mary with the young child; first steps (in a photograph of a *bas relief*); "Lord hear my prayer" (a mother teaches her child how to pray); "The wounded Cupid"; a mother shows affection to her child; etc. The "female profile" topic is treated in several extraordinarily successful shots. One of them shows a young girl deep in thought—in her dreams a male figure [ ].

[ ] an unclear silhouette in the background, as if a shadow from out of her own mind) expression of the face is exceptionally successful—in it there is both indecisiveness and the awareness of the seriousness of the issue, and the dream about a future, hopefully happy, life. Another photo, based on the text of the Gospel from St. Luke, chapter 1, "Behold the Handmaid of the Lord: be it unto me according to Thy word," represents the Virgin Mary in white clothing with a lily in her hand, suffused with holiness and dedicated to the service of God; in her there is not one single trait linking her to the mundane world; even the outlines, full of a certain lack of clarity and lightness, carry the viewer away from the everyday world to another world, far away. In the lighted background, the outline of a cross is barely evident. The entire picture conveys a lighted character: there is nothing dark, nothing clear, sharp, or distinct.

In terms of artistic design and composition, the American collection is of special interest. The artistic taste is evident in the choice of models; in the lighting used; and in the attempt to cross over into the world of ideas and evade the exact and real representation of reality, as photography by its very nature is so very much inclined to do. For this, the American women amateurs almost intentionally distort that which objectivity and the photographic plate provide; either making the image not sharp, not clear or giving the character of a sketch, or a completely darkened model, or one clearly lighted. These artists paid great attention to the correctness of the chiaroscuro, and have attained, not a cheap, surface effect, but rather the truth. In several pictures, the fidelity of transmission of the half-tones is so great that the image appears with hints of color.

The first impression of the American photographs, perhaps not appropriate for them but a whole series of pictures, full of the individuality of the authors, overshadows the impression, and even to the connoisseur of photography, the photographic interest recedes into second place under the influence of the ideas in the photo and its subject. How is this peculiar beauty achieved? With what technical methods has the author managed to approach the task of pure art, to transmit in a photo not a single, random image, but something typical from life, and even to evoke in the viewer the desired mood? Until very recently, the unreal world seemed to be inaccessible to photography, given the very nature of the technology. Here in several photographs, however, we see not portraits of persons, but images that serve as the incarnation of ideas that capture the attention of viewers by the very existence of the photographs. These sometimes unclear and weak outlines, hiding in their shadows only the most noticeable details—the folds of a skirt, distant objects—all are accomplished artistically. Faced with such talent and taste for forming impressions, the most important thing we can wonder about is, with what means, with what technical methods are these effects not accessible in photography! It is amazing that these effects do not cry out. In almost all the works in the collection there is a hint of calm—there is neither lifelessness nor blank spots nor deadly darkness, nor tawdry shininess and gloss. The matt-like quality of all the pictures and the softness of the shadows allow for the perception of peace. It seems that in the very darkest, most overlooked shadows you will gradually see more and more detail.

We must give due recognition to the young American women and their artistic taste and talent, as they have completely mastered the technical aspects of photography. They have succeeded in capturing unique images, and in passing from the real world to the world of ideas.

"First Photographic Exhibition of Artistic Photography in Moscow," trans. Thomas Hoisington, *Photography Review*, 7:6 (1902).

The Photography Society of Texas has sent very good photos, but this collection, which the Photography Society of New England has exhibited, really ought to be compared with the one that Mr. Sreznewsky presented last year at one of the RPS [Russian Photography Society's] meetings. Both these collections show what heights artistic photography has reached, especially portrait photography in America.

The following bibliography was compiled specifically for this publication from materials provided by each of the contributors. It is not a comprehensive bibliography of women photographers of this period, but rather focuses on sources that were most relevant to the research of this project. The references have been divided between unpublished sources, books and articles and followed by a section listed by photographer that corresponds with the biographies.

Unpublished Sources

Frances Benjamin Johnston Papers, Manuscripts Division, Library of Congress, Washington, D.C.

F. Holland Day Archives, Norwood Historical Society, Norwood, MA.

Stieglitz Archives, Collection of American Literature, Beinecke Rare Book and Manuscript Library, Yale University, New Haven, CT.

Books and Exhibition Catalogues

Catalogue of Exhibitors in the United States Sections of the International Universal Exposition, Paris, 1900. Paris: Imprimeries Lemercier, 1900.

Cauldwell, John B. United States Sections of the International Universal Exposition, Paris, 1900. Boston: George E. Ellis, 1900: XV.

Daniel, Pete and Raymond Smock. A Talent for Detail. The Photographs of Miss Frances Benjamin Johnston 1889–1910. New York: Harmony Books, 1974.

Danly, Susan and Cheryl Liebold. Eakins and the Photograph. Philadelphia: The Pennsylvania Academy of the Fine Arts, 1994.

Davidov, Judith Fryer. Women's Camera Work/Self/Body/Other in American Visual Culture. Durham and London: Duke University Press, 1998.

Davis, Kate. Camera Notes: Indices. Chicago: Kate Davis, 1978.

Fink, Loïs. Paris Bound: Americans in Art Schools, 1868–1918 (exh. cat.). Paris: Réunion des Musées Nationaux, 1990.

Fischer, Diane Pietrucha. "The "American School" in Paris: The Repatriation of American Art at the Universal Exposition of 1900" (Ph.D. diss.). New York: City University of New York, 1993.

—, ed. Paris 1900: The "American School" at the Universal Exposition (exh. cat.). New Brunswick, NJ: Rutgers University Press, 1999.

Fulton, Marianne, ed. Pictorialism into Modernism: The Clarence H. White School of Photography. Rochester, NY: George Eastman House, 1996.

Gover, Jane C. The Positive Image: Women Photographers in Turn of the Century America. Albany: State University of New York, 1988.

Hannum, Gillian Greenhill. The Outsiders: the Salon Club of America and the Popularization of Pictorial Photography. Ann Arbor, MI: University Microfilms International, 1986.

—. Coming to Light: Frances Benjamin Johnston and the Foremost Women Photographers in America. Forthcoming.

Homer, William Innes. Alfred Stieglitz and the Photo-Secession. Boston: New York Graphic Society, 1983.

—. Pictorial Photography in Philadelphia: The Pennsylvania Academy's Salons 1898–1901. Philadelphia: Pennsylvania Academy of the Fine Arts, 1984.

Lee, Mack. Naturalist Photography, 1880–1920. Winchester, MA: Lee Gallery, September 1998.

Moeller, Madelyn. Women Photographers: A New Dimension in Leisure. Norwalk, CT: The Lockwood-Mathews Mansion Museum, 1987.

Naef, Weston. Fifty Pioneers of Modern Photography: The Collection of Alfred Stieglitz. New York: The Metropolitan Museum of Art, 1978.

Palmquist, Peter. Camera Fiends & Kodak Girls: 50 Selections by and about Women in Photography, 1840–1930. New York: Midmarch Arts Press, 1989.

—. Shadowcatchers: A Directory of Women in California Photography Before 1901. Arcata, CA: Peter E. Palmquist, 1990.

—. Camera Fiends & Kodak Girls II: 60 Selections by and about Women in Photography, 1855–1965. New York: Midmarch Arts Press, 1995.

—. Bibliography of Articles by and about Women in Photography 1840–1990. Arcata, CA: The Women in Photography International Archive, 2000.

Pector, Sosthène. Congrès International de Photographie, tenu à Paris du 23 au 28 juillet 1900. Procès-verbaux sommaires. Ministère du Commerce, de l'Industrie, des Postes et des Télégraphes. Exposition Universelle Internationale de 1900. Paris: Imprimerie Nationale, 1900.

—. Congrès international de photographie, procès-verbaux, rapports, notes et documents divers. Paris: Gauthier-Villars, 1901.

Peterson, Christian A. Alfred Stieglitz's: Camera Notes. Minneapolis: The Minneapolis Institute of Arts, 1993.

—, ed. Index to the American Annual of Photography. Printed privately in Minneapolis, 1996.

Régnal, G. Comment la femme peut gagner sa vie. Paris: J. Tallandier, 1908.

Report of the Commissioner General for the United States to the International Exposition, Paris, 1900, 6 vols. Washington, D.C.: Government Printing Office, 1901.

Reyner, Albert. L'Année photographique 1901. Paris: C. Mendel, 1901.

Rosenblum, Naomi. A History of Women Photographers. New York: Abbeville Press, 1994.

Sandweiss, Martha. Photography in Nineteenth-Century America. Fort Worth: Amon Carter Museum; New York: Abrams, 1991.

Schweizer, Alfred. Les États-Unis à l'Exposition Universelle de 1900. Paris: Imprimerie P. Dubreuil, 1900.

Steele, Chris. A Directory of Massachusetts Photographers, 1839–1900. Camden, ME: Picton Press, 1993.

Sternberger, Paul Spencer. Between Amateur & Aesthete: The Legitimation of Photography as Art in America, 1880–1900. Albuquerque: University of New Mexico Press, 2001.

Ulehla, Karen Evans. The Society of Arts and Crafts, Boston: Exhibition Record 1897–1927. Boston: Boston Public Library, 1981.

Tucker, Anne. The Woman's Eye. New York: Knopf, 1973.

Weisberg, Gabriel P. and Jane R. Becker, ed. Overcoming All Obstacles: The Women of the Académie Julian. New York: Dahesh Museum; New Brunswick, NJ: Rutgers University Press, 1999.

Wexler, Laura. Tender Violence: Domestic Visions in an Age of U.S. Imperialism. Chapel Hill and London: The University of North Carolina Press, 2000.

Willard, Frances E. Occupations for Women. New York: The Success Co., 1897.

Articles

Abel, Juan C. "Women Photographers and their Work." The Delineator 58, part 1 (September 1901): 406–11; part 2 (October 1901): 574–79; part 3 (November 1901): 747–51.

Allan, Sidney. "The Exhibition of the Photo-Secession." The Photographic Times Bulletin 36, no. 3 (March 1904): 101.

Barnes, Catherine Weed. "Why Ladies Should be Admitted to Membership in Photographic Societies." The American Amateur Photographer 1, no. 6 (December 1889): 223–24.

—. "Women as Photographers." American Amateur Photographer 3 (September 1891): 338.

Bennett, Jeanne E. "First American Photographic Salon." Camera Craft 10, no. 1 (January 1905): 36.

Bentzon, Th. "Woman at the Paris Exhibition." The Outlook 66 (29 September 1900): 258.

Bisland, Margaret. "Women and Their Cameras." Outing 17 (October 1890): 36–8.

Bisland, Mary L. "Women." The Illustrated American 7, no. 69 (13 June 1891): 185.

Breck, Henrietta S. "California Women and Artistic Photography." Overland Monthly 43, no. 2 (February 1904): 88–97.

Coburn, A.L. "American Photographs in London." Photo Era 6, no. 1 (January 1901): 209–15.

Crane, Frank W. "American Women Photographers." Munsey's Magazine 2 (July 1894): 398–408.

Cunha, A. de. "Les Photographes à l'Exposition de 1900." Photo-Gazette (25 July 1900): 161–69.

Davie, Helen L. "The Los Angeles Exhibition, Its History and Success and Those Responsible for It." Camera Craft 5, no. 2 (June 1902).

—. "Women in Photography." Camera Craft 5, no. 4 (August 1902): 130–38.

Davison, George. "The Photographic Salon." The American Amateur Photographer 5 (November 1893): 495–98.

Day, F. Holland. "Photography as a Fine Art." Photo-Era (March 1900): 91.

Déambulator. "Les Anglais et les Américains à l'exposition du Photo-Club." Bulletin du Photo-Club de Paris (June 1898): 185–202.

Delaney, Michelle Anne. "The 1896 Washington Salon and Art Photography." American Art Review 9, no. 1 (1997): 110–15.

Demachy, Robert. "Conclusion." Bulletin du Photo-Club de Paris (December 1900): 392–93.

—. "L'Exposition des Artistes Américaines." Bulletin du Photo-Club de Paris (April 1901): 107–13.

—. "The American New School of Photography in Paris." Camera Notes 5, no. 1 (July 1901): 33–42.

—. "Artistic Photography in France." Photograms of the Year (1901): 7–9.

Doherty, Amy S. "Frances Benjamin Johnston, 1864–1952." History of Photography 4, no. 2 (April 1980): 97–111.

"The English Exhibitions and the 'American Invasion.'" Camera Notes 4 (January 1901): 162–75.

"Frances Benjamin Johnston Collection." In Washingtoniana Photographs: Collections in the Prints and Photographs Division of the Library of Congress, ed. by Kathleen Collins, 126–133. Washington, D.C.: Library of Congress, 1989.

Gastine, M.L. "La Femme Photographe." Bulletin du Photo-Club de Paris (1902): 268–71.

Hersey, Héloise. "The Educated Woman of Tomorrow." The Outlook (August 1, 1903): 841.

Hines, Richard, Jr. "Women and Photography." The American Amateur Photographer 11, no. 3 (March 1899): 118–24.

—. "Women in Photography." *Wilson's* 36 (March 1899): 137–41.

—. "Women and Photography." *The American Amateur Photographer* 11, no. 4 (April 1899): 144–52.

Horsley-Hinton, Alfred. "À l'Étranger. 'L'École Américaine.'" *Bulletin du Photo-Club de Paris* (1901): 16–17.

—. "L'École Américaine." *Le Photogramme* 5, no. 3 (March 1901): 46–48.

Johnston, Frances Benjamin. "What a Woman Can Do with a Camera." *The Ladies' Home Journal* 14 (September 1897): 6–7.

—, ed. "The Foremost Women Photographers of America. A Series of Picture-pages Showing What Women Have Done with the Camera." *Ladies' Home Journal*, Gertrude Käsebier, 18, no. 6 (May 1901): 1; Mathilde Weil, no. 7 (June 1901): 9; Frances and Mary Allen, no. 8 (July 1901): 13; Emma J. Farnsworth, no. 9 (August 1901): 1; Eva Lawrence Watson (Mrs. Martin Schultze [*sic*]), no. 11 (October 1901): 5; Zaïda Ben-Yusuf, no. 12 (November 1901): 13; Elizabeth Brownell, no. 19 (January 5, 1902): 3.

Klary, C. "L'Exposition Photographique des Artistes Américaines." *Le Photogramme* 5, no. 3 (March 2001): 48.

—. "L'Exposition des œuvres de M.F. Holland Day et des Artistes de la Nouvelle École Américaine." *Le Photogramme* 5, no. 4 (April 1901): 63–64.

Moore, Clarence Bloomfield. "Women Experts in Photography." *Cosmopolitan* 14 (March 1893): 556.

Pascaline. "La Femme-photographe." *La Photographie* 2 (1903): 28–30.

Peterson, Anne E. "Nineteenth-Century Profile: Frances Benjamin Johnston. The Early Years, 1888–1908." *Nineteenth Century Magazine of the Victorian Society in America* (spring 1980): 58–61.

"La Photographie comme profession féminine." *Photo Pêle-Mêle* (March 3, 1906): 66–69.

"Photography at the Paris Exhibition." *British Journal of Photography* 12 (June 7, 1900): 380–86.

Poivert, Michel. "La Photographie artistique à l'Exposition universelle de 1900." *Histoire de l'Art* 13–14 (May 1991): 55–65.

—. "Le Sacrifice du présent—pictorialisme et modernité." *Études photographiques* 8 (November 2000): 92–110.

"Progress in Photography. Collections of Specimens for the Paris Exposition. All the Work of American Women—A Proposed Exhibit in This City." *The Evening Star* (July 6, 1900): 1, 11.

Przyblyski, Jeanne M. "American Visions at the Paris Exposition, 1900: Another Look at Frances Benjamin Johnston's Hampton Photographs." *Art Journal* 57, no. 3 (fall 1998): 60–68.

Puyo, Constant. "La Photographie artistique aux États-Unis." *Le Monde moderne* 13 (May 1901): 641–49.

Quitslund, Toby. "Her Feminine Colleagues—Photographs and Letters Collected by Frances Benjamin Johnston in 1900." In *Women Artists in Washington Collections*, ed. by Josephine Withers, 97–143. College Park, MD and Women's Caucus for Art, 1979.

Rayne, M.L. "Women as Photographers." In *What Can A Woman Do?* St. Louis: F. B. Dickerson and Company, 1884. Reprint New York: Arno, 1974.

Reyner, A. "La Femme et la photographie." *Le Nord Photographe* 7 (1907): n.p.

Sheldon, S.L. "The International Congress of Photography at Paris." *The Photographic Times* 32 (December 1900): 558.

"The Social World." *The Evening Star* (June 30, 1900): 7.

Sreznewsky, W.I. "The Collection of Photographs Taken by American Women Amateur Photographers." *Fotograficheskoe obozrienie* 1 (1901): 1–5.

Staley, Kathryn. "Photography as a Fine Art." *Munsey's* 14 (February 1896): 582–91.

Stieglitz, Alfred. "American Photography at the Paris Exposition." *The American Photographer* 12, no. 4 (September 1900): 411–14.

—. "Modern Pictorial Photography." *Century Magazine* 64 (October 1902): 822–25.

"Three Gold Medals." [Rochester, New York] *Post Express* (February 21, 1901): 12.

"The Two Exhibitions—the Ninth Annual Exhibition of the Photographic Salon." *Photography* 13 (October 3, 1901): 659–70.

Varigny, C. de. "La Femme aux États-Unis." *Revue des Deux Mondes* (January 15, 1893): 391–428.

Vidal, Léon. "L'Exposition des artistes américains [*sic*] au Photo-Club de Paris." *Le Moniteur de la photographie* 4 (1901): 49–51.

Wallon, Étienne. "L'Exposition des Artistes Américaines au Photo-Club." *Photo-Gazette* (February 25, 1901): 61–64.

Wasburne, Marion Foster. "A New Profession for Women: Photography and the Success Which Follows Earnest Endeavor and Diligent Work." *Godey's Magazine* 134 (February 1897): 123–28.

Wexler, Laura. "Black and White and Color: American Photographs at the Turn of the Century." *Prospects: An Annual of American Culture Studies* 13 (1988): 356–57.

"Woman's Work in Photography." *The Photographic Times and the American Photographer* 17, no. 287 (March 18, 1887): 127–28.

Photographers

MARY ELECTA AND FRANCES STEBBINS ALLEN

Allen, Mary E. "Blue-and-White Needlework." *House Beautiful* 3 (April 1898): 166–69.

Crenshaw, Karen. "Images of Childhood: The Photography of Mary and Frances Allen." In unpublished paper, Collection of Historic Deerfield Summer Fellowship Program, 1979.

Douglas, Ed. Polk. "Frances and Mary Allen: A Biography." In unpublished paper, Collection of Historic Deerfield Summer Fellowship Program, 1969.

Flynt, Suzanne. *Pictorial Ideals: Allen Sisters Photographs*. Deerfield, MA: Pocumtuck Valley Memorial Association. Forthcoming.

"A Group of Photographic Studies." *The Craftsman* 8 (May 1905): 221–22.

Hannum, Gillian Greenhill. "Frances and Mary Allen." In *Coming to Light: Frances Benjamin Johnston and the Foremost Women Photographers in America*. Forthcoming.

Kelly, Jain. "Frances S. Allen" and "Mary E. Allen." In *A History of Women Photographers*, Naomi Rosenblum. New York: Abbeville Press, 1994.

Moeller, Madelyn. *Nineteenth-Century Women Photographers: A New Dimension in Leisure*. Norwalk, CT: The Lockwood-Mathews Mansion Museum, 1987.

Quitslund, Toby. "Frances Stebbins Allen and Mary Electa Allen." In *Women Artists in Washington Collections*, ed. by Josephine Withers. College Park, MD: University of Maryland Art Gallery and Women's Caucus for Art, 1979.

Illustrations for

Abbott, Katharine M. *Old Paths and Legends of the New England Border—Connecticut, Deerfield, and the Berkshires*. New York and London: G. P. Putnam's Sons, 1909 [first published: New York: Knickerbocker Press, 1907].

Earle, Alice Morse. *Home Life in Colonial Days*. New York: MacMillan Company, 1898.

Holme, Charles, ed. *Colour Photography*. London, New York: Offices of The Studio, 1908.

Moore, N. Hudson. *The Old Furniture Book*. New York: Frederick A. Stokes Company, 1903.

Sheldon, George. *The Little Brown House on the Albany Road*. Deerfield, MA: George Sheldon, 1915.

Warner, Charles F., ed. *Picturesque Franklin*. Northampton, MA: Wade, Warner and Co., 1891.

Unpublished Sources

Allen Papers, Pocumtuck Valley Memorial Association Library, Deerfield, MA.

Frances Benjamin Johnston Papers, Manuscripts Division, Library of Congress, Washington, D.C.: Six letters from Mary E. Allen to Frances Benjamin Johnston, 1897–1901; four letters from Mary E. Allen to Frances Benjamin Johnston, n.d.

ALICE AUSTIN

Hines, Richard, Jr. "Women in Photography." *Photo-Era* 17, no. 3 (September 1906): 141–53.

Kelly, Jain. "Alice Austin." In *A History of Women Photographers*, Naomi Rosenblum. New York: Abbeville Press, 1994.

Meister, Laura Ilise. "Alice Austin." In "Missing from the Picture: Boston Women Photographers 1880–1920" (M.A. thesis). Tufts University, 1998.

Quitslund, Toby. "Alice Austin." In *Women Artists in Washington Collections*, ed. by Josephine Withers. College Park, MD: University of Maryland Art Gallery and Women's Caucus for Art, 1979.

Unpublished Sources

Frances Benjamin Johnston Papers, Manuscripts Division, Library of Congress, Washington, D.C.: One letter from Alice Austin to Frances Benjamin Johnston with accompanying biographical sketch, June 8, 1900; one letter, with enclosures: one photographic portrait of Austin by Arthur Gleason and one advertising pamphlet, June 21, 1900.

F. Holland Day Papers, Norwood Historical Society, Norwood, MA: One letter from Alice Austin to F. Holland Day, July 11, 1906.

MARY A. BARTLETT

Bartlett, Mary A. *Old Friends with New Faces*. Boston: Joseph Knight Company, 1893. [photographs on tissue by Mrs. N. Gray Bartlett]

—. *Mother Goose of '93: Photographic Illustrations by Mrs. N. Gray Bartlett*. Boston: Joseph Knight Company, 1893.

Crane, Frank W. "American Women Photographers." *Munsey's* 11 (July 1894): 404.

Humphrey, Marmaduke. "Triumphs in American Photography—Mrs. N. Gray Bartlett." *Godey's Magazine* 136, no. 814 (April 1898): 368–78.

Kelly, Jain. "Mary Bartlett." In *A History of Women Photographers*, Naomi Rosenblum. New York: Abbeville Press, 1994.

Moore, Clarence B. "Women Experts in Photography." *Cosmopolitan* 14 (March 1893): 580–90.

Morrill, Frederick K. "The Ladies of the Chicago Camera Club." *The American Amateur Photographer* 3, no. 11 (November 1891): 416–17.

Quitslund, Toby. "Her Feminine Colleagues—Photographs and Letters Collected by Frances Benjamin Johnston in 1900." In *Women Artists in Washington Collections*, ed. by Josephine Withers, 114. College Park, MD: University of Maryland Art Gallery and Women's Caucus for Art, 1979.

Wyatt, Marian L. *A Girl I Know*. Boston: Joseph Knight, 1894. [Photographically illustrated by Mary A. Bartlett.]

Unpublished Sources

Frances Benjamin Johnston Papers, Manuscripts Division, Library of Congress, Washington, D.C.: Two letters from Mary Bartlett to Frances Benjamin Johnston, June, 6 and 20 [1900].

ZAIDA BEN-YUSUF

Abel, Juan C. "Women Photographers and Their Work. Paper the First." *The Delineator* 58 (September 1901): 406–11.

Allan, Sidney (Sadakichi Hartmann). "A Few American Portraits." *Wilson's Photographic Magazine* 49 (October 1912): 457–59.

"An Artist-Photographer." *Current Literature* 34 (January 1903): 21.

Ben-Yusuf, Zaida. "Japan Through My Camera." *Photo-Era* 12 (May 1904): 77–79.

—. "Period of Daikan." *Architectural Record* 19 (February 1906): 145–50.

—. "Honorable Flowers of Japan." *Century* 73 (March 1907): 697–705.

Hannum, Gillian Greenhill. "The Salon Club of America and the Popularization of Pictorial Photography." University Microfilms International, 1986.

—. "Zaida Ben-Yusuf." In *Coming to Light: Frances Benjamin Johnston and the Foremost Women Photographers in America*. Forthcoming.

Hartmann, Sadakichi. "Zaida Ben-Yusuf: A Purist." *Photographic Times* 31 (October 1899): 449–55. Also reprinted in Lawton, Harry W. and George Knox, eds. *The Valiant Knights of Daguerre: Selected Critical Essays on Photography and Profiles of Photographic Pioneers*. Berkeley: University of California Press, 1978: 167–72.

—. "Portrait Painting and Portrait Photographers." *Camera Notes* 3, no. 1 (July 1899): 3–22.

Hines, Richard, Jr. "Women in Photography." *Wilson's Photographic Magazine* 36, no. 507 (March 1899): 137–41. Reprint of address delivered before the Art League of Mobile, Alabama, January 19, 1899.

Johnston, Frances Benjamin. "The Foremost Women Photographers of America. Sixth Article: Zaida Ben-Yusuf." *The Ladies' Home Journal* 18, no. 12 (November 1901): 13.

Kelly, Jain. "Zaida Ben-Yusuf." In *A History of Women Photographers*, Naomi Rosenblum. New York: Abbeville Press, 1994.

Murray, William F. "Miss Zaida Ben-Yusuf's Exhibition." *Camera Notes* 2 (April 1899): 168–72.

Naef, Weston J. "Zaida Ben-Yusuf." In *The Collection of Alfred Stieglitz: Fifty Pioneers of Modern Photography*. New York: Metropolitan Museum of Art and Viking Press, 1978.

Poulson, Elizabeth. *Zaida*. Tempe, AZ: Arizona State University, School of Art, 1985.

Quitslund, Toby. "Zaida Ben-Yusuf." In *Women Artists in Washington Collections*, ed. by Josephine Withers. College Park, MD: University of Maryland Art Gallery and Women's Caucus for Art, 1979.

Unpublished Sources

Frances Benjamin Johnston Papers, Manuscripts Division, Library of Congress, Washington, D.C.: One letter and accompanying biographical sketch from Zaida Ben-Yusuf to Frances Benjamin Johnston, May 31, 1900.

Stieglitz Archives, Collection of American Literature, Beinecke Rare Book and Manuscript Library, Yale University, New Haven, CT: Three letters from Zaida Ben-Yusuf to Alfred Stieglitz and one from Alfred Stieglitz to Zaida Ben-Yusuf, 1897–1915, two undated.

ELIZABETH BROWNELL

Brownell, Elizabeth. *Posters of the Vision Children of Childhood*. Chicago: American Plate and Picture Co., 1902.

—. *Really Babies*. Chicago: Rand; New York: McNally and Company, 1908.

—, ed. *Dream Children*. With an introduction by Clara E. Laughlin. Indianapolis: The Bowen-Merrill Company, 1901. [Illustrated by Brownell]

Chicago Historical Society. *Chicago Photographers 1847 through 1900*. Chicago: Chicago Historical Society, 1958.

Hannum, Gillian Greenhill. "Dream Children." Unpublished manuscript, Manhattanville College, 1999.

—. "Elizabeth Brownell." In *Coming to Light: Frances Benjamin Johnston and the Foremost Women Photographers in America*. Forthcoming.

Johnston, Frances Benjamin. "The Foremost Women Photographers in America. Seventh Article: Elizabeth Brownell." *The Ladies' Home Journal* 19, no. 2 (January 1902): 1.

Laughlin, Clara E. *Traveling Through Life*. Boston, New York: Houghton Mifflin Company, 1934.

ROSE CLARK AND ELIZABETH FLINT WADE

Abel, Juan C. "Women Photographers and Their Work. Concluding Paper." *The Delineator* 58 (September 1901): 747–51.

Allen, Sidney. "The Exhibition of the Photo-Secession." *The Photographic Times* 36, no. 3 (March 1904): 101.

Bannon, Anthony. "Rose Clark" and "Elizabeth Flint Wade." In *The Photo-Pictorialists of Buffalo*. Buffalo, NY: Media Study, 1981.

Caffin, Charles H. "Exhibition of Prints by Miss Rose Clark and Mrs. Elizabeth Flint Wade." *Camera Notes* (January 1901): 186.

Hitchcock, Lucious W. "Pictorial Photography." *Photo-Beacon* 14 (July 1902): 198–201.

Mallett, Daniel Trowbridge. "Rose Clark." In *Mallet's Index of Artists, International Biography*. New York: Peter Smith, 1948.

"Miss Rose Clark, Artist is Dead at Age 90." *Buffalo Evening News* (November 20, 1942).

Naef, Weston J. "Rose Clark and Elizabeth Flint Wade." In *The Collection of Alfred Stieglitz: Fifty Pioneers of Modern Photography*, 298–99. New York: Metropolitan Museum of Art and Viking Press, 1978.

Naylor, Maria. "Rose Clark." In *The National Academy of Design Exhibition Record, 1861–1900*. New York: Kennedy Galleries, 1973.

"Obituary Record: Mrs. Elizabeth Flint Wade." *Norwalk Hour* (December 3, 1915).

Peterson, Christian A. "Rose Clark and Elizabeth Flint Wade." In *Alfred Stieglitz's Camera Notes*. Minneapolis: Minneapolis Institute of Arts and W.W. Norton & Company, 1993.

Quitslund, Toby. "Rose Clark and Elizabeth Flint Wade." In *Women Artists in Washington Collections*, ed. by Josephine Withers. College Park, MD: University of Maryland Art Gallery and Women's Caucus for Art, 1979.

"Rose Clark." In *Dictionnaire critique et documentaire des peintres, sculpteurs, dessinateurs et graveurs*, ed. by Emmanuel Bénézit. Paris: Libraire Gründ, 1976.

"Rose Clark" In *Dictionary of Women Artists: an International Dictionary of Women Artists Born before 1900*, ed. by Chris Petteys. Boston: G.K. Hall, 1985.

Stieglitz, Alfred. "Modern Pictorial Photography." *Century Magazine* (October 1902).

Wade, Elizabeth Flint. "Artistic Pictures, Suggestions How to Make Them." *The American Amateur Photographer* 5 (October 1893): 441–47.

—. "Amateur Photography Through Women's Eyes." *The Photo-American* 5 (March 1894): 235–38.

—. "The Camera as a Source of Income Outside the Studio." *The Photographic Times* 24 (June 8, 1894): 358–61.

—. "Photography—Its Marvels." *St. Nicholas* 20 (September 1898): 952–59.

—. "The Round Robin Guild." *Photo-Era* 7 (November 1901) to 31 (September 1912). [monthly column]

—. "The Nation's Landmarks." *Photo-Era* 11 (July 1903): 243–45.

—. "Coloring Lantern Slides." *Photo-Era* 16 (March 1906): 151–54.

—. "Portrait Photography." *Photo-Era* 18, no. 3 (March 1907): 155.

Unpublished Sources

Frances Benjamin Johnston Papers, Manuscripts Division, Library of Congress, Washington, D.C.: One letter from Rose Clark and Elizabeth Flint Wade to Frances Benjamin Johnston, June 11, [1900]; one letter from Rose Clark to Frances Benjamin Johnston, June 22, 1900.

Stieglitz Archives, Collection of American Literature, Beinecke Rare Book and Manuscript Library, Yale University, New Haven, CT: Five letters from Rose Clark to Alfred Stieglitz, 1900–1902; two letters from Elizabeth Flint Wade to Alfred Stieglitz, October 12, 1898, one undated.

ANNIE N. CROWELL

"Annie Crowell dies at 87." *San Francisco Examiner* (October 7, 1949). [Errantly listed as Annie M. Crowell]

"A Few Words of Criticism Upon the Work of Each Exhibitor, Leveled in a Kindly Spirit by the Editor." *Camera Craft* 4, no. 3 (January 1902): 124.

Hughes, Edan Milton. "Crowell, Anne Nelson." In *Artists in California: 1786–1940*. San Francisco: Hughes Publishing Company, 1986.

Palmquist, Peter. "Annie Nelson Crowell." In *Shadowcatchers: A Directory of Women in California Photography 1900–1920*. Arcata, CA: Peter E. Palmquist, 1991.

"Prize Winning Pictures at the Salon." *Camera Craft* 2, no. 4 (February 1901): 321. [Errantly listed as Mrs. A. M. Crowell.]

Quitslund, Toby. "Her Feminine Colleagues—Photographs and Letters Collected by Frances Benjamin Johnston in 1900." In *Women Artists in Washington Collections*, ed. by Josephine Withers, 117. College Park, MD: University of Maryland Art Gallery and Women's Caucus for Art, 1979.

San Francisco City Directory.

Schwartz, Ellen. *Nineteenth Century San Francisco Art Exhibition Catalogs*. Davis, CA: Library Associates, University Library, University of California, Davis, 1981.

ANNA DESMOND

Davie, Helen L. "The Los Angeles Exhibition, Its History and Success and Those Responsible for It." *Camera Craft* 5, no. 2 (June 1902): 47.

Desmond, Anna & Co. "Florence." *Camera Craft* 4, no. 8 (June 1902): 73.

—. "Baby." *Camera Craft* 4, no. 10 (August 1902): 135.

Palmquist, Peter. "Anna Desmond." In *Shadowcatchers: A Directory of Women in California Photography 1900–1920*. Arcata, CA: Peter E. Palmquist, 1991.

MARY DEVENS

Downes, William Howe. "Artistic Photography: Memorial Exhibition of Works by Miss Mary Devens in Gallery of Society of Arts and Crafts." *Boston Evening Transcript* (January 18, 1921): 6.

Hartmann, Sadakichi. "The Photo-Secession Exhibition at the Carnegie Art Galleries, Pittsburgh, PA." *Camera Work* 6: 50.

Meister, Laura Ilise. "Mary Devens." In "Missing from the Picture: Boston Women Photographers 1880–1920" (M.A. thesis). Tufts University, 1998.

"Miss Mary Devens of Cambridge." [obituary] *Boston Evening Transcript* (March 15, 1920).

Naef, Weston J. "Mary Devens." In *The Collection of Alfred Stieglitz: Fifty Pioneers of Modern Photography*. New York: Metropolitan Museum of Art, 1978.

"Old Cambridge Camera Club." *Photo-Era* 2, no. 4 (March 1899): 261.

Peterson, Christian A. "Mary Devens." In *Alfred Stieglitz's Camera Notes*. Minneapolis: Minneapolis Institute of Arts, W.W. Norton & Company, 1993.

Quitslund, Toby. "Mary Devens." In *Women Artists in Washington Collections*, ed. by Josephine Withers. College Park, MD: University of Maryland Art Gallery and Women's Caucus for Art, 1979.

Robinson, William F. "Devens, Mary." In *A Certain Slant of Light: The First 100 Years of New England Photography*. Boston: New York Graphic Society, 1980.

Wells, James A. *A Short History of the Old Cambridge Photographic Club*. Boston: Alfred Mudge & Son, 1905.

Unpublished Sources

Frances Benjamin Johnston Papers, Manuscripts Division, Library of Congress, Washington, DC.: One letter from Mary Devens to Frances Benjamin Johnston, August22, 1901.

F. Holland Day Archives, Norwood Historical Society, Norwood, MA. Twelve letters from Mary Devens to F. Holland Day, 1898–1907.

Stieglitz Archives, Collection of American Literature, Beinecke Rare Book and Manuscript Library, Yale University, New Haven, CT: Ten letters from Mary Devens to Alfred Stieglitz, 1899–1904.

SARAH JANE EDDY

Eddy, Sarah J. "A Good Use for the Camera." *American Annual of Photography and Photographic Times Almanac for 1894* (1894): 186–88.

—. *Friends and Helpers*. Boston: Ginn and Co., 1899.

—. *Songs of Happy Life*. Silver, Burdett and Co., 1901.

—. *Amigos y auxiliares del hombre; cuentos comp. Por S. J. Eddy*. Boston: Ginn and Co., 1901.

—. *The Robin's Nest*. Bristol Ferry, RI, n.d.

—. *Alexander and Some Other Cats*. Boston: Marshall Jones, 1929.

—. *Happy Cats and Their Care: Compiled and Arranged by Sarah J. Eddy.* Norwood, MA: privately printed by the Plimpton Press, 1938.

Hickman, W. Albert. "A Recent Exhibition: Tenth Annual Composition Exhibition, 1898, Boston Camera Club." *Photo-Era* 1 (May 1898): 11–13.

Hines, Richard, Jr. "Women in Photography." *Wilson's Photographic Magazine* 36, no. 507 (March 1899): 137–41. Also published in *American Amateur Photographer* 11, no. 3 (March 1899): 121–22. Reprints of address delivered before the Art League of Mobile, AL, January 19, 1899.

Kelly, Jain "Sarah J. Eddy." In *A History of Women Photographers*, Naomi Rosenblum. New York: Abbeville Press, 1994.

Meister, Laura Ilise. "Sarah Jane Eddy." In "Missing from the Picture: Boston Women Photographers 1880–1920" (M.A. thesis). Tufts University, 1998.

"Miss Sarah A. [*sic*] Eddy." [Obituary] *New York Times* (March 31, 1945): 19.

"The Providence Camera Club," *Photo-Era* (May 1900): 156.

"Providence, R.I., Camera Club." *Photo-Era* 2 (April 1900): 289–90.

Quitslund, Toby. "Sarah Jane Eddy." In. *Women Artists in Washington Collections*, ed. by Josephine Withers. College Park, MD: University of Maryland Art Gallery and Women's Caucus for Art, 1979: 118.

"Sarah James [*sic*] Eddy." In *Dictionary of Women Artists: an International Dictionary of Women Artists Born before 1900*, ed. by Chris Petteys. Boston: G.K. Hall, 1985.

"Sarah James [*sic*] Eddy." In *Mantle Fielding's Dictionary of American Painters, Sculptors & Engravers*, ed. by Glenn B. Opitz. Poughkeepsie, NY: Apollo, 1986.

Unpublished Sources

Frances Benjamin Johnston Papers, Manuscripts Division, Library of Congress, Washington, D.C.: Six letters from Sarah J. Eddy to Frances Benjamin Johnston, 1895–1904.

Frederick Douglass Papers, Manuscripts Division, Library of Congress, Washington, D.C.: Eight letters from Sarah Jane Eddy to Frederick Douglass, 1882–1890.

FANNIE ELTON

Cleveland, Ohio City Directories, 1893–1912.

"Elton, Fannie L." In *Artists in Ohio, 1787–1900: A Biographical Dictionary*, ed. by Mary Sayre Haverstock, et al. Kent, OH: The Kent State University Press, 2000.

Gagel, Diane VanSkiver. *Ohio Photographers 1839–1900*. Nevada City: Carl Mautz Publishing, 1998.

Quitslund, Toby. "Her Feminine Colleagues—Photographs and Letters Collected by Frances Benjamin Johnston in 1900." In *Women Artists in Washington Collections*, ed. by Josephine Withers. College Park, MD: University of Maryland Art Gallery and Women's Caucus for Art, 1979: 118.

Unpublished Sources

Frances Benjamin Johnston Papers, Manuscripts Division, Library of Congress, Washington, D.C.: Two letters from Fannie Elton to Frances Benjamin Johnston, June 16 and 23, 1900.

EMMA J. FARNSWORTH

Abel, Juan C. "Women Photographers and Their Work. Second Article." *The Delineator* 58 (September 1901): 574–79.

Farnsworth, Emma Justine. *In Arcadia*. New York: George M. Allen Co., 1892.

—. *Sunshine and Playtime: verses by the Rt. Rev. William Croswell Doane*. New York: Dutton, 1893.

Hannum, Gillian Greenhill. "Emma J. Farnsworth." In *Coming to Light: Frances Benjamin Johnston and the Foremost Women Photographers in America*. Forthcoming.

Hines, Richard, Jr. "Women in Photography." *Wilson's Photographic Magazine* 36, no. 507 (March 1899): 137–41. Also published in *American Amateur Photographer* 11, no. 3 (March 1899): 119–20. Reprints of address delivered before the Art League of Mobile, AL, January 19, 1899.

Johnston, Frances Benjamin. "Foremost Women Photographers in America, Fourth Article: Emma J. Farnsworth." *The Ladies' Home Journal* 18, no. 9 (August 1901): 1.

Kelly, Jain. "Emma J. Farnsworth." In *A History of Women Photographers*, Naomi Rosenblum. New York: Abbeville Press, 1994.

Murray, William M. "The Farnsworth Exhibition." *Camera Notes* (January 1898): 82–83.

Peterson, Christian A. "Emma J. Farnsworth." *Alfred Stieglitz's Camera Notes*. Minneapolis: Minneapolis Institute of Arts, W.W. Norton & Company, 1993.

Quitslund, Toby. "Emma Justine Farnsworth." In *Women Artists in Washington Collections*, ed. by Josephine Withers. College Park, MD: University of Maryland Art Gallery and Women's Caucus for Art, 1979.

Unpublished Sources

Frances Benjamin Johnston Papers, Manuscripts Division, Library of Congress, Washington, D.C.: One letter from Emma J. Farnsworth to Frances Benjamin Johnston, June 24, [1900].

Stieglitz Archives, Collection of American Literature, Beinecke Rare Book and Manuscript Library, Yale University, New Haven, CT: Ten letters from Emma J. Farnsworth to Alfred Stieglitz, n.d.

EMMA FITZ

Fitz, Emma. "Photography as a Fine Art." *The American Amateur Photographer* 6, no. 12 (December 1894): 543–48.

Hines, Richard, Jr. "Women in Photography." *Wilson's Photographic Magazine* 36, no. 507 (March 1899): 137–41. Also published in *American Amateur Photographer* 11, no. 3 (March 1899): 122–23. Reprints of address delivered before the Art League of Mobile, AL, January 19, 1899.

Meister, Laura Ilise. "Emma Fitz." In "Missing from the Picture: Boston Women Photographers 1880–1920" (M.A. thesis). Tufts University, 1998.

"Miss Emma J. Fitz Dead." *Boston Evening Transcript* (June 7, 1926).

Quitslund, Toby. "Emma J. Fitz," In *Women Artists in Washington Collections*, ed. by Josephine Withers. College Park, MD: University of Maryland Art Gallery and Women's Caucus for Art, 1979.

"'Royal Medals' Won by Americans." *Camera Notes* 2, no. 3 (January 1899): 100.

Unpublished Sources

Frances Benjamin Johnston Papers, Manuscripts Division, Library of Congress, Washington, D.C.: One letter from Emma Fitz to Frances Benjamin Johnston, June 21, 1900.

FLORIDE GREEN

"California Camera Club." *The American Amateur Photographer* (December 1894): 581–82.

"California Camera Club." *The American Amateur Photographer* (May 1896): 227.

"Green, Floride."[Obituary] *San Francisco Chronicle* (October 25, 1896): 5.

Green, Floride. *Some Personal Recollections of Lillie Hitchcock Coit*. San Francisco: The Grabhorn Press, 1935.

—. "Mrs. Lillie Hitchcock Coit." *Quarterly of the California Historical Society* 12 (1933): 366–67.

—. "Annie King Dutton."[Obituary] *Quarterly of the California Historical Society* 12 (1933): 372.

Hines, Richard, Jr. "Women in Photography." *Wilson's Photographic Magazine* 36, no. 507 (March 1899): 138–39. Also published in *American Amateur Photographer* 11, no. 3 (March 1899): 122. Reprints of address delivered before the Art League of Mobile, AL, January 19, 1899.

"In Memorium. Floride Green. 1863–1936." *California Historical Society Quarterly* 15 (1936): 383–84.

New York City Directories, 1897–1901.

Palmquist, Peter E. "Pioneer Women Photographers in Nineteenth-Century California." *California History* 71, no. 1 (spring 1992): 71–110.

—. "Floride Green." In *Shadowcatchers: A Directory of Women in California Photography Before 1901*. Arcata, CA: Peter E. Palmquist, 1990. Reprinted in Palmquist, *Shadowcatchers:*

A Directory of Women in California Photography 1900–1920. Arcata, CA: Peter E. Palmquist, 1991.

Quitslund, Toby. "Floride Green." In *Women Artists in Washington Collections*, ed. by Josephine Withers, 122. College Park, MD: University of Maryland Art Gallery and Women's Caucus for Art, 1979.

San Francisco City Directories, 1885–1890 and 1907–1936.

Unpublished Sources

Frances Benjamin Johnston Papers, Manuscripts Division, Library of Congress, Washington, D.C.: One letter from Floride Green to Frances Benjamin Johnston, June 19, 1900; one letter from Floride Green to Frances Benjamin Johnston with list of photographs, n.d.; press clipping: "Special Photography: Miss Floride Green's Striking Success." In *Occupations for Women: Society Women in Business*. n.d.: 105–6.

ESTELLE HUNTINGTON HUGGINS

Gagel, Diane VanSkiver. *Ohio Photographers 1839–1900.* Nevada City: Carl Mautz Publishing, 1998.

New York City Directories, 1901–1902, 1920–1921.

Unpublished Sources

Frances Benjamin Johnston Papers, Manuscripts Division, Library of Congress, Washington, D.C.: One advertising pamphlet, c. 1900.

GERTRUDE STANTON KÄSEBIER

Bunnell, Peter C. "Gertrude Käsebier." *Arts in Virginia* 16 (fall 1975): 2–15, 40.

Caffin, Charles. "Mrs. Käsebier and the Artistic–Commercial Portrait." *Everybody's Magazine* 4 (May 1901): 480–95.

—. "Mrs. Käsebier's Work—An Appreciation." *Camera Work* 1 (January 1903): 19.

Cram, R.A. "Mrs. Käsebier's Work." *Photo-Era* 4 (May 1900): 131–36.

Demachy, Robert. "Mrs. Käsebier et son œuvre." *La Revue de Photographie* 4 (October 1906): 289–95.

Dow, Arthur W. "Mrs. Gertrude Käsebier's Portrait Photographs." *Camera Notes* 3 (July 1899): 22–23.

Edgerton, Giles (pseud. Mary Fanton Roberts). "Photography as an Emotional Art: A Study of the Work of Gertrude Käsebier." *The Craftsman* 12, no. 1 (April 1907): 80–93.

Hannum, Gillian Greenhill. "Gertrude Käsebier." In *Coming to Light: Frances Benjamin Johnston and the Foremost Women Photographers in America*. Forthcoming.

Hartmann, Sadakichi. "Gertrude Käsebier." *Photographic Times* 32 (May 1900): 195–99.

Hervey, Walter L. "Gertrude Käsebier—Photographer." *Photo-Era* 62 (March 1929): 131–32.

Holm, Ed. "Gertrude Käsebier's Indian Portraits" *The American West* 10 (July 1973): 38–41.

Homer, William Innes. "Gertrude Käsebier: American Pictorial Photographer." *Art & Antiques* (January–February 1980): 78–85.

Johnston, Frances Benjamin. "The Foremost Women Photographers of America. First: The Work of Mrs. Gertrude Käsebier." *The Ladies' Home Journal* 18, no. 6 (May 1901): 1.

—."Gertrude Käsebier, Professional Photographer." *Camera Work* 1 (January 1903): 20.

Käsebier, Gertrude. "Peasant Life in Normandy." *The Monthly Illustrator* 3 (March 1895): 269–75.

—. "An Art Village." *The Monthly Illustrator* 4 (April 1895): 9–17.

—. "Studies in Photography." *The Photographic Times* 30 (June 1898): 269–72.

—. "To Whom It May Concern." *Camera Notes* 3 (January 1900): 121–22.

Keiley, Joseph T. "Gertrude Käsebier." *Camera Work* 20 (October 1907): 27–31.

—. "Mrs. Käsebier's Prints." *Camera Notes* 3 (July 1899): 34.

Kelly, Jain. "Gertude Käsebier" In *A History of Women Photographers*, Naomi Rosenblum. New York: Abbeville Press, 1994.

Lohmann, Helen. "Gertrude Käsebier—Photographer." *Abel's Photographic Weekly* 3 (February 20, 1909): 130.

Ménard, Cyrille. "Les Maîtres de la photographie—Gertrude Käsebier." *Photo-Magazine* 23 (1909): 177–84; 24 (1909): 185–92.

Michaels, Barbara. "Rediscovering Gertrude Käsebier." *Image* (summer 1976): 21.

—. *Gertrude Käsebier*. New York: Abrams, 1992.

Naef, Weston J. "Gertrude Käsebier." In *The Collection of Alfred Stieglitz: Fifty Pioneers of Modern Photography*. New York: Metropolitan Museum of Art and Viking Press, 1978.

Peterson, Christian A. "Gertude Käsebier." In *Alfred Stieglitz's Camera Notes*. Minneapolis: Minneapolis Institute of Arts, W.W. Norton & Company, 1993.

Quitslund, Toby. "Gertrude Käsebier." In *Women Artists in Washington Collections*, ed. by Josephine Withers. College Park, MD: University of Maryland Art Gallery and Women's Caucus for Art, 1979.

Stieglitz, Alfred. "Our Illustrations." *Camera Notes* 3 (July 1899): 24.

Tighe, Mary Ann. "Gertrude Käsebier Lost and Found." *Art in America* 65 (March 1977): 94–98.

Tucker, Anne. "Gertrude Käsebier." In *The Woman's Eye*. New York: Alfred A. Knopf, 1973.

Ward, H. Snowden. "Gertrude Käsebier and Her Work." *Amateur Photographer and Photographic News* 52 (December 13, 1910): 590–91.

Unpublished Sources

Frances Benjamin Johnston Papers, Manuscripts Division, Library of Congress, Washington, D.C.: Five letters from Gertrude Käsebier to Frances Benjamin Johnston, 1892–1903; two letters.

Stieglitz Archives, Collection of American Literature, Beinecke Rare Book and Manuscript Library, Yale University, New Haven, CT: Twenty-one letters from Gertrude Käsebier to Alfred Stieglitz, 1899–1912.

EDITH HAGGIN LOUNSBERY

Bisland, Margaret. "Women and their Cameras." *Outing* 17 (October 17, 1890): 36–43.

"Charitable Photography." *The American Amateur Photographer* (May 1893): 222–23.

Lounsbery, Edith C. "D'après Chapelin." *The Photogram* 1, no. 2 (1894): 40.

"The New York Camera Club's Exhibition of Pictures." *The Photographic Times* (April 15, 1892): 205–7.

New York City Directories, 1894–1934.

Quitslund, Toby. "Edith Haggin Lounsbery." In *Women Artists in Washington Collections*, ed. by Josephine Withers. College Park, MD: University of Maryland Art Gallery and Women's Caucus for Art, 1979.

"Richard R. Lounsbery." [Obituary] *New York Times* (October 24, 1911): 13.

Unpublished Sources

Frances Benjamin Johnston Papers, Manuscripts Division, Library of Congress, Washington, D.C.: Two letters from Edith Haggin Lounsbery to Frances Benjamin Johnston, June 13, [1900] and June 18, 1900.

EMILY MEW

Quitslund, Toby. "Emily Mew." In *Women Artists in Washington Collections*, ed. by Josephine Withers. College Park, MD: University of Maryland Art Gallery and Women's Caucus for Art, 1979.

Washington, D.C. City Directories, 1894–1941.

Unpublished Sources

Frances Benjamin Johnston Papers, Manuscripts Division, Library of Congress, Washington, D.C.: One letter from Emily Mew to Frances Benjamin Johnston, November 12, 1894; two letters from Emily Mew to Frances Benjamin Johnston, n.d., and June 30, [1900].

MARY F. CARPENTER PASCHALL

"Alfred Paschall Dies Very Suddenly." *Bucks County Intelligencer* (January 16, 1912).

Battle, J.H., ed. "The Paschall Brothers." In *History of Bucks County Pennsylvania*. Spartanburg, SC: The Reprint Company, Publishers, 1985.

Panzer, Mary. "Mary F.C. Paschall." In *Philadelphia Naturalistic Photography, 1885–1906*. New Haven: Yale University Art Gallery, 1982.

Quitslund, Toby. "Mary F.C. Paschall." In *Women Artists in Washington Collections*, ed. by Josephine Withers. College Park, MD: University of Maryland Art Gallery and Women's Caucus for Art, 1979.

Unpublished Sources

Frances Benjamin Johnston Papers, Manuscripts Division, Library of Congress, Washington, D.C.: Two letters from Mary Paschall to Frances Benjamin Johnston, June, 16 and 22 [1900].

ANNE K. PILSBURY

Boston City Directories, 1899–1903

Meister, Laura Ilise. "Anne K. Pilsbury." In "Missing from the Picture: Boston Women Photographers 1880–1920" (M.A. thesis). Tufts University, 1998.

Quitslund, Toby. "Annie K. Pilsbury." In *Women Artists in Washington Collections*, ed. by Josephine Withers, 136. College Park, MD: University of Maryland Art Gallery and Women's Caucus for Art, 1979.

Unpublished Sources

Family Papers of Jane Loring Winsor, Schlesinger Library, Radcliffe College, Cambridge, MA: Five photographs by Anne K. Pilsbury.

VIRGINIA M. PRALL

Abel, Juan C. "Women Photographers and Their Work. Second Article." *The Delineator* 58 (September 1901): 574–79.

Cummings, Evaire H. "The Exhibition of Work by Women Photographers at the Hartford Camera Club." *Photo-Era* 16 (May 1906): 329–30.

Hartmann, Sadakichi. "Exhibition of Prints by Virginia M. Prall." *Camera Notes* 4 (April 1901): 276–77.

Nicol, Dr. John. "Holiday Work with the Camera." *Outing* (August 1899): 512–20.

"Notes from the Secretary's Desk." *Camera Notes* 3, no. 3 (January 1900): 126.

Quitslund, Toby. "Virginia Prall." In *Women Artists in Washington Collections*, ed. by Josephine Withers. College Park, MD: University of Maryland Art Gallery and Women's Caucus for Art, 1979.

Watson-Schütze, Eva. "Some Fragmentary Notes on the Chicago Salon." *Camera Notes* 4, no. 4 (January 1902): 200–3.

Unpublished Sources

Frances Benjamin Johnston Papers, Manuscripts Division, Library of Congress, Washington, D.C.: One letter from Virginia Prall to Frances Benjamin Johnston, June 3, 1900.

ADDIE K. ROBINSON

Boston City Directory, 1901.

Bryant, Sarah Cone. "Addie K. Robinson—Artist-Photographer." *Photo-Era* 3, no. 3 (August 1899): 386–89.

"Corliss Art and Camera Club Exhibit." *Photo-Era* (May 1900): 157.

Meister, Laura Ilise. "Addie K. Robinson." In "Missing from the Picture: Boston Women Photographers 1880–1920" (M.A. thesis). Tufts University, 1998.

Quitslund, Toby. "Fr[?]y Gercher" and "Addie Kilburn Robinson." In *Women Artists in Washington Collections*, ed. by Josephine Withers. College Park, MD: University of Maryland Art Gallery and Women's Caucus for Art, 1979.

"Robinson, Addie Kilburn." [Obituary] *Boston Evening Transcript* (January 31, 1935).

Unpublished Sources

Frances Benjamin Johnston Papers, Manuscripts Division, Library of Congress, Washington, D.C.: Two letters and accompanying biographical sketch from Addie K. Robinson to Frances Benjamin Johnston, June 14, [1900], one undated.

MARY TOWNSEND SHARPLES SCHÄFFER

Beck, Janice Sanford. *No Ordinary Woman: the Story of Mary Schäffer Warren*. Calgary, Alberta: Rocky Mountain Books, 2001.

Hart, E.J., ed. *A Hunter of Peace: Mart T.S. Schäffer's Old Indian Trails of the Canadian Rockies/including a previously unpublished account/the 1911 expedition to Maligne Lake and Yahe-Weha—Mountain Woman: A Portrait of Mary Schaeffer. Warren* Banff, Alberta, Canada: The Whyte Foundation, 1980.[Illustrated with photos by Mary T.S. Schäffer.]

Panzer, Mary. "Mary Townsend Sharples Schaeffer [*sic*]." In *Philadelphia Naturalistic Photography, 1885–1906*. New Haven: Yale University Art Gallery, 1982.

Quitslund, Toby. "Mary F.S. [*sic*] Schäffer." In *Women Artists in Washington Collections*, ed. by Josephine Withers. College Park, MD: University of Maryland Art Gallery and Women's Caucus for Art, 1979.

Schäffer, Mary T.S. *Old Indian Trails of the Canadian Rockies*. New York: G. P. Putnam's Sons, 1912 [Illustrated with 100 photos by the author and by Mary W. Adams].

— and Stewardson Brown. *Alpine Flora of the Canadian Rocky Mountains*. New York: G. P. Putnam's, 1907.

Unpublished Sources

Frances Benjamin Johnston Papers, Manuscripts Division, Library of Congress, Washington, D.C.: One letter and accompanying biographical sketch from Mary T.S. Schäffer to Frances Benjamin Johnston, June 12, [1900]; one letter, n.d. [June 24, 1900].

Mary Townsend Sharples Schäffer Papers and Photographs, Whyte Museum of the Canadian Rockies, Banff, Alberta.

SARAH C. SEARS

Allan, Sidney. [Hartmann, Sadakichi] "Pictorial Criticism: Constructive, not Destructive—Portrait of Julia Ward Howe by Sarah C. Sears." *The Photographer* 1 (June 11, 1904): 104–5.

Barter, Judith, et al. *Mary Cassatt: Modern Woman*. Chicago: The Art Institute of Chicago; New York: Abrams, 1998.

Hickman, W. Albert. "A Recent Exhibition." *Photo-Era* 1 (May 1898): 11–13.

Hirschler, Erica E. *A Studio of Her Own: Women Artists in Boston, 1870–1940*. Boston: Museum of Fine Arts Publications, 2001.

Kelly, Jain. "Sarah C. Sears." In *A History of Women Photographers*, Naomi Rosenblum. New York: Abbeville Press, 1994.

McKenna, Maureen A. "Sarah C. Sears." In *Catalogue of Photography: The Cleveland Museum of Art*, Tom E. Hinson. Cleveland: Cleveland Museum of Art, 1996.

Meister, Laura Ilise. "Sarah Sears." In "Missing from the Picture: Boston Women Photographers 1880–1920" (M.A. thesis). Tufts University, 1998.

"Mrs. Sarah Sears Dies at Age 77." *Boston Herald* (September 27, 1935).

Naef, Weston J. "Sarah C. Sears." In *The Collection of Alfred Stieglitz: Fifty Pioneers of Modern Photography*. New York: Metropolitan Museum of Art and Viking Press, 1978.

Quitslund, Toby. "Sarah Choate Sears." In *Women Artists in Washington Collections*, ed. by Josephine Withers. College Park, MD: University of Maryland Art Gallery and Women's Caucus for Art, 1979.

"Recent Exhibitions." *Photo-Era* 2 (March 1899): 260–61.

"Sarah C. Sears." *Who's Who* 5 (1908–1909): 1688.

Sarah C. Sears. "The English Exhibition and the 'American Invasion.'" *Camera Notes* 4 (January 1901): 162–75.

Unpublished Sources

Frances Benjamin Johnston Papers, Manuscripts Division, Library of Congress, Washington, D.C.: Two letters from Sarah C. Sears to Frances Benjamin Johnston, June 1, [1900] and June 26, 1900; one letter from Frank W. Birchall on behalf of Sarah C. Sears to Frances Benjamin Johnston, June 19, 1900.

F. Holland Day Papers, Norwood Historical Society, Norwood, MA (Reel 3566 in the Archives of American Art, Smithsonian Institution): Eleven letters from Sarah C. Sears to F. Holland Day, 1899–1904; one letter from Sarah C. Sears to F. Holland Day, n.d.

Stieglitz Archives, Collection of American Literature, Beinecke Rare Book and Manuscript Library, Yale University, New Haven, CT: Six letters from Sarah C. Sears to Alfred Stieglitz, n.d.

EMILY AND LILLIAN SELBY

Gover, Jane C. "New Profession." *The Positive Image: Women Photographers in Turn of the Century America*. Albany, NY: State University of New York Press, 1988: 24–25, 30.

"John Bartlett's Criticism." *Bulletin of Photography* 9, no. 219 (October 18, 1911): 265–68.

"Lily Selby." In "Survey of Soft Focus Lenses—Professional Opinions." *The Photo-Miniature* 16, no. 184: 184.

New York City Directories, 1894–1925 and 1931–1934.

"Prof. Miller's Criticism." *Bulletin of Photography* 9, no. 219 (October 18, 1911): 263–64.

Quitslund, Toby. "Emily Selby and [?] Selby." In *Women Artists in Washington Collections*, ed. by Josephine Withers. College Park, MD: University of Maryland Art Gallery and Women's Caucus for Art, 1979: 139.

Unpublished Sources

Frances Benjamin Johnston Papers, Manuscripts Division, Library of Congress, Washington, D.C.: Three letters from Emily Selby to Frances Benjamin Johnston, n.d., June, 12 and 23 [1900].

VIRGINIA GUILD SHARP

"Death of Mrs. Sharp." *Nantucket Inquirer and Mirror* (July 6, 1946).

Quitslund, Toby. "Virginia G. Sharp." In *Women Artists in Washington Collections*, ed. by Josephine Withers. College Park, MD: University of Maryland Art Gallery and Women's Caucus for Art, 1979.

Unpublished Sources

Frances Benjamin Johnston Papers, Manuscripts Division, Library of Congress, Washington, D.C.: Three letters from Virginia G. Sharp to Frances Benjamin Johnston, 1900–1902.

Virginia Sharp Papers, Private collection: One letter to Virginia Sharp from William B. Dyer, April 8, 1900; one letter to Virginia Sharp from Edmund Stirling, April 12, 1900; one letter to Virginia Sharp from Eva Lawrence Watson, n.d. [April 1900].

ALTA BELLE SNIFF

Columbus, Ohio, City Directories, 1885, 1886–1909, 1910.

Gagel, Diane VanSkiver. *Ohio Photographers 1839–1900*. Nevada City: Carl Mautz Publishing, 1998.

Quitslund, Toby. "Alta Belle Sniff." In *Women Artists in Washington Collections*, ed. by Josephine Withers. College Park, MD: University of Maryland Art Gallery and Women's Caucus for Art, 1979.

"Sniff, Alla [Alta]." In *Artists in Ohio, 1787–1900: A Biographical Dictionary*, ed. by Mary Sayre Haverstock, et al. Kent, OH: The Kent State University Press, 2000.

Unpublished Sources

Frances Benjamin Johnston Papers, Manuscripts Division, Library of Congress, Washington, D.C.: Two letters from Alta Belle Sniff to Frances Benjamin Johnston, June 22 and 23, 1900.

EMA SPENCER

"Ema Spencer." In *Woman's Who's Who of America: A Biographical Dictionary of Contemporary Women of U.S. and Canada, 1914–1915*, ed. by John William Leonard. New York: American Commonwealth Co., 1914. Reprint, Detroit: Gale Research, 1976.

Erwin, Kathleen. "Ema Spencer." In *Pictorialism into Modernism: The Clarence H. White School of Photography*, ed. by Marianne Fulton. Rochester, NY: George Eastman House, 1996.

Fels, Thomas Weston. "Ema Spencer." In *Catalogue of Photography: The Cleveland Museum of Art*, Tom E. Hinson. Cleveland: Cleveland Museum of Art, 1996.

—. "Ema Spencer." In *O Say Can You See: American Photographs, 1839–1900*. Pitsfield, MA: Berkshire Museum; Cambridge, MA: MIT Press, 1989. [Ill., "Girl at Table with Peaches": 73, bio.: 130]

Neely, Ruth. *Women of Ohio: A Record of Their Achievements in the History of the State*, Vol. 3. S.J. Clarke Publishing Company, sponsored by the Ohio Newspaper Women's Association, n.d.

Quitslund, Toby. "Ema Spencer." In *Women Artists in Washington Collections*, ed. by Josephine Withers. College Park, MD: University of Maryland Art Gallery and Women's Caucus for Art, 1979.

Spencer, Ema. "The White School." *Camera Craft* 3, no. 3 (July 1901): 85–92.

—. "The Newark Camera Club." *Brush and Pencil* 3, no. 2 (November 1898): 93–99.

"Spencer, Ema." In *Artists in Ohio, 1787–1900: A Biographical Dictionary*, ed. by Mary Sayre Haverstock, et al. Kent, OH: The Kent State University Press, 2000.

Unpublished Sources

Stieglitz Archives, Collection of American Literature, Beinecke Rare Book and Manuscript Library, Yale University, New Haven, CT: Six letters from Ema Spencer to Alfred Stieglitz,1907–1908.

KATHARINE S. STANBERY AND MARY R. STANBERY

Homer, William Innes. *Pictorial Photography in Philadelphia: The Pennsylvania Academy's Salons 1898–1901*. Philadelphia: The Pennsylvania Academy of the Fine Arts, 1984. [Ill., "The Miniature": 26]

Stanbery, Katharine Sheward. "Platinum Printing." *The Photo-American* 10, no. 9 (July 1899): 261–64.

—. "Leaves from an Amateur's Notebook." *The Photo Miniature* 8, no. 96 (December 1908): 518–62. [Illustrated with photos by the author]

"Stanbery [*sic*] Sheward" and "Stanbery, Mary R." In *Artists in Ohio, 1787–1900: A Biographical Dictionary*, ed. by Mary Sayre Haverstock, et al. Kent, OH: The Kent State University Press, 2000.

Zanesville, Ohio, City Directories 1900–1919 (1917–1918 not published).

Unpublished Sources

Frances Benjamin Johnston Papers, Manuscripts Division, Library of Congress, Washington, D.C.: One letter from Katharine Sheward Stanbery to Frances Benjamin Johnston, 9 September 1897.

Stieglitz Archives, Collection of American Literature, Beinecke Rare Book and Manuscript Library, Yale University, New Haven, CT: Eight letters from Katherine Sheward Stanbery to Alfred Stieglitz, 1901–1906.

AMELIA VAN BUREN

"Amelia C. Van Buren." In *Dictionary of Women Artists: an International Dictionary of Women Artists Born before 1900*, ed. by Chris Petteys. Boston: G.K. Hall, 1985.

Detroit City Directories 1890–1891, 1898–1917.

"Amelia C. Van Buren." In *Artists of Early Michigan: A Biographical Dictionary of Artists Native to or Active in Michigan, 1701–1900*, ed. by Arthur Hopkin Gibson. Detroit: Wayne State University Press, 1975.

Kelly, Jain. "Amelia C. Van Buren." In *A History of Women Photographers*, Naomi Rosenblum. New York: Abbeville Press, 1994.

Quitslund, Toby. "Amelia C. Van Buren." In *Women Artists in Washington Collections*, ed. by Josephine Withers. College Park, MD: University of Maryland Art Gallery and Women's Caucus for Art, 1979.

Unpublished Sources

Frances Benjamin Johnston Papers, Manuscripts Division, Library of Congress, Washington, D.C.: One letter from Amelia Van Buren to Frances Benjamin Johnston, June 7, 1900; one letter, n.d.

EVA WALBORN

Quitslund, Toby. "Eva Gamble Walborn." In *Women Artists in Washington Collections*, ed. by Josephine Withers. College Park, MD: University of Maryland Art Gallery and Women's Caucus for Art, 1979.

"Walbron [*sic*], Eva Gamble." In *Artists in Ohio, 1787–1900: A Biographical Dictionary*, ed. by Mary Sayre Haverstock, et al. Kent, OH: The Kent State University Press, 2000.

Unpublished Sources

Frances Benjamin Johnston Papers, Manuscripts Division, Library of Congress, Washington, D.C.: One letter from Eva Gamble Walborn to Frances Benjamin Johnston, June 21, 1900.

EVA L. WATSON-SCHÜTZE

Abel, Juan C. "Women Photographers and Their Work. Second Article." *The Delineator* 58 (September 1901): 574–79.

Block, Jean F. *Eva Watson-Schütze: Chicago Photo Secessionist*. Chicago: The University of Chicago Library, 1985.

Dyer, W.B. "Eva L. Watson, Artistic Photographer." *Brush and Pencil* 6, no. 6 (September 1900): 263–72. [Illustrated with nine photos by Watson-Schütze].

"Eva Lawrence Watson-Schütze, 1867–1935." In *Philadelphia: Three Centuries of American Art*, 476–77. Philadelphia: Philadelphia Museum of Art, 1976.

Hannum, Gillian Greenhill. "Eva Watson-Schütze." In *Coming to Light: Frances Benjamin Johnston and the Foremost Women Photographers in America*. Forthcoming.

Johnston, Frances Benjamin. "The Foremost Women Photographers in America. Fifth Article: Eva Lawrence Watson (Mrs. Martin Schultze [*sic*])." *The Ladies' Home Journal* 18, no. 11 (October 1901): 5.

Keiley, Joseph T. "Eva Watson-Schütze." *Camera Work* 9, no. 9 (January 1905): 23–26.

—. "And!?" *Camera Notes* 6, no. 1 (July 1902): 57–58.

—. "Exhibition of Prints by Eva L. Watson." *Camera Notes* 4, no. 2 (October 1900): 122–23.

Kelly, Jain. "Eva Watson-Schütze." In *A History of Women Photographers*, Naomi Rosenblum. New York: Abbeville Press, 1994.

McKenna, Maureen A. "Eva Watson-Schütze." In *The Cleveland Museum of Art Catalogue of Photography*, Tom E. Hinson, 478. Cleveland: The Cleveland Museum of Art, 1996.

Naef, Weston J. "Eva Watson-Schütze." In *The Collection of Alfred Stieglitz: Fifty Pioneers of Modern Photography*, 477–78. New York: Metropolitan Museum of Art and Viking Press, 1978.

Panzer, Mary. "Eva Lawrence Watson-Schütze." In *Philadelphia Naturalistic Photography, 1885–1906*. New Haven: Yale University Art Gallery, 1982.

Peterson, Christian A. "Eva Watson-Schütze." In *Alfred Stieglitz's Camera Notes*. Minneapolis: Minneapolis Institute of Arts, Norton & Company, 1993.

Quitslund, Toby. "Eva Watson-Schütze." In *Women Artists in Washington Collections*, ed. by Josephine Withers. College Park, MD: University of Maryland Art Gallery and Women's Caucus for Art, 1979.

Watson-Schütze, Eva. "Gertrude Käsebier." *American Amateur Photographer* 12 (May 1900): 219–20.

—. "Photography." *American Amateur Photographer* 13 (January 1901): 10–17. Also published in *Anthony's Photographic Bulletin* 32, no. 1 (January 1901): 9–11.

—. "Photography as Art." *Anthony's Photographic Bulletin* 32, no. 1 (January 1901): 9–11.

—. "Some Fragmentary Notes on the Chicago Salon." *Camera Notes* 5, no. 3 (January 1902): 200–2.

—. "Signatures." *Camera Work* 1 (January 1903): 35–36.

—. "Salon Juries." *Camera Work* 2 (April 1903): 46–47.

—. "Eva Watson-Schütze." In *Art of Today*, ed. by J.Z. Jacobson. Chicago: L.M. Stein, 1933.

—. "Forward to the Series." In *Plastic Redirections in 20th-Century Painting*, James Johnson Sweeney. Chicago: University of Chicago Press, 1934.

Yellott, Osborne I. "The Eva Lawrence Watson Exhibit." *Photo-Era* 4 (February 1900): 42–44.

Unpublished Sources

Frances Benjamin Johnston Papers, Manuscripts Division, Library of Congress, Washington, D.C.: Five letters from Eva Watson to Frances Benjamin Johnston, 1897–1900; two letters, June 10, [1900] and June 19, [1900]; five letters, n.d.

F. Holland Day Papers, Norwood Historical Society, Norwood, MA (Reel 3366 in the Archives of American Art, Smithsonian Institution): Four letters from Eva Watson-Schütze to F. Holland Day, 1899–1905.

Martin Schütze Papers, Department of Special Collections, The University of Chicago Library, Chicago.

Stieglitz Archives, Collection of American Literature, Beinecke Rare Book and Manuscript Library, Yale University, New Haven, CT: Fifty-four letters from Eva Watson-Schütze to Alfred Stieglitz, 1900–1905.

Watson-Schütze, Eva. "A Sketch of Mr. Joseph T. Keiley." Seven pages of typescript, Beinecke Rare Book and Manuscript Library, Yale University, New Haven, CT, n.d.

MATHILDE WEIL

Johnston, Frances Benjamin. "The Foremost Women Photographers in America: Miss Mathilde Weil." *Ladies' Home Journal* 18 (June 1901): 9.

Hannum, Gillian Greenhill. "Mathilde Weil." In *Coming to Light: Frances Benjamin Johnston and the Foremost Women Photographers in America*. Forthcoming.

Hines, Richard, Jr. "Women in Photography." *Wilson's Photographic Magazine* 36, no. 507 (March 1899): 137–41. Reprint of address delivered before the Art League of Mobile, AL, January 19, 1899.

Kelly, Jain. "Mathilde Weil." In *A History of Women Photographers*, Naomi Rosenblum. New York: Abbeville Press, 1994.

"Miss Mathilde Weil and Her Work." *Wilson's* 34, no. 548 (August 1902): 313–14.

Peterson, Christian A. "Mathilde Weil." In *Alfred Stieglitz's Camera Notes*. Minneapolis: Minneapolis Institute of Arts, W.W. Norton & Company, 1993.

"Photography Criticism. The Embroidery Frame. By Mathilde Weil." *Photography* 12 (July 5, 1900): 450–51.

Quitslund, Toby. "Mathilde Weil." In *Women Artists in Washington Collections*, ed. by Josephine Withers. College Park, MD: University of Maryland Art Gallery and Women's Caucus for Art, 1979.

Weil, Mathilde. "Outdoor Portraiture." *The Photo-Miniature* 5, no. 58 (January 1904): 441–64.

—. "Home Portraiture Book #1: Written from the Pictorial Viewpoint." *The Photo-Miniature* 6, no. 65 (August 1904): 244–80. [Illustrated with photos by Weil.]

—. "Outdoor Portrait Photography." *Country Life in America* 10 (May 1906): 47.

"Weil, Miss Mathilde: 1907." In *The Annual Exhibition Record of the Pennsylvania Academy of the Fine Arts, 1876–1913*. Philadelphia: Pennsylvania Academy of the Fine Arts. [With photo illustrated advertisement.]

Yellott, Osborne I. "Mathilde Weil—Artist Photographer." *Photo Era* 3 (June 1899): 323–28.

Unpublished Sources

Frances Benjamin Johnston Papers, Manuscripts Division, Library of Congress, Washington, D.C.: One letter from Mathilde Weil to Frances Benjamin Johnston, June 8, 1900; one letter, n.d. [February 12].

Stieglitz Archives, Collection of American Literature, Beinecke Rare Book and Manuscript Library, Yale University, New Haven, CT: Six letters from Mathilde Weil to Alfred Stieglitz, 1901 and n.d.

MYRA WIGGINS

Abel, Juan C. "Women Photographers and Their Work. Paper the First." *The Delineator* 58 (September 1901): 406–11.

Callahan, Kenneth. "Tiny, Energetic Mrs. Wiggins Was Vital, Dedicated Artist." *Seattle Times* (January 22, 1956).

Funk, Goldie Robertson. "Mrs. Wiggins of Toppenish Wash—One of the State's Most Remarkable Women." *Seattle Times* (March 9, 1930).

Glauber, Carole. *Witch of Kodakery: The Photography of Myra Albert Wiggins 1869–1956*. Pullman, WA: Washington State University Press, 1997.

—. "A Wandering Lens. Myra Albert Wiggins: Photographer, Artist and Mentor." *Northwest Art History* (March–April 1996): 33–35.

—. "Myra Albert Wiggins: Arts & Crafts Photographer." *Style 1900, The Quarterly Journal of the Arts & Crafts Movement* 12, no. 2 (Spring/Summer 1999): 34–40.

Hull, Roger. "Myra Wiggins and Helen Gatch: Conflicts in American Pictorialism." *History of Photography* 16, no. 2 (summer 1992): 152–69.

Kelly, Jain. "Sarah J. Eddy." In *A History of Women Photographers*, Naomi Rosenblum. New York: Abbeville Press, 1994.

"Mrs. Myra Albert Wiggins." In *The American Federation of Arts. American Art Annual 30*. Washington, D.C.: The American Federation for the Arts, 1933.

"Myra Albert Wiggins." In *Dictionary of Women Artists: an International Dictionary of Women Artists Born before 1900*, ed. by Chris Petteys. Boston: G.K. Hall, 1985.

Quitslund, Toby. "Myra Albert Wiggins." In *Women Artists in Washington Collections*, ed. by Josephine Withers. College Park, MD: University of Maryland Art Gallery and Women's Caucus for Art, 1979.

Widrig, Charlotte. "Dean of Northwest Painters." *Seattle Times* (December 13, 1953).

Wiggins, Myra Albert. "Amateur Photography Through Women's Eyes." *The Photo-American* 15 (March 1894): 193.

—. "Bedtime Stories told by the Light of the Moon." *Salem Oregon-Statesman* (June 6, 1897).

—. "Alone in Holland." *American Annual of Photography and Photographic Times Almanac* (1903): 227–31.

—. *Letters from a Pilgrim*. Salem: Statesman Publishing Company, 1904.

—. "The Log Cabin. Mrs. Wiggins Defends Oregon's Building at Stieglitz. St. Louis World's Fair." *Oregon Statesman* (July 5, 1904): 3.

—. "Trials and Triumphs of an Amateur Photographer." *American Magazine of Art* 17 (September 1926): 481–85.

"Wiggins, Myra Albert (Mrs.)." In *Who Was Who in American Art: 1564–1975*, ed. by Peter Hastings Falk. New York: Sound View Press, 1999.

Unpublished Sources

Frances Benjamin Johnston Papers, Manuscripts Division, Library of Congress, Washington, D.C.: Two letters and accompanying biographical sketch from Myra Wiggins to Frances Benjamin Johnston, June 3, [1900] and June 25, 1900.

Stieglitz Archives, Collection of American Literature, Beinecke Rare Book and Manuscript Library, Yale University, New Haven, CT: Six letters from Myra Wiggins to Alfred Stieglitz, 1905–1909.

MABEL OSGOOD WRIGHT

Austen, Barbara E. and Rebecca L. Abbott. *The Friend of Nature, Mabel Osgood Wright*. Fairfield, CT: Fairfield Historical Society, 1998.

Begg, Virginia Lopez. "Mabel Osgood Wright: The Friendship of Nature and the Commuter's Wife." *Journal of the New England Garden History Society* 5 (fall 1977).

Braun, Elizabeth T. "Mabel Osgood Wright and the Audubon Movement: Success of Sentimentality in Reform." Senior essay, Yale University College, 1987.

Chapman, Frank. "Appreciation." *Bird-Lore* 36 (July 1934): 280.

"Connecticut Audobon Society." *Bird-Lore* (November–December 1934): 427–28. [Memoriam of Mabel Osgood Wright]

"Mabel Osgood Wright Recalls Pleasures and Adventures of a Busy Literary Life." *Bridgeport Sunday Post* (March 8, 1925).

"Mabel Osgood Wright, 1859–1934." *Bird-Lore* (July–August 1934).

Obituary, *Publisher's Weekly* 12 (July 28, 1934): 286.

Obituary, *New York Times* (July 18, 1934).

Philippon, Daniel J. "The Garden, You, and I: Mabel Osgood Wright and the National Audubon Society." Introduction to *The Friendship of Nature by Mabel Osgood Wright* Washington, D.C.: Johns Hopkins, 1999.

Wright, Mabel Osgood. "A Photographic Question." *The American Annual of Photography and Photographic Times Almanac* (1894): 113–15.

—. *The Friendship of Nature*. New York: MacMillan, 1894. [Illustrated with photos by the author]

—. *Flowers and Ferns and Their Haunts*. New York: MacMillan, 1901. Illustrated with photos by the author]

—. *Dogtown*. New York: MacMillan, 1902. [Illustrated with photos by the author]

—. "A Poor Man's Paradise." *The Country Calendar* (August 1905).

—. *The Making of Birdcraft Sanctuary*. Self-published pamphlet, n.d. [with illustrations by author]

Wright, Mrs. James Obsorne. "Photographic Simplicity." *American Annual of Photography and Photographic Times Almanac* (1893): 49–52.

Illlustrations for

Abbott, Katharine M. *Trolley Trips: The Historic New England Coast*. 1899.

Child, Frank S. *An Old New England Town*. 1895.

—. *Friend or Foe*. 1900.

—. *An Unknown Patriot*. 1900.

—. *Fairfield Ancient and Modern*. 1909.

Earle, Alice Morse. *Old Time Gardens*. 1902.

McCauley, Jena May. *The Joy of Gardens*. n.d.

Unpublished Sources

Frances Benjamin Johnston Papers, Manuscripts Division, Library of Congress, Washington, D.C.: One letter from Mabel Osgood Wright to Frances Benjamin Johnston, June 19, [1900], one card, n.d.

Joel Asaph Allen Papers, American Museum of Natural History, Washington, D.C.: Letters from Mabel Osgood Wright to Joel Asaph Allen, Chairman of the Joint Department of Birds and Mammals.

Mabel Osgood Wright Papers and Photographs, Fairfield Historical Society, Fairfield, CT.

The MacMillan Collection, New York Public Library, New York: letters from Mabel Osgood Wright to George Brett.

The index covers all parts of the book except such supplementary apparatus as the preface, notes and selected bibliography. Page number in *italic* refer to illustrations and plates. Page numbers in **bold type** refer to biographies of selected photographers.

Abbott, Berenice, 46

Abel, Juan C., 28

Allen, Frances Stebbins, 10, *20*, 21, 28, 36, **138**, *138, 139, 140, plates 1–4*

Allen, Mary Electa, 10, *15, 20*, 21, 28, 36, **138**, *138, 139, 140, plates 1–4*

Allen, Sidney, *See* Hartmann, Sadakachi

Anthony, Susan B., 36

Austin, Alice, 10, *18, 20*, 28, *35*, 41, **141**, *141, 142, 177, plates 5–7*

Bain, George Grantham, 27, 34

Bartlett, Mary A. (Mrs. N. Gray Bartlett), 10, 21, 22, 39, 134, *135*, **142**, *142, 143, plates 8–10*

Beckwith, James Carroll, 157

Ben-Yusuf, Zaida, 10, 20, 28, *35*, 36, 41, 44, **144**, *144, 145*, 170, 174, *plates 11–16*

Binder-Mestro, Louise, 48, *48*

Bisland, Margaret, 14, 160

Bok, Edward, 17, 36

Brownell, Elizabeth, 36, **146**, *146, 147*

Bucquet, Antoinette, 48

Bunker, Dennis Miller, 168

Brush, George De Forest, 168, 185

Cabot, Elise Pumpelly, 10, 28, 44, 149

Calloway, Thomas J., 33

Cameron, Julia Margaret, 39, 144

Cassatt, Mary, 168, 169

Chase, William Merrit, 185

Clark, Rose, 10, 21, 28, 29, 41, **147, 148**, *148, plate 17*

Coburn, Alvin Langdon, *35*, 45, 46, 149, 168

Cox, Kenyon, 157, 185

Crane, Frank W., 142, 187

Crowell, Annie Nelson, **149**

Daguerre, Louis Jacques, 132, 133

Davison, George, 144

Day, F. Holland, 18, 28, *28*, 29, *35*, 36, 40, 42, 44, 45, 131, 141, 149, 163, 164, 168, 173

DeCamp, Joseph, 168

Degas, Edgar, 168

Demachy, Robert, 10, *35*, 38, 41–43, *42*, 45–47, *46, 47*, 132, 149, 158, 178

DeMeyer, Adolf, *157*, 158

Demuth, Charles, 168

Desmond, Anna, 21, **149**, *149*

Devens, Mary, 10, 28, 29, 41, 44, 147, 149, **150**

Dewey, George, 25, 31

Dillaye, Frédéric, 40

Douglass, Frederick, 33, 150

Du Bois, W. E. B., 33

Dyer, William B., 146, 171, 178, 179

Eakins, Thomas, 176, *176*, 179

Eastman, George, 14, 30

Eddy, Sarah Jane, 10, 14, 20, 21, 28, 41, **150, 151**,

150, 151, 152, plates 18–23

Eickemeyer, Rudolf, 40

Elton, Fannie L. (Mrs. Elton Saunders), 10, 20, *19*, 21, 29, **153**, *153*

Emerson, P. H., 130

Farnsworth, Emma Justine, 10, 20, *20*, 28, 36, 40, **153, 154**, *153, 154, 155, plates 24–30*

Fitz, Emma L., 29, **155, 156**, *156, plate 31*

Gastine, Louis, 43, *43*, 44, 48

Gercher, F., 165, *166*

Green, Floride, 10, 41, **156**, *156*

Gover, Jane C., 170

Hartmann, Sadakichi (also known as Sidney Allen), 144, 147, 164

Henrotin, Ellen Charles, 17, 27

Hines, Richard Jr., 141, 148, 155, 183

Horsley Hinton, Alfred, 41

Hügl, Arthur von, 131, 132

Huggins, Estelle Huntington, 20, **157**, *157*

Johnson, Eastman, 19, 171

Johnston, Frances Antoinette Benjamin (mother), 9, 26, 34, 137

Johnston, Frances Benjamin, 8–10, 12, 14, 17–22, 24–37, *24, 25, 26, 28, 32, 34*, 36, 38, 40, 41, 44, 46, 129, 134, 137, 138, 141, 144, 146, 148–150, 153, 155, 156, 158, 160, 161, 164, 165, 167, 168, 170–172, 174, 176, 178, 179, 183, 185, 187, 188, 190

Käsebier, Gertrude Stanton, 10, 18, 20, 21, 28, *28*, 29, 36, 41, 42, 44–49, *47, 48*, 141, 147, **157–159**, *157, 159*, 168, 173, *185, plates 32–34*

Keiley, Joseph, 29, 179

La Farge, John, 168

Laguarde, Céline, 48, 49, *49*

Laughlin, Clara E., 146

Lounsbery, Edith C. Haggin (Mrs. Richard P. Lounsbery), 10, 41, **160**, *160, plates 35–36*

Marin, John, 168

Mathieu, Emmanuel, 39, 40, *40*

McKinley, William, 17, 25

Ménard, Cyrille, 47, 48, *48*

Mew, Emily, 10, 41, **161**, *161, plates 37–38*

Minns, H. W., 178, *178*

Murray, William M., 144, 153

Palmer, Bertha Honoré Potter, 17, 22, 27

Paschall, Mary Frances Carpenter, 10, *21*, 28, 29, 36, **162**, *162, plates 39–43*

Paschall, Alfred (husband), *21*, 162

Peck, Ferdinand W., 17

Pilsbury, Anne K., 10, 41, **163**, *163, plates 44–45*

Poitevin, Louis Adolphe, 132, 133

Powell, William Bramwell, 31

Prall, Virginia M., 10, **164**, *164, 165, plates 46–48*

Puyo, Constant, 44–47, 161

Reyner, Albert, 45, 46, 48

Robinson, Addie Kilburn, 10, 20, 28, **165**, *165, 166, plate 49*

Rodin, Auguste, 46, 158

Russell, Margaret, 28, 29, 44, 149

Sargent, John Singer, 19, 168, 176

Saunders, William W., 153

Schäffer, Mary Townsend Sharples, 10, 28, 36, **167**, *167, 168, plates 50–53*

Sears, Sarah Carlisle Choate (Mrs. Joshua Montgomery Sears), 10, 19, 28, 35, *35*, 41, 44, **168, 169**, *168, 169, 170*

Selby, Emily, 10, 21, 28, 41, 144, **170**, *170, 171, plates 54–56*

Selby, Lillian, 10, 21, 28, 41, 144, **170**, *170, 171, plates 54–56*

Sharp, Virginia Guild, 10, 19, 22, 28, **171**, *171*

Smillie, Thomas W., 30, 161

Sniff, Alta Belle, 19, 21, 29, **172**, *172, plate 57*

Spencer, Ema, 21, 44, **173**, *173, 174*

Sreznewsky, Wiacheslav Izmilovitch, 9, 24, 33, 34, 188, 190, 191

Stanbery, Katharine Sheward (Mrs. Levi J. Burgess), 21, 137, **174, 175**, *174, 175, 176*

Stanbery, Mary R. (Mrs. George A. Stanbery), 21, 44, **174, 175**, *174, 175*

Steichen, Edward, 44, 45, 46, 147, 149

Stein, Gertrude, 169

Stieglitz, Alfred, 18, 20, 28, 29, 34, 35, 40, 41, 44–47, 144, 147, 149, 150, 153, 157, 158, 168, 173, 174, 179, 183, 185

Talbot, Henry Fox, 132, 133

Tarbell, Edmund C., 168

Tonnesen, Beatrice, 27

Troth, Henry, 28, *28*

Turner, Hermine, 158

Twachtman, John Henry, 157, 185

Van Buren, Amelia C., 10, *18, 20*, 21, 28, 36, 41, **176**, *176, 177*, 179, *plates 58–59*

Vidal, Léon, 42, 43

Wade, Elizabeth Flint, 14, 21, 147, **148**, *148, plate 17*

Walborn, Eva Gamble, 10, 21, 28, 41, 134, *136*, **178**, *178, plates 60–63*

Wallon, Étienne, 20, 41–43, 45

Ward, Catherine Weed Barnes, 14, 28

Ward, Snowden, 28

Watson, Eva Lawrence (Mrs. Watson-Schütze), 10, 14, 19, 21, 22, 28, 29, 36, 44, 147, 171, 176, **179, 180**, *179, 181, 182, 183, plates 64–69*

Weil, Mathilde, 10, 21, 28, 36, 41, 44, **183, 184**, *183, 184, plates 70–74*

White, Clarence H., *28*, 45, 158, 173

Wiggins, Myra Albert, 10, 20, 28, 130, **185, 186**, *185, 186, 187, plates 75–76*

Wright, Mabel Osgood (Mrs. James Osborne Wright), 10, 22, 28, 40, **187**, *187, plate 77*

Photography Credits
The photographic material in this catalogue has been provided through the courtesy of the owners or custodians of the work, who are credited in the captions accompanying the images.